Fifty Classic French Films 1912–1982

A Pictorial Record

Anthony Slide

DOVER PUBLICATIONS, INC.
New York

Also by Anthony Slide and published by Dover:

Fifty Great American Silent Films, 1912–1920: A Pictorial Survey (with Edward Wagenknecht)
Great Radio Personalities in Historic Photographs
Fifty Classic British Films, 1932–1982: A Pictorial Record

Copyright © 1987 by Anthony Slide.
All rights reserved under Pan American and International Copyright Conventions.

Published in Canada by General Publishing Company, Ltd., 30 Lesmill Road, Don Mills, Toronto, Ontario.

Published in the United Kingdom by Constable and Company, Ltd., 10 Orange Street, London WC2H 7EG.

Fifty Classic French Films, 1912–1982: A Pictorial Record is a new work, first published by Dover Publications, Inc., in 1987.

Book design by CBG Graphics.
Manufactured in the United States of America
Dover Publications, Inc., 31 East 2nd Street, Mineola, N.Y. 11501

Library of Congress Cataloging-in-Publication Data

Slide, Anthony.
  Fifty classic French films, 1912–1982.

  Bibliography: p.
  1. Moving-pictures—France. 2. Moving-pictures—France—Pictorial works. I. Title. II. Title: 50 classic French films, 1912–1982.
PN1993.5.F7S56 1987   791.43′75′0944   86-11521
ISBN 0-486-25256-6

FOREWORD

"In France, as in no other country, it has been the custom to view motion pictures with critical intelligence and with a sense of their historical value," wrote Iris Barry in *Tricolor* (June 1944). "In France, as nowhere else, motion pictures have been esteemed as an instrument of communication and expression rather than as a lucrative manufactured commodity."

France has always been at the forefront of film production since the days when it vied with the United States as the country in which the motion picture was invented. It has been a country of great film critics, such as André Bazin, and of great film theorists, such as Roland Barthes or Christian Metz. The film archives movement may well be argued to have its roots in France with the 1936 establishment of the Cinémathèque Française. It is a country of great pioneers: Louis and Auguste Lumière, George Méliès, Charles Pathé, Emile Cohl, Ferdinand Zecca and Léon Gaumont. Of great comedians: Max Linder, Jacques Tati and Pierre Etaix. Of great experimenters: Louis Delluc, Jean Epstein and Germaine Dulac. Of great innovators: Jean-Luc Godard, Alain Resnais, Marguerite Duras, Abel Gance and Robert Bresson. Of great entertainers: Sacha Guitry, René Clair, Julien Duvivier, Marcel Pagnol and Jacques Feyder. And of some of the world's greatest artists and screen poets: Jean Renoir, Jean Vigo, Jean Cocteau and François Truffaut.

The golden age of French cinema may well have been from the late Twenties through the late Thirties, but French films have been popular in the United States since the turn of the century, and, indeed, up to the First World War French films were as important as American productions at the box office. There have never been barren years in French cinema. Even during the Second World War, with half of the country occupied by the Germans, its film industry could still create major works by Robert Bresson, Henri-Georges Clouzot, Jacques Becker and Marcel Carné; while, in exile, Jean Renoir, René Clair and Max Ophüls (who is certainly an honorary French filmmaker) continued to entrance filmgoers.

In the early Fifties, the French New Wave, or Nouvelle Vague, heralded a new era for French cinema, as the theorists of *Cahiers du Cinéma* became the practitioners of film art. And in the Seventies and Eighties, French cinema remained high in international regard, thanks to the work of Moshe Mizrahi, Constantin Costa-Gavras, Jean-Jacques Annaud, Jean-Jacques Beineix and Bertrand Blier; while François Truffaut took over the mantle vacated by Jean Renoir as the grand old (or in Truffaut's case it seemed perennially young) man of French cinema.

Included here are fifty major French films from *Queen Elizabeth* to *Diva*. They have been selected not only as classics in their own right, but also because many are representative of a particular director, star or movement. For each film, I have provided detailed credits, a synopsis and a short essay offering historical background, critical evaluation and a sampling of contemporary American critical commentary.

My thanks to the Margaret Herrick Library of the Academy of Motion Picture Arts and Sciences (Robert Cushman), John Belton, Eddie Brandt, The British Film Institute (Elaine Burrows and Elaine Crowther), Robert Gitt, The Museum of Modern Art (Mary Corliss), Kit Parker and the UCLA Film Archives. Special thanks to Dido Renoir for reading the manuscript and checking my French grammar, and to Christian Tual and Unifrance Film for help in Paris. The photographs of Henri-Georges Clouzot, Jean-Luc Godard and François Truffaut, and the scene stills from *King of Hearts, Madame Rosa, I Sent a Letter to My Love* and *Diva* are reproduced by courtesy of Unifrance Film. Many of the films discussed in this book are available for rental in 16mm from Kit Parker Films, 1245 Tenth Street, Monterey, Calif. 93940-3692.

A. S.

This book is for Jean and Dido Renoir

Dido and Jean Renoir, photographed by Beulah Bondi while filming *The Southerner* (1945).

CONTENTS

Queen Elizabeth Les Amours de la Reine Elisabeth (1912)	1
The Miracle of the Wolves Le Miracle des Loups (1924)	4
The Italian Straw Hat Un Chapeau de Paille d'Italie (1927)	7
Napoléon (1927)	10
The Passion of Joan of Arc La Passion de Jeanne d'Arc (1928)	13
The Blood of a Poet Le Sang d'un Poète (1930)	16
The Golden Age L'Age d'Or (1930)	19
Le Million (1931)	22
The "Marius" Trilogy: Marius (1931), Fanny (1932), César (1936)	25
Zero for Conduct Zéro de Conduite (1933/1945)	28
Carnival in Flanders La Kermesse Héroïque (1935)	31
A Day in the Country Une Partie de Campagne (1936/1946)	34
Grand Illusion La Grande Illusion (1937)	37
The Pearls of the Crown Les Perles de la Couronne (1937)	40
Pépé le Moko (1937)	43
The Baker's Wife La Femme du Boulanger (1938)	46
La Marseillaise (1938)	49
Port of Shadows Quai des Brumes (1938)	52
Daybreak Le Jour Se Lève (1939)	55
Volpone (1939)	58
The Rules of the Game La Règle du Jeu (1939)	61
Children of Paradise Les Enfants du Paradis (1945)	64
Beauty and the Beast La Belle et la Bête (1946)	67
Monsieur Vincent (1947)	70
Orpheus Orphée (1950)	73
La Ronde (1950)	76
Diary of a Country Priest Journal d'un Curé de Campagne (1951)	79
Le Plaisir (1952)	82
Mr. Hulot's Holiday Les Vacances de Monsieur Hulot (1953)	85
The Wages of Fear Le Salaire de la Peur (1953)	88
The Sheep Has Five Legs Le Mouton a Cinq Pattes (1954)	91
Only the French Can French Cancan (1955)	94
And God Created Woman Et Dieu . . . Créa la Femme (1957)	97
The Lovers Les Amants (1958)	100
The Cousins Les Cousins (1959)	103
The 400 Blows Les Quatre Cents Coups (1959)	106
Hiroshima, Mon Amour (1959)	109
Breathless A Bout de Souffle (1960)	112
Last Year at Marienbad L'Année Dernière à Marienbad (1961)	115
Jules and Jim Jules et Jim (1962)	118
Judex (1963)	121
The Umbrellas of Cherbourg Les Parapluies de Cherbourg (1964)	124
King of Hearts Le Roi de Cœur (1966)	127
Belle de Jour (1967)	130
Z (1969)	133
Day for Night La Nuit Américaine (1973)	136
Madame Rosa La Vie Devant Soi (1977)	139
La Cage aux Folles (1978)	142
I Sent a Letter to My Love Chère Inconnue (1980)	145
Diva (1981)	148
Select Bibliography	151
Alphabetical List of Films	152

QUEEN ELIZABETH
LES AMOURS DE LA REINE ÉLISABETH

Producer: Histrionic Film. *Released:* 1912, Gaumont (France); 1912, Famous Players (U.S.). *Running Time:* 4 reels.

Director: Louis Mercanton. *Associate Director:* Henri Desfontaines. *Screenplay:* Based on a play by Emile Moreau. *Art Director:* Théâtre Sarah-Bernhardt, Paris.

CAST: Sarah Bernhardt (*Queen Elizabeth*); Lou Tellegen (*Robert Devereux, Earl of Essex*); Mlle. Romani (*Countess of Nottingham*); M. Maxudian (*Earl of Nottingham*); M. Chameroy (*Lord Bacon*); M. Decœur (*Sir Francis Drake*); and the actors of the Théâtre Sarah-Bernhardt. Paris.

SYNOPSIS: Sir Francis Drake brings Queen Elizabeth and her court news of the English victory over the Spanish Armada, and a celebratory performance of *The Merry Wives of Windsor* is held, after which Elizabeth congratulates Shakespeare. When a female soothsayer prophesies the execution of Elizabeth's favorite, the Earl of Essex, the Queen gives the Earl a ring as a token of trust. Jealous of the attention that Essex is paying to his wife, the Earl of Nottingham arranges for the former's exile to Ireland, from where, for eleven years, Essex corresponds with Elizabeth. Upon the Earl's return, Nottingham and Bacon conspire against him, and Elizabeth sees Essex with the Countess of Nottingham. She orders the Earl arrested and taken to the Tower of London, but relents and asks the Countess of Nottingham to request the return of the ring as a mark of Essex's penitence. However, the Earl of Nottingham seizes the ring from his wife and throws it into the Thames. After Essex's execution, Elizabeth discovers that the ring is missing and learns the truth from the Countess of Nottingham. Full of remorse, Elizabeth dies, before the entire court, in her throne room.

COMMENTARY: On March 25, 1907, a new French production company, Film d'Art, was founded, dedicated to the ideal that the cinema was primarily an art form, as opposed to an industry or an entertainment. The leading figures behind the company were associated with the Comédie Française, such as the actor Charles Le Bargy and the playwright Henri Lavedan. The latter provided the script for the first Film d'Art production, *The Assassination of the Duke de Guise,* which was co-directed by and starred Le Bargy, and also boasted a score by composer Camille Saint-Saëns.

Film d'Art produced *Tosca* in 1909, featuring Cécile Sorel, and in 1911 filmed Réjane in *Madame Sans-Gêne,* but it was the 1912 production of *Queen Elizabeth,* starring Sarah Bernhardt, that made the biggest impact on world cinema. Adolph Zukor purchased the film for American release and used it to launch his Famous Players organization, which was eventually to become Paramount.

Queen Elizabeth was not the first film venture of Sarah Bernhardt (1844-1923)—she had made three earlier films and was to make four more, including *Adrienne Lecouvreur* (1913), also for Film d'Art—but it was the film for which she will be best remembered. When the feature opened in New York, James C. Metcalfe, drama critic for *Life,* gave his first formal recognition of the motion picture. In a full-page review, published in the November 7, 1912 edition, he commented:

"Ever since moving pictures have been presented, usually at very popular prices, and with the idea of catching the nickels of the populace, we've heard a lot about their possible educational value. The educational purpose seems almost invariably to have been to keep the exhibitions down to the lowest level of intelligence.

"The little drama of *Queen Elizabeth* is on an entirely different basis and perhaps marks a new epoch in the moving picture business. It is in the first place a complete, although condensed, historical play. Played with spoken lines, it would last out an evening, but the essential story told in pantomime takes about an hour. As the principal attraction we have Mme. Bernhardt in the title role, herself in everything but the sound of her voice. She as well as the other actors of her company were evidently impressed with the importance of what they were doing before the camera, and their every motion was apparently up to the best that they could do.

"French actors are of course better schooled in pantomimic values than those of the English-speaking stage, so in this instance the absence of speech is less noticeable than it might be with people of our own theatre. With the admirable work of every member of the large company clearly shown, the illusion of seeing an interesting play well performed was almost complete.

"The usual 'movie' audience may not care for the Bernhardt films. Those who admire the great artist and those who have never seen her will find this play in dumb show a most interesting exhibition of her powers in her later years. With such material the moving pictures possess a real educational value."

Directing *Queen Elizabeth* and making his debut in the medium was Louis Mercanton, whose background was in the theatre, and who was to direct Bernhardt's next three features. Swiss-born, Mercanton (1879-1932) was at times a heavy-handed director, but he did demonstrate an understanding of the medium in some of his later films, notably *Monkeynuts* (1928), starring Betty Balfour, and he was an important enough director to be assigned features with other important stars.

The problem with the Film d'Art movement and the reason for its demise are, of course, obvious. Rather than create a cinematic language and technique, it borrowed too heavily from a totally different medium, the stage. As Georges Sadoul commented, "Its films were theatre in celluloid, every scene was shot straight through from the same camera position, and [Film d'Art] simply presented the resulting series of images with no attempt to edit sequences."

ABOVE: Lou Tellegen as the Earl of Essex and Sarah Bernhardt as Queen Elizabeth. BELOW: "So superb is the art of Sarah Bernhardt that she made her conception, which is that of a passionate woman, dominated wholly by her affections, seem not impossible," W. Stephen Bush in *The Moving Picture World* (August 3, 1912).

ABOVE: The execution of the Earl of Essex. BELOW: Elizabeth's remorse after Essex's death.

THE MIRACLE OF THE WOLVES
LE MIRACLE DES LOUPS

Producer: Raymond Bernard for Société des Romans Historiques Filmés. *Released:* 1924, Société des Romans Historiques Filmés (France); 1925, under the auspices of a committee composed of Barron Collier, Rodman Wanamaker, William Wrigley, Jr., William Ziegler, Jr., Cornelius Vanderbilt, Jr., R. A. C. Smith, Myron T. Herrick and General Coleman DuPont (U.S.). *Running Time:* 13 reels (France); 113 minutes, and subsequently cut to 73 minutes (U.S.).

Director: Raymond Bernard. *Screenplay:* A. Paul Antoine (based on the novel by Henry Dupuis-Mazuel). *Photography:* Forster, Bujard and Batton. *Art Director:* M.-R. Mallet-Stevens. *Music:* Henri Rabaud. *Costumes:* Job.

CAST: Charles Dullin (*Louis XI*); Vanni-Marcoux (*Charles, Duke of Burgundy*); Romuald Joubé (*Robert Cottereau*); Yvonne Sergyl (*Jeanne Hachette*); Mailly (*Philip the Good*); Philippe Hériat (*Tristan L'Ermite*); Gaston Modot (*Count de Lau*); Armand Bernard (*Bische*); Maujain (*Fouquet*).

SYNOPSIS: In this complex historical drama set in fifteenth-century France, Louis XI battles for control of the country with Charles the Bold, Duke of Burgundy. Robert Cottereau, a knight in the Duke's service, is in love with Jeanne, who is also desired by the Count de Lau. Jeanne and her father attempt to help Louis, who is being kept prisoner by Charles at Péronne, by bringing a document that will prove him innocent of the Duke's charges of insurrection. De Lau kills the father and chases Jeanne across the snowy mountains. Just as she is about to be caught, she is surrounded by a pack of wolves who protect the praying girl and attack her pursuers. Some years later, the army of the Duke, led by Robert Cottereau and de Lau, attack the city of Beauvais, where Jeanne is now living. She incites the townspeople to defend their city, joining in the fighting with an axe and thus acquiring her name of Hachette. Robert kills de Lau while defending Jeanne. In view of Robert's faithful past service to him, the Duke refuses to kill the couple. The King eventually arrives on the scene, and once more France is united.

COMMENTARY: It is only in recent years that *The Miracle of the Wolves* has gained its rightful reputation. Georges Sadoul wrote in his 1953 book, *French Film,* that it was "authentic, polished and stately, with the right degree of pomp and splendor." Film historian William K. Everson first saw it at the Cinémathèque Française in the early Seventies and hailed it as "a staggering and often lyrical film," but it was not until the feature's screening at the 1978 New York Film Festival that *The Miracle of the Wolves* was once again recognized as a major production in the history of the silent screen.

The film was highly regarded in its native land, receiving its premiere at the Paris Opéra on November 13, 1924, before an audience that included the President of France, but in the U.S. its initial critical reception was far different. That first American presentation took place on February 23, 1925, at New York's Criterion Theatre, where the film was presented under the auspices of a special committee, but by the film's first arthouse release screening it had been cut from 113 to 73 minutes.

"*The Miracle of the Wolves,*" reported *Variety* (February 23, 1925), "was viewed for the first time at the Criterion Monday night by an audience that far from filled the little theatre . . . There was nothing to grow enthusiastic about. The big scene from which the production derives its name resolves itself into seven police dogs, well trained in protection, and the fight they put up with the men was to all appearances a real one. . . . In the cast of French players there is no one that offers anything in particular any American producer would want with the possible exception of the leading lady, who while a little mature for ingenue leads in this country, might develop as a vamp type." *Photoplay* (May 1925) was equally caustic in its comments, reporting only that "More than half of this picture should have been cut out, the rest of it edited in good American fashion and then made over." The only enthusiastic American response to *The Miracle of the Wolves* came from Mordaunt Hall, in *The New York Times* (February 24, 1925), who, while critical of the subtitles and the confusing plot, did describe it as "a wonderful picture in many respects."

To be sure, there can be little argument that the plot is confusing and convoluted, demanding more knowledge of medieval French history than the average audience possesses. However, what do impress are the battle scenes, particularly the siege of Beauvais, and the protection of Jeanne by the pack of wolves. It is doubtful than any other silent film has depicted anything as vicious as the wolves' attack on Jeanne's pursuers. Yvonne Sergyl is adequate as Jeanne, but far more assured is Charles Dullin (1885-1949) as Louis XI. Although a major French theatrical figure, Dullin unfortunately bore a marked similarity to cowboy star William S. Hart, which damaged his chances of gaining much appeal in the United States. In his superb study *French Cinema: The First Wave, 1915-1929* (1984), Richard Abel has compared *The Miracle of the Wolves,* in its realism, to *Napoléon* and to Orson Welles's *Chimes at Midnight.* It might well be argued that *The Miracle of the Wolves* is closer to D. W. Griffith's *Intolerance,* not only in the splendor of its battles, but in the emotional warmth that it generates.

The Miracle of the Wolves was filmed between December 1923 and August 1924 at the Levinksy studios at Joinville, on the outskirts of Paris. Because the city of Beauvais no longer had its medieval battlements, the siege was filmed at the walled city of Carcassonne in the south of France, with the French military providing the soldiers.

Raymond Bernard (1891-1977) was the son of the playwright Tristan Bernard, and in 1916 played the son of Sarah Bernhardt in *Jeanne Doré,* based on a play by his father. Bernard worked as an assistant to Jacques Feyder, and made his directorial debut with *Le Ravin sans Fond* (1917). *The Miracle of the Wolves* is Bernard's most important film in a career that lasted through the late Fifties, and includes the 1934 version of *Les Misérables.*

RIGHT: Charles Dullin as Louis XI. BELOW: "The producer has attempted to put too much into this film instead of telling one interesting episode coupled with his romance, and the result is bewildering to the spectators," Mordaunt Hall in *The New York Times* (February 24, 1925).

ABOVE: The Miracle: Yvonne Sergyl as Jeanne.
LEFT: The siege of Beauvais.

THE ITALIAN STRAW HAT
UN CHAPEAU DE PAILLE D'ITALIE

Producer: Albatros Films. *Released:* 1927, Albatros (France); 1931, Moviegraphs (U.S.). *Running Time:* 7 reels.

Director: René Clair. *Screenplay:* René Clair (based on the comedy by Eugène Labiche and Marc Michel). *Photography:* Maurice Desfassiaux and Nicolas Roudakoff. *Artistic Director:* Alexandre Kamenka. *Film Editor:* Henry Dobb. *Set Designer:* Lazare Meerson. *Costumes:* Souplet.

CAST: Alice Tissot (*a cousin*); Alexis Bondi (*anther cousin*); Marise Maïa (*the bride*); Yvonneck (*Nonancourt*); Albert Préjean (*Fadinard, the bridegroom*); Pré fils (*Cousin Bobin*); Vital Geymond (*Lieutenant Tavernier*); Olga Tschechowa (*Anaïs Beauperthuis*); Paul Olivier (*Uncle Vézinet*); Alex Allin (*Félix*); Volbert (*the mayor*); Jim Gérald (*Beauperthuis*).

SYNOPSIS: Prior to his wedding, Fadinard is going for a carriage drive in the Bois de Vincennes when his horse eats the hat of a lady strolling with a soldier. It transpires that the soldier is not the lady's husband, and unless the hat is replaced the real husband will suspect something is wrong. The couple follow Fadinard to his house, where they are hidden as the wedding guests arrive. The wedding party drives to the town hall, but as the mayor is late for the ceremony, Fadinard goes to a milliner's to buy a replacement hat, only to be dragged away by his fiancée's father. After the wedding, Fadinard goes to the home of a lady who was the last person to buy a hat similar to the one eaten by his horse, but it is *the* lady's home and Fadinard inadvertently discusses his problem with her husband, Beauperthuis. To further add to the confusion, Fadinard's new father-in-law has followed him and accidentally changes shoes with Beauperthuis. The latter rushes off to Fadinard's house, where the guests have now arrived and are being refused admission. The bride's father is ready to call off the wedding and the guests are about to take back their presents when Uncle Vézinet opens his to reveal the exact hat for which Fadinard has been searching. Meanwhile the guests are being taken to the police station because of their suspicious behavior, and as Beauperthuis arrives at the house, his wife and the soldier escape, go to the police station and retrieve Vézinet's hat. Madame Beauperthuis returns home with the hat and is in bed before her husband comes back, while Fadinard explains everything to his new wife.

COMMENTARY: Nowhere in French silent cinema is there a more perfect example of bedroom farce, complete with mistaken identity and erring wife, than René Clair's *The Italian Straw Hat*.

Although, according to some of his colleagues, René Clair (1898-1981) was an exceedingly dull and boring person, he has an enviable reputation for producing some of the brightest comedy films of the century, beginning with *Paris Qui Dort/The Crazy Ray* (1923), and continuing with *Le Million* (1931), *Quatorze Juillet/July 14th* (1933), *The Ghost Goes West* (1935), *I Married a Witch* (1942) and *It Happened Tomorrow* (1943). He had a lightness of touch, a Gallic charm to his direction, which not even the Hollywood studio system could entirely diminish. Even as late as 1952, *Les Belles de Nuit/Beauties of the Night* offered a delightful example of Clair's particular whimsy.

The basis for *The Italian Straw Hat* is a nineteenth-century stage farce by Eugène Labiche, who also was responsible for *Les Deux Timides/The Two Timid Souls*, filmed by Clair in 1928. The Labiche original contained music, which of course Clair was forced to reject, but he added to the farce exaggerated comedy in the style of Mack Sennett, as well as moving the story up from the mid- to the late 1800s. Clair served Labiche well, but in return he was well served by his author, in that Labiche's play has not aged badly.

Despite its popularity in France, *The Italian Straw Hat* was perhaps a little too Gallic for other nationalities. It was not seen in England until its screening by the Film Society there. In the United States, it was not until the success of Clair's *Le Million* and *Sous les Toits de Paris/Under the Roofs of Paris* that *The Italian Straw Hat* gained a release under the uncommercial title of *The Horse Ate the Hat* and with a synchronized music score. *Variety* (September 8, 1931) branded it as "Hardly worth commenting on since American distributors will probably ignore it . . . of no importance today, except as a yard stick on how far the French have advanced." After noting a slight similarity between the chase for the hat in *The Italian Straw Hat* and the chase for the coat in *Le Million, Variety* concluded, "It's like comparing *City Lights* with an early Keystone Chaplin." Mordaunt Hall in *The New York Times* (September 1, 1931) was a little more sympathetic, but he did comment that "it is scarcely one [film] that boosts the stock of mute productions, for there are times when the players cavort about the screen with about as much rhythm and grace as hens on a hot griddle."

It should be noted that *The Italian Straw Hat* offers Albert Préjean (1893-1979) a perfect role as Fadinard, and it is easy to see why he became Clair's favorite actor, featured in *Paris Qui Dort/The Crazy Ray, Le Fantôme du Moulin Rouge/The Phantom of the Moulin Rouge* (1924), *Le Voyage Imaginaire/The Imaginary Voyage* (1925) and *Sous les Toits de Paris/Under the Roofs of Paris*. His best-known non-Clair role is as Mack the Knife in the French-language version of *Die Dreigroschenoper/The Three Penny Opera* (1931, G. W. Pabst).

ABOVE: The horse eats the hat: Albert Préjean as Fadinard. BELOW: At the milliner's, Fadinard tries to find a substitute hat.

RIGHT: The wedding breakfast. BELOW: The farce continues: Beauperthuis and the bride's father at the former's home.

NAPOLÉON

Producer: Société Générale de Films. *Released:* 1927, Gaumont-Metro-Goldwyn (France); 1929, M-G-M (U.S.). *Running Time:* 5 hours (France); 70 minutes (U.S.).

Director: Abel Gance. *Screenplay:* Abel Gance. *Photography:* Jules Kruger. *Additional Photography:* Léonce-Henry Burel. *Art Directors:* Alexandre Benois, Schildknecht, Lochavoff, Jacouty, Meinhardt and Eugène Lourié. *Film Editors:* Marguerite Beaugé and Henriette Pinson. *Music:* Arthur Honegger. *Special Effects:* W. Percy Day. *Costumes:* Charmy, Sauvageau, Mme. Augris and Jeanne Lanvin.

CAST: Albert Dieudonné (*Napoléon Bonaparte*); Abel Gance (*Saint-Just*); Philippe Hériat (*Salicetti*); Nicolas Koline (*Tristan Fleuri*); Alexandre Koubitzky (*Danton*); Maxudian (*Barras*); Antonin Artaud (*Marat*); Edmond van Daële (*Robespierre*); Gina Manès (*Joséphine de Beauharnais*); Annabella (*Violine Fleuri*); Marguerite Gance (*Charlotte Corday*); Vladimir Roudenko (*Napoléon as a child*).

SYNOPSIS: Part One opens with a snowball fight at the military academy of Brienne, where Napoléon is the victor in the fight but basically unhappy except for the companionship of a pet eagle. In 1789, the revolution begins in Paris, and Lieutenant Napoléon Bonaparte is there. He returns to his native Corsica, but cannot win the inhabitants over to the revolutionary cause, and is forced to flee in a small boat, using the tricolor as a sail. At the siege of Toulon (1793), Napoléon replaces the incompetent General Carteaux and is able to force the withdrawal of Admiral Hood and the British fleet. Napoléon sleeps, his head on a drum, while the eagle of destiny watches over him.

Part Two has Napoléon returning to Paris and the Terror. Marat is stabbed. Napoléon's loyalty is questioned by the Committee of Public Safety, and he is imprisoned. Danton is sent to the guillotine, and Joséphine de Beauharnais is accused, but her estranged husband takes her place on the scaffold. Saint-Just brings an end to the reign of terror in 1794, but Napoléon refuses to fight the royalists because they are Frenchmen just like him. However, when the royalists threaten the government, in October of 1794, Napoléon is asked to take command. He saves the revolution, and meets Joséphine at a celebration, the Bal des Victimes. Joséphine makes an arrangement with her protector, Barras, who is anxious to be rid of her. In return for his promoting Napoléon to the command of the Alps, she will marry him. Napoléon and Josephine are married on March 9, 1796. In the foothills of the Alps, the French troops are hungry, ill-clothed and unpaid. However, Napoléon rouses them with his dream of a march into Italy and new glory for France. Napoléon leads his troops across the Alps, while the eagle of destiny again hovers over his head.

COMMENTARY: "It's more difficult to make epics," said Abel Gance. "One must rise to the level of the heroes one wants to depict." With *Napoléon*, Gance achieved a high in filmmaking which he himself was never to achieve again; and at the same time he laid the groundwork for a high in media exploitation that was to take place some 53 years after *Napoléon*'s initial release, and that was to give the film a fame and an importance out of all proportion to its worth.

Certainly *Napoléon* is a major film in the history of the motion picture, not only in France, but on an international level. It is an epic of extraordinary proportions, of breathtaking technical virtuosity and astonishing craftsmanship. The fast cutting and camera wizardry of the opening snowball fight give promise of what the rest of the film has to offer from a purely technical standpoint. At the same time, *Napoléon* is a film that lacks warmth, that fails to move its audience adequately. One never gets particularly close to Napoléon, the man. The audience does not care about this French upstart, whether he wins or loses, whether he marries Joséphine or not.

Many years ago, the French critics and historians, led by Jean Mitry, suddenly discovered Thomas H. Ince, the pioneer American producer, and lauded him out of all proportion to his importance, largely because it was a way of denigrating the achievements of D. W. Griffith, who was a little too conservative for the naturally left-wing intelligentsia. The rush of critics eager to praise *Napoléon* and to push to one side Griffith's *Intolerance* stems from much the same ideology. Yet, in the long run, hopefully, Griffith's *Intolerance* will be the survivor, not Gance's *Napoléon*. And the reason is simple. *Intolerance* makes one care about its characters.

Napoléon was first released in the United States in 1929, in a seventy-minute version, missing the famed three-screen triptych or Polyvision sequences. The trade papers were not overly enthusiastic as to the film's potential. *Variety* (January 23, 1929) complained that Napoléon looked like William Randolph Hearst (a not inappropriate comparison), and that the film "doesn't mean anything to the great horde of picture house goers over here."

The feature was reissued by Paramount in a sound version, edited by Gance, in 1935, and there was a second sound version, this time with dialogue, released by Cinelde in 1955. In 1971, Films 13 presented a new sound reissue with additional footage by Abel Gance, under the patronage of Claude Lelouch. However, through the years, Kevin Brownlow was at work, attempting with almost messianic zeal to restore the film to Gance's original concept. (And any criticism that I may have of the film must be tempered with total praise and admiration for Brownlow's efforts.)

Brownlow's work in progress was seen at least twice in the United States—at the American Film Institute Theatre in Washington, D.C. (1973) and at the Telluride Festival (1979)—before its climactic presentation by Francis Ford Coppola at the Radio City Music Hall, January 23-25, 1980. This was an event comparable to Hitler's manipulation of the masses at the Nuremberg Rally. Peter Pappas, in *Cineaste* (Vol. 11, No. 2, 1981), summed it all up perfectly as "yet another of those massive pseudo-cultural diversions for the new urban gentry which have become the signature of our times." The critics lost all sense of proportion, with the award for sheer stupidity going to Charles Champlin of the Los Angeles *Times* (July 16, 1981), who described *Napoléon* as "a film against which all the others have to be measured, now and forever."

In fact, the hoopla and ballyhoo has probably, in the long run, damaged the reputation of Abel Gance (1889-1981). It will make it harder for scholars to take seriously the important films in a career that began in the early 'teens and includes several major works.

ABOVE: The death of Marat (Antonin Artaud). BELOW: The arrest of Joséphine (Gina Manès) and her incarceration.

LEFT: Albert Dieudonné as Napoléon Bonaparte. BELOW: Two views from the triptych sequence with which the film concludes: Napoléon prepares to march into Italy.

THE PASSION OF JOAN OF ARC
LA PASSION DE JEANNE D'ARC

Producer: Société Générale de Films. *Released:* 1928, Société Générale de Films (France); 1929, M. J. Gourland (U.S.). *Running Time:* 110 minutes.

Director: Carl Theodor Dreyer. *Screenplay:* Joseph Delteil and Carl Theodor Dreyer. *Photography:* Rudolf Maté. *Art Directors:* Hermann Warm and Jean Hugo. *Film Editor:* Carl Theodor Dreyer. *Costumes:* Jean and Valentine Hugo. *Historical Consultant:* Pierre Champion.

CAST: Maria Falconetti (*Joan of Arc*); Eugène Silvain (*Bishop Pierre Cauchon*); Maurice Schutz (*Nicholas Loyseleur*); Michel Simon (*Jean Lemaître*); Antonin Artaud (*Massieu*); Ravez (*Jean Beaupère*); André Berley (*Jean d'Estivet*); Jean d'Yd (*Guillaume Evrard*); Jean Hemm, André Lurville, Jacques Arma, Alexandre Mihalesco, Robert Narlay, Henri Maillard, Jean Ayme, Léon Larive, Paul Jorge, Henri Gaultier (*the judges*); Sommaire, Radin (*clerks of the court*); Granowski, Rouf (*executioners*); Dalleu, Dacheux, Persitz, Derval, Bac, Valbret, Fromet, Argentin, Piotte, Polonsky, Dmitrieff, Marnay, Gitenet, Fournez, Goffard, Ridez, Beri, Delauzac, le Flon, Velsa, Nikitino, Bazaine (*additional judges*).

SYNOPSIS: Following her capture, Joan of Arc (1412-1431) is brought to trial. She cannot remember her exact age, refuses to recite the Lord's Prayer and states she will exchange her male attire for a dress only when her work is completed. The judges refuse Joan's request to be tried by the Pope. They trick her into trusting a hostile priest and refuse her request to hear Mass. Tortured, Joan accepts the court's condemnation of her as a heretic and sorcerer, but later recants. Her head shaved, she is burnt at the stake, as the crowds riot and accuse the judges of killing a saint. She dies with Jesus' name on her lips. (Joan of Arc was rehabilitated at a new trial in 1456 and canonized in 1920.)

COMMENTARY: Richard Watts, Jr. made an interesting comment concerning *The Passion of Joan of Arc* in his review of the film in the April 12, 1929 issue of *The Film Mercury*. "A Dane directed it, it is true," wrote Watts, "but the work is completely French in style, acting and locale. It comes, therefore, as a sort of tragic irony that one of the hitherto most backward nations in silent film manufacture arrives with something great, just as America, the home of the cinema, is gleefully giving up the medium."

Watts's remarks indicate the low regard in which French cinema was held by Americans in the Twenties. To the majority of American critics, the French film industry had reached its zenith in the early 'teens with the releases of Pathé and Gaumont.

The Passion of Joan of Arc is, of course, French in theme, but Watts is incorrect in heralding it as French in style. The style is very much that of Carl Theodor Dreyer (1889-1968). The best known of Dreyer's nine silent films, *The Passion of Joan of Arc* contains much of the cold, dramatic intensity to be found in the director's later films, particularly *Vredens Dag/Day of Wrath* (1943), *Ordet/The Word* (1954) and *Gertrud* (1961). The production is heavily stylized not only in terms of the acting, but in the director's decision to concentrate the trial and execution of Joan into one day, rather than the eighteen months over which the events actually took place.

There is a harsh, almost naked quality to the film. The suffering of Joan is brutally forced into the consciousness of the audience. Each shot is carefully composed, but the images do not particularly blend together into a whole. The film is also painfully slow, with too many close-ups and too little action. The great strength of Dreyer's masterpiece lies in its ability to treat its noble theme with sincerity and nobility.

Initially Carl Dreyer had been invited to France by the Société Générale de Films, and had suggested three topics for his first production, Marie Antoinette, Catherine de Médicis or Joan of Arc. Dreyer had sought to make the film with sound, but supposedly because the necessary equipment was not available (a somewhat unlikely excuse) settled for a silent production. The film was shot between the spring and winter of 1927 at the Billancourt Studios and on location at a specially constructed castle set. The cast includes a young Michel Simon, Antonin Artaud from the avant-garde theatre and Maria Falconetti from the Comédie Française in the title role. Of Falconetti (1901-1946), Dreyer is reported to have said, "I found in her face exactly what I had been seeking for Joan of Arc: a rustic woman, very sincere, who was also a woman who had suffered."

American critics were split in their response to the production. Harry Alan Potamkin, in *Exceptional Photoplays* (January 1929), considered the film neither a costume picture nor a religious drama: "Life, it urges, is transcendent. It is a transcendent film." Harshest was Sime Silverman in *Variety* (April 10, 1929), who announced, "This *Passion of Joan of Arc* isn't worth a dollar to any commercial regular picture theatre in the U.S." Curiously there were those in the American film industry who took notice of the brilliant camerawork of Rudolf Maté, notably Arthur Miller, a major American cinematographer, who wrote a lengthy article on the film in the *Los Angeles Times* (September 22, 1929).

The Passion of Joan of Arc has suffered through the years from excessive cutting and the distribution of inferior prints. In 1983 the Danish Film Museum restored the film as close as possible to Dreyer's original. Unfortunately the Danes also commissioned a new musical score by Ole Schmidt, which is totally out of keeping with the mood of the film and detracts *and* distracts from Dreyer's work.

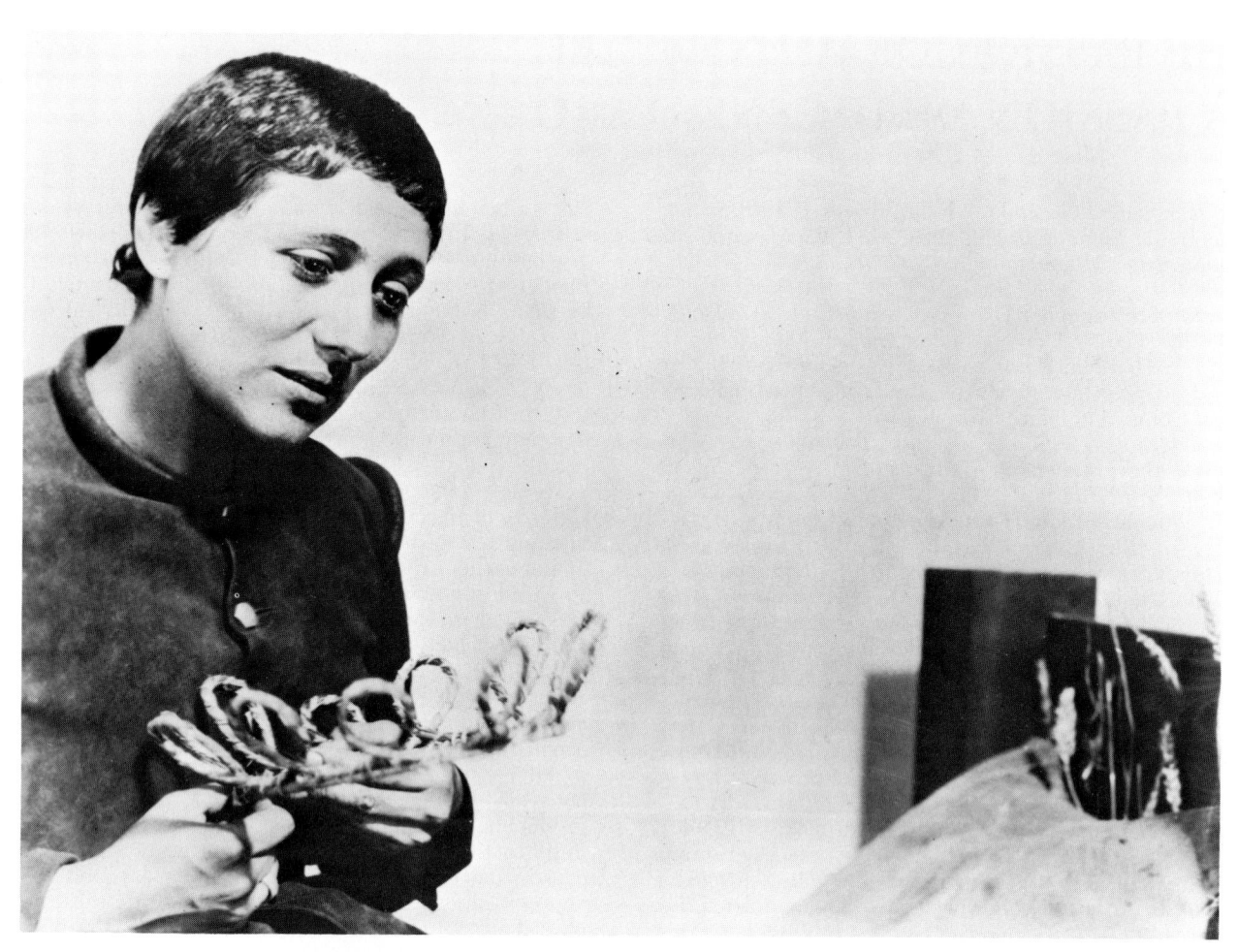

ABOVE: Maria Falconetti as Joan of Arc. BELOW: Antonin Artaud (right) as Massieu.

ABOVE: The trial. BELOW: A good example of the stark, effective quality of the sets.

THE BLOOD OF A POET
LE SANG D'UN POÈTE

Producer: Jean Cocteau. *Released:* 1931, Jean Cocteau (France); 1933, Edward Ricci (U.S.). *Running Time:* 60 minutes.

Director: Jean Cocteau. *Screenplay:* Jean Cocteau. *Photography:* Georges Périnal. *Technical Director:* Michel J. Arnaud. *Settings, Montage and Commentary:* Jean Cocteau. *Sound:* Henri Labrely. *Set Construction:* Y.-G. d'Eaubonne. *Accessories:* La Maison Berthelon. *Plaster Casts:* La Plastikos. *Music:* Georges Auric.

CAST: Lee Miller (*the Statue*); Enrique Rivero (*the Poet*); Pauline Carton (*child's tutor*); Feral Benga (*black angel*); Jean Desbordes (*the character of Louis XV, masked*); Barbette (*woman in box/at balcony*); Fernand Deschamps; Lucien Jager; Odette Talazac.

SYNOPSIS: The film is divided into four episodes: (1) The Washed Hand or the Scar of a Poet, (2) Do Walls Have Ears?, (3) The Battle of the Snowballs, (4) The Stolen Card. A chimney begins to fall. A painter is horrified to discover that the mouth of his painting is moving. He erases the mouth, but as he washes his hands, the mouth reappears on one of his palms. The painter transfers the mouth to a statue, which comes to life and urges him to go through the mirror. On the other side of the mirror, the painter encounters a corridor in a hotel, where he views, through the keyholes of various doors, a surrealistic view of Mexico, of China, of childhood and of surrealism. Returning through the mirror, the painter destroys the statue and is, in turn, transformed into a statue. Out in the street, children engage in a snowball fight around a statue, which is apparently made of snow and destroyed by the kids. One of the boys throws a snowball at another boy and kills him. An elegant couple play at cards by the dead boy's side, while the balconies overlooking the street become like boxes at the opera, inhabited by elegant playgoers. The woman at the card game tells her partner he is lost without the ace of hearts, which the man retrieves from the dead boy. A black man enters as the boy's guardian, removes the boy and takes back the card from the man, who is killed. The audience in the balcony applaud. The woman becomes a statue and walks off. Following various surrealistic images, the chimney is seen making its final fall.

COMMENTARY: When *The Blood of a Poet* opened at New York's Fifth Avenue Playhouse on November 3, 1933, the theatre offered a prize of $25 to any patron who could offer an explanation as to the film's meaning. There were no takers among this "nuttiest of the arty audiences" (as *Variety* described them).

Jean Cocteau also has offered little help in deciphering his film. "My connection to the work was that of a cabinet-maker," he has written, "who assembles the parts of a table, and whom the spirits, having made that table turn, consult." Is it a surrealistic exercise? Cocteau disputes that, maintaining that surrealism did not exist when he created the film, but this is not true, as surrealism dates back to 1924. However, perhaps it is surrealistic to claim that surrealism does not exist, for existence is reality, and reality is not part of surrealism or Cocteau's film. Is the film a work of eccentricity? Undoubtedly. But eccentricity is acceptable from a poet, whereas it is madness when expressed by an ordinary human being. Could it be that *The Blood of the Poet* is nothing more than a homosexual wet dream? The tower is certainly a phallic symbol, and its collapse signifies the close of the film. The poet/painter, stripped to the waist, is a classic homosexual beauty, and as he wanders dreamlike through the hotel corridor he is spying on what might be considered sado-masochistic rites. There is also the presence of Barbette, the great transvestite trapeze artiste, in full drag and pouting most prettily in the best female impersonator tradition.

"Can I blame anyone for misunderstanding a film that I understand so poorly?" asked Cocteau. *The Blood of a Poet* does not necessarily seek an understanding, but rather, like any great visual work, asks only that the viewer appreciate the beauty of the images, the poetry on film which Cocteau has created. *The Blood of a Poet* deserves no criticism as a work of art; the only criticism to be leveled against it, as a film, is that it is a talkie that fails to utilize sound. There are too many descriptive subtitles, too many words from narrator Cocteau. If the images are to speak for themselves, then there should be no sound—other than music—or else the sound should emanate from the images, not from a writer's pen or an unseen voice.

Both *The Blood of a Poet* and Buñuel's *L'Age d'Or* were commissioned by the Viscount de Noailles in 1930, but not shown publicly—at the Vieux Colombier—until a year later. The film, as Cocteau wrote, "badly printed, badly cut, and badly projected, provoked scandals and battles without being able to defend itself by its distinction." The doyen of French critics, Georges Sadoul, wrote, "Cocteau's film, supreme expression of decadence, was the pillar of salt left beside the ruins of the surrealist avant-garde."

The Blood of a Poet is of primary importance in the history of French cinema because it was the first film by Jean Cocteau (1889-1963), arguably the greatest French intellectual of this century, and paved the way for a career in films that was to last until 1965, and include such important works as *La Belle et La Bête/Beauty and the Beast, L'Aigle à Deux Têtes/The Eagle Has Two Heads* (1948), *Les Enfants Terribles/The Storm Within* (1948), *Orphée/Orpheus* and *Le Testament d'Orphée/The Testament of Orpheus* (1960). The use of the mirror in *The Blood of a Poet* is an obvious carry-over to *Orpheus*. Although Cocteau's later films were commercial successes both in his native France and abroad, he was a filmmaker who always worked outside of the system, and thus was able to create works of a highly personal nature, which have transformed the motion picture into an art form in its purest sense.

ABOVE: Enrique Rivero as the Poet. BELOW: Lee Miller as the Statue.

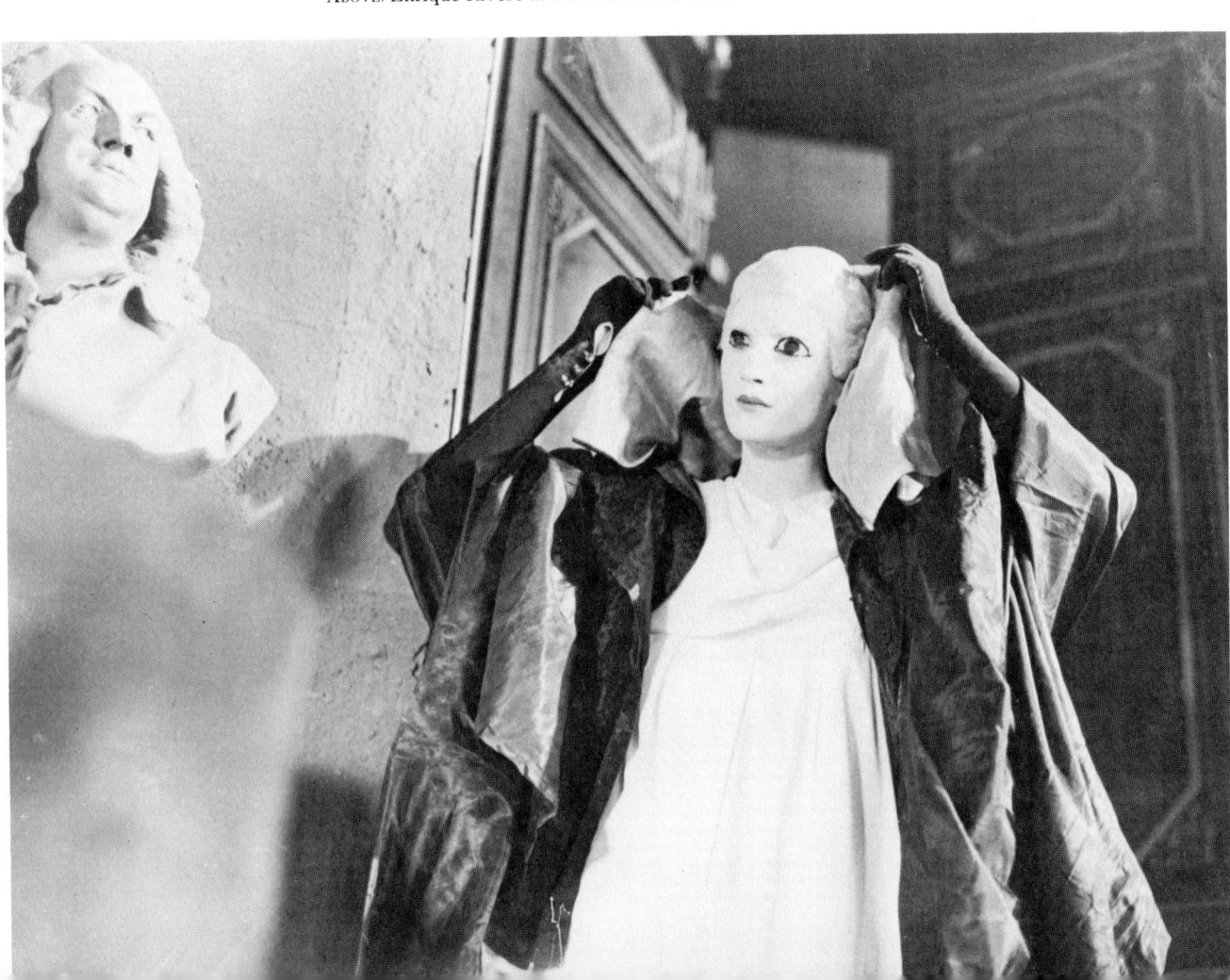

ABOVE: One of the surrealistic images from the film's closing scene. BELOW: The Poet (Lee Miller) after he has taken the journey through the mirror.

THE GOLDEN AGE
L'AGE D'OR

Producer: Vicomte Charles de Noailles. *Released:* 1930 (France); 1980, Corinth Films (U.S.). *Running Time:* 65 minutes.

Director: Luis Buñuel. *Screenplay:* Luis Buñuel and Salvador Dali. *Photography:* Albert Dubergen. *Art Director:* Schilzneck. *Music:* Georges van Parys, and selections from Wagner, Debussy, Beethoven and Mendelssohn. *Film Editor:* Luis Buñuel.

CAST: Gaston Modot (*the man*); Lya Lys (*the girl*); Max Ernst; Pierre Prévert; Jose Artigas; Cardinal de Lamberdesque; Jacques Brunius.

SYNOPSIS: After a discourse on the habits of two scorpions, a bandit watches on a rocky shore as four archbishops perform religious rites. He tells his companions that the Majorcans are here, but when the bandits reach the shore, the archbishops have become skeletons. Various establishment figures arrive in boats, and as the Governor speaks a man and a woman, fully clothed, are discovered making love in the mud. They are dragged away. The title "Imperial Rome" introduces shots of the Vatican; the title "Sometimes on Sunday" introduces shots of houses being destroyed; the title "Various Picturesque Views of the Metropolis" introduces shots of a man kicking a violin, an elderly man walking with a stone on his head, etc. As the man is dragged away by police, we see images of his mistress, her father and her mother announcing, "Hurry, the Majorcans will come at nine o'clock." In her bedroom, the woman finds a cow on her bed and polishes her nails while viewing clouds in the mirror of her dressing table. At an elegant party, the guests ignore a farm cart, laborers, a screaming maid and a gamekeeper shooting his son. The man arrives and he and the woman are oblivious to what is happening around them. As they walk in the garden, an orchestra prepares to play the "Liebestod" from *Tristan and Isolde*, but the man is called away to speak on the telephone to the Minister of the Interior and the girl sucks the toe of a statue. After the Minister has accused the man of causing the deaths of hundreds, the Minister's body is seen lying dead on the ceiling. The man returns to the woman, the orchestra stops and the conductor is embraced by the woman. The man hurts his head and rushes into the woman's room, from which he expels an archbishop, a plough, a bishop's crook, a stuffed giraffe and feathers. The feathers become snow outside a medieval castle in which according to titles, orgies take place. The gates open, and four participants in the orgy leave. The final shot is of a snow-covered cross, decorated with women's scalps.

COMMENTARY: Luis Buñuel (1900–1983) was one of the truly unique, independent and iconoclastic filmmakers, whose influence and importance stretched over a period of fifty years. He was a veritable "enfant terrible" of cinema, thanks to his first two surrealistic films, *Un Chien Andalou/An Andalusian Dog* (1928) and *L'Age d'Or*. Spanish-born—he was once included with Pablo Casals and Pablo Picasso among "the three living Spanish giants"—Buñuel came to Paris in the mid-Twenties and became infatuated with cinema and with surrealism. He worked as an assistant to Jean Epstein before making *Un Chien Andalou* with his collaborator Salvador Dali. Aside from *Las Hurdes/Land without Bread* (1932), Buñuel directed nothing of importance until 1950 and *Los Olvidados/The Young and the Damned;* it was followed by *Nazarín* (1958), *Viridiana* (1961), *El Angel Exterminador/The Exterminating Angel* (1962), *Le Journal d'une Femme de Chambre/Diary of a Chambermaid* (1964), and *Le Charme Discret de la Bourgeoisie/The Discreet Charm of the Bourgeoisie* (1972), among others.

Although it does not have the same shock appeal as *Un Chien Andalou*, which opens with the famous shot of a woman's eye being slit with a razor, *L'Age d'Or* is generally considered the greatest work of surrealist filmmaking. It is certainly the first surrealist feature and, arguably, the last from a purist, unadulterated viewpoint. Unlike Cocteau's *Blood of a Poet*, it has stood the test of time fairly well, and is considerably easier to understand. Buñuel leaves the viewer in little doubt as to who the villains of his world are: the Catholic Church in particular and religion in general, and the bourgeoisie, as represented by established forms of government. The heroic theme of *L'Age d'Or* is "free love," that old bête noire of anti-Communist agitators in America of the late 'teens and early Twenties.

L'Age d'Or, like *The Blood of a Poet*, was financed by the Vicomte de Noailles, and filmed, in one month, at the Billancourt-Epinay Studios. The film received its premiere at Studio 28 in Paris, the site, shortly thereafter, of a violent demonstration staged by the League of Patriots and the Anti-Semitic League, who threw stink bombs and destroyed paintings by Dali, Max Ernst and Man Ray. The controversy over *L'Age d'Or* followed Buñuel and hurt him, in a curious way, years later when he was working, in a minor position, at The Museum of Modern Art. Salvador Dali publicly discussed Buñuel's involvement with the film, and word reached the ears of the Rockefeller hierarchy, who were not happy to learn of Communists in their midst. In November of 1942, Buñuel was forced to leave the Museum, and never forgave Dali, whose contribution to *L'Age d'Or* he later dismissed as minor.

Although *L'Age d'Or* had been seen at private screenings and in 1961 at George Eastman House (in Rochester, N.Y.), the film was never publicly shown in the United States until the 1964 New York Film Festival, when it was teamed with Buñuel's latest feature, *Diary of a Chambermaid*. "At this late date," wrote Eugene Archer, in *The New York Times* (September 22, 1964), "the film's outstanding quality is not its defiance of traditional mores but its wit, which is savage, scabrous and frequently hilarious."

The film eventually gained an American commercial release in 1980. It broke the house record at the Roxie Theatre in San Francisco, and, in London, at the 240-seat ICA Cinema, grossed a record $7,340 in its opening four days. David Denby, in *New York* (May 5, 1980), hailed *L'Age d'Or* as "a great nasty high—perhaps the most entertaining avant-garde experiment in movie history."

ABOVE: The archbishops become skeletons. RIGHT: The girl (Lya Lys) sucks the phallic toe of the statue.

20

ABOVE: The man (Gaston Modot) in the girl's bedroom; he is about to discard a wooden plough. RIGHT: The final shot of a snow-covered cross, decorated with women's scalps.

LE MILLION

Producer: Tobis. *Released:* 1931, Tobis (France); 1931, American Tobis (U.S.). *Running Time:* 89 minutes (France); 80 minutes (U.S.).

Director: René Clair. *Screenplay:* René Clair (based on the play by Georges Berr and Marcel Guillemaud). *Photography:* Georges Périnal. *Art Director:* Lazare Meerson. *Costumes:* Georges K. Benda. *Music:* Armand Bernard, Philippe Parès and Georges van Parys. *Film Editor:* René Le Hénaff. *Sound:* Hermann Storr.

CAST: Annabella (*Béatrice*); René Lefèvre (*Michel*); Vanda Gréville (*Vanda*); Paul Olivier (*Crochard, aka Père-la-Tulipe*); Louis Allibert (*Prosper Bénévant*); Constantin Stroesco (*Sopranelli*); Odette Talazac (*Mme. Ravellina*); Pitouto (*stage manager*); Raymond Cordy (*taxi driver*); Jane Pierson (*grocer*); André Michaud (*butcher*); Armand Bernard (*conductor*).

SYNOPSIS: An impoverished artist, Michel, learns that his lottery ticket, one of two purchased by him and his friend Prosper, is the winning ticket. He had left the ticket in the pocket of an old jacket, which his girl friend Béatrice was mending, but she has given the coat to a criminal named Père-la-Tulipe. As Prosper and Michel set out, separately, to find the jacket, it is learned that the jacket has been purchased by a famous operatic tenor, Sopranelli. Michel is mistakenly arrested for Père-la-Tulipe, while Prosper heads for the opera, where Béatrice is a dancer, and where Michel also goes after his release. Vanda, a former girlfriend of Michel, is there, now working with Prosper, as are Père-la-Tulipe and his gang. A soccer game-cum-fight breaks out on stage as each character tries to grab the jacket. Michel and Béatrice are finally given the jacket by Père-la-Tulipe, but when they arrive home they discover the ticket is missing; Père-la-Tulipe has it and had not handed it over earlier because Béatrice had expressed an interest in the jacket only. The story is told in flashback and ends as it began—with a joyful party.

COMMENTARY: In *The Italian Straw Hat* it was a hat, in *Le Million* it is a lottery ticket. In both films, René Clair creates wild and hilarious chase sequences, unsurpassed for their inventiveness and sophistication, with *Le Million* having the edge on the earlier film thanks to the brilliance of the opera sequence, climaxing with the players turning the stage into a soccer field as they run, scrimmage and tackle for the coat supposedly containing the missing ticket. With *Le Million*, the René Clair characters have become even further removed from reality; they behave exactly as if they were participants in a musical comedy. The fantasy is further aided by Clair's use of sound, with the players continually and unexpectedly bursting into song. Lewis Jacobs, in the February 1936 issue of *New Theatre*, wrote that René Clair "juggles sound with the same dexterity as images and relates both to a rhythmic continuity which emerges as an integrated and complete sound-image unity, each dependent upon the other for life and meaning," and stated that Clair had only one equal in that respect: Walt Disney. Up to a point, Jacobs was correct, but certainly there were other directors in the States eager to experiment with Clair's "tricks," notably Frank Tuttle with *This Is the Night* and Rouben Mamoulian with *Love Me Tonight*, both released a year after *Le Million*, and both bringing a new sophistication to the medium of film musicals.

Love Me Tonight opens with the camera roaming through an awakening Paris; *Le Million* has the camera exploring the rooftops of Paris as it goes to bed—at midnight. The sets created by art director Lazare Meerson at the Tobis Studios at Epinay-sur-Seine have a sense of reality that is in direct contrast to the story and the actions of the players. In this sense, René Clair is creating very much his own, personal view of Paris; his sets illustrate his love for the city that *is*, while the story tells of the gaiety and fantasy of the Paris that Clair feels in his heart.

Sous les Toits de Paris, Le Million and *Quatorze Juillet* represent—as Gavin Lambert has suggested in *Sequence* (Winter 1948/49)—a trilogy of Parisian life. "They take us," wrote Lambert, "into the heart of the world of Clair. In each, a pair of young lovers are the central figures, and their vicissitudes, misunderstandings and ultimate reconciliations set the slender moving pattern of the film; round them is composed an exquisitely romanticised picture of lower middle-class life." The three films illustrate Clair's coming to terms with the sound motion picture. "Sound is the death of film," René Clair had initially announced, but for Clair it breathed new life into his work. In those few early years of the Thirties, René Clair created a comedic fantasy world that thrived on the use of sound for effect; he utilized the new medium not to maintain it as an insular affair but rather to transform the motion picture once again into an international art form. In so doing, he became an internationally renowned director, and, to a certain extent, lost much of the potency demonstrated by those early talkies. The techniques might be similar, but in his later American films, such as *It Happened Tomorrow* (1944), Clair became Americanized and the internationality was gone, to be recaptured again only after his return to France in the late Forties.

You had to be American to appreciate Clair's American films, but as *Photoplay* (August 1931) commented, "You don't have to be French to get all the fun and flavor out of this French musical farce [*Le Million*]." In *The New York Times* (May 21, 1931), Mordaunt Hall hailed *Le Million* as "a scintillating entertainment," adding, "It is a combination of farce, burlesque, travesty and satire, all of which is sharpened with keen wit."

ABOVE: The tradespeople celebrate the good fortune of Michel (René Lefèvre). BELOW: Michel and Vanda (Vanda Gréville) in his studio.

ABOVE: Michel (René Lefèvre) and Béatrice (Annabella) unhappy after a lover's quarrel. BELOW: The chase gets rough.

THE "MARIUS" TRILOGY

MARIUS

Producer: Marcel Pagnol, for Paramount Joinville. *Released:* 1931, Paramount (France); 1933, Paramount (U.S.). *Running Time:* 125 minutes (France); 103 minutes (U.S.).

Director: Alexander Korda. *Screenplay:* Marcel Pagnol (based on his own play). *Photography:* Ted Pahle. *Music:* Francis Gromon. *Film Editor:* Roger Spiri-Mercanton.

CAST: Raimu (*César Olivier, also "Fanny" and "César"*); Pierre Fresnay (*Marius, also "Fanny" and "César"*); Orane Demazis (*Fanny, also "Fanny" and "César"*); Fernand Charpin (*Honoré Panisse, also "Fanny" and "César"*); Alida Rouffe (*Honorine Cabanis, also "Fanny" and "César"*); Robert Vattier (*M. Brun, also "Fanny" and "César"*); Paul Dullac (*Félix Escartefigue, also "César"*); Alexandre Mihalesco (*Piquoiseau*); Edouard Delmont (*the second mate*); Maupi (*the stoker*).

FANNY

Producer: Marcel Pagnol, for Braunberger-Richebé. *Released:* 1932, Marcel Pagnol (France); 1948, Siritzky International (U.S.). *Running Time:* 142 minutes (France); 125 minutes (U.S.).

Director: Marc Allégret. *Screenplay:* Marcel Pagnol (based on his own play). *Photography:* Nicolas Toporkoff, André Dantan, Roger Hubert, Georges Benoit and Coutelen. *Music:* Vincent Scotto. *Film Editor:* Raymond Lamy.

CAST: Auguste Mouriès (*Félix Escartefigue*); Milly Mathis (*Claudine Foulon, also "César"*); Maupi (*the chauffeur, also "César"*); Edouard Delmont (*Dr. Félicien Venelle, also "César"*).

CÉSAR

Producer: Marcel Pagnol. *Released:* 1936, Marcel Pagnol (France); 1949, Siritzky International (U.S.). *Running Time:* 170 minutes (France); 120 minutes (U.S.).

Director: Marcel Pagnol. *Screenplay:* Marcel Pagnol. *Photography:* Willy. *Music:* Vincent Scotto. *Film Editors:* Suzanne de Troeye and Jeanette Ginestet.

CAST: André Fouché (*Césariot*); Doumel (*Fernand*); Thommeray (*The Priest*); Robert Bassac (*Pierre Dromard*).

SYNOPSES: *Marius:* Working in a Marseilles bar and yearning to go to sea, Marius irritates his father César with his lack of spirit, and is in love with Fanny, who is, in turn, loved by Panisse, a middle-aged widower. After some months of lovemaking, unrevealed to either César or Fanny's mother, Honorine, Marius is told by Piquoiseau that a berth is available on the ship *Malaise*, and that only Fanny is holding him back. When Honorine discovers Marius and Fanny in bed together, she rushes to César, who urges Marius to marry, but Fanny knows that he will be unhappy, pretends that she plans to marry Panisse and watches sadly as an angry Marius sails off.

Fanny: The film begins where *Marius* leaves off, with César hurt at his son's departure and Fanny being asked to marry Panisse, which she does, upon discovering her pregnancy, despite a desire to wait for Marius' return. César initially believes that Fanny is marrying Panisse for his money, but eventually learns the truth, as does Panisse, who is not concerned that the son will not be his (and even agrees to name him César-Marius Panisse). A year after the marriage, Marius returns on a visit; he and Fanny realize their continuing love for each other, and Marius demands the return of his son. However, Fanny tells him that the son is not ethically his, despite her love, and César orders his son out of the house.

César: Marius' son, Césariot, is now eighteen and, after Panisse's death, Fanny tells him of his natural father, whom Césariot goes to visit at the garage in Toulon where Marius works. Disliking the young man, the owner, Fernand, pretends that Marius is involved in opium smuggling, which outrages Césariot, until he later learns the truth. He and Marius have a confrontation with Fanny and César, during which various accusations are made by all parties. Césariot goes off to perform his military service, Marius opens a marine motor business near Marseilles, and is eventually able to overcome his concern that he would be marrying Fanny for Panisse's money. César is happy that Marius and Fanny are reunited at last.

COMMENTARY: In its obituary on Marcel Pagnol (1895-1974), *The Times* of London (April 19, 1974) observed that "Pagnol was always a man of Marseilles and the South—many of his stars, among them Raimu and Fernandel, came originally from the Marseilles music-hall—and in his films, derived from this rich background, he created something of lasting value." A noted playwright, Pagnol's greatest screen achievements are *The Baker's Wife* and the "Marius" trilogy (sometimes known as the Marseilles trilogy), consisting of *Marius*, *Fanny* and *César*. Despite Pagnol's only directing the last, all are very much his personal work—he wrote and produced all three—and all are set in the Marseilles that he loved.

Pagnol's films are rich in characterizations, in studies of the friendly folk to be found in César's bar. The Marius trilogy is very much a series relying on great actors to give great performances, and Pagnol was lucky in that he took the actors who had originally appeared in the 1929 stage production of *Marius* (an even bigger success than Pagnol's earlier *Topaze*). These actors were, without exception, able to adapt to the new medium.

Following the stage and screen success of *Marius*, Pagnol wrote a second stage play in 1931, *Fanny*, which formed the basis for the second feature. The third, *César*, was written for the screen. The first film was shot, at a reported budget of $80,000, at Paramount's Joinville Studios in French, German and Swedish-language versions. *Fanny* was filmed at the Billancourt Studios and on location in Marseilles. *César*, like *Fanny*, was produced by Pagnol's own company, and this time at the director's own studio in Marseilles. (If there are any major faults to be found in the three films, it is that *César* spends too much of the time recapping what has happened in the earlier productions. As a trilogy, the features are somewhat unique in being both self-contained in their own right and with their working as a collective whole—indeed *Fanny* follows on immediately with the story from *Marius*.)

ABOVE: *Marius:* Fanny and Marius (Orane Demazis and Pierre Fresnay). BELOW: *Fanny:* Panisse (Fernand Charpin) announces that Fanny has given birth to a boy. César (Raimu) is at the right.

RIGHT: *César:* Raimu in the title role. BELOW: *César:* Césariot (André Fouché), right, sails off to find his father.

ZERO FOR CONDUCT
ZÉRO DE CONDUITE

Producer: Jacques-Louis Nounez. *Released:* 1945, Gaumont (France); 1947, Cine Classics in Association with French Ideal Films (U.S.). *Running Time:* 47 minutes.

Director: Jean Vigo. *Screenplay:* Jean Vigo. *Photography:* Boris Kaufman. *Music:* Maurice Jaubert. *Film Editor:* Jean Vigo.

CAST: Louis Lefebvre (*Caussat*); Gilbert Pruchon (*Colin*); Gérard de Bédarieux (*Tabard*); Constantin Goldstein-Kehler (*Bruel*); Jean Dasté (*Huguet*); Robert Le Flon (*M. Parrain*); Delphin (*the principal*); Du Verron (*the assistant principal*); Léon Larive (*the chemistry master*); Henri Storck (*the priest*); Louis de Gonzague-Frick (*the police commissioner*); Michèle Fayard (*the daughter*).

SYNOPSIS: Two boys return, by train, to their boarding school. As tension builds and the adults are seen as the children perceive them, the audience is introduced to the dormitory, the playground, the Sunday walk in the town, a science lesson with a skeleton, and the various masters at the school. A revolt in the dormitory leads to a pillow fight and a teacher being tied to his bed, which is then raised rather like a crucifix. The skull and crossbones are raised on the roof of the school, from where the leaders of the revolt bombard visiting dignitaries with tiles and chamber pots.

COMMENTARY: Jean Vigo (1883-1939) holds a unique position in the history of the cinema. He made only four films, only one of them feature-length, and yet three of those productions—*A Propos de Nice* (1930), *Zéro de Conduite* and *L'Atalante* (1934)—are major, original works, while the remaining film, *Taris* (1931), is not lacking in interest. Vigo's films have suffered more than most from cutting and re-editing, and certainly, it has taken many years for them to gain in appreciation; *Zéro de Conduite* was not released in the United States until some eight years after its maker's death. Despite his small output, Vigo has been the subject of two book-length studies in English, not to mention at least three volumes in French. His films are surprisingly dissimilar, borrowing—as John M. Smith has noted—from the French, American and Soviet cinemas, and—as William G. Simon has written—"the diversity in their conception and structural principles is almost unprecedented in film history."

Simon writes: "*Zéro de Conduite* is Vigo's masterpiece, his most original contribution to film art. It is his first narrative film in the most basic sense of being the first film in which he was involved with telling a story." It followed *A Propos de Nice* and *Taris*, and was based on a script by Vigo, titled *Les Cancres*, which had its origins in the director's schooldays. Producer Jacques-Louis Nounez arranged for financing, and the film was shot between December 24, 1932 and January 22, 1933 on location at Saint-Cloud and at the G-F-F-A Studio, located at Buttes-Chaumont. *Zéro de Conduite* was completed and ready for its first private screening by April of 1933.

The film was promptly banned by the French censor, and was not shown in France publicly until 1945. In a speech, delivered in Belgium, on October 17, 1933, Vigo joked, "'You know,' they told me, smacking their lips, 'we love it so much we can't bear the idea of anyone else seeing it.' What touching possessiveness! You must admit it would be wrong for me to complain. All I can hold against them is that they are being a trifle selfish, however excellent their judgement."

The censor was concerned that *Zéro de Conduite* was a vicious attack on the French educational system, and certainly it is as much of an attack as *If*... is an attack on the British public school system. Vigo's anarchist background is very apparent in the production, as he presents what can best be described as a child's view of authority. But it is also a surrealistic work, blending fantasy and reality. The film reaches its zenith with the pillow fight in the dormitory, filmed in slow motion, a triumph of youthful fantasy over adult reality.

The children of *Zéro de Conduite* are basically uninteresting. It is the adults who capture the imagination: the grotesque midget of a principal running the school along military lines; the kindly master who impersonates Chaplin in the classroom. The adults are caricatures, but with an alarming closeness to reality. There is little question as to where Vigo's sympathies lie—his schoolboys are the heroes of the piece (unlike, say, Lindsay Anderson's public schoolboys in *If*..., who do not automatically gain the continuing respect of the viewer).

The atmospheric effects of Vigo's cinematography and staging are enhanced by Maurice Jaubert's score. In the July 1936 issue of *World Film News,* Jaubert recalled, "I had to write music to a procession of small boys by night, the occasion being a dormitory rebellion. The sequence in itself was highly fantastic and shot in slow motion. In order to follow out this atmosphere of unreality, I recorded my music and then reversed the sound track. The effect of running it backwards was to retain the broad outline of the melody, but as each single note was heard backwards an atmosphere of strangeness was achieved."

When *Zéro de Conduite* first opened in England—at the Everyman Theatre, Hampstead—in 1936, it was greeted with caustic sarcasm by most critics. In *The Observer*, C. A. Lejeune made the famous comment, "Nought for direction. Nought for acting. Nought for story. Nought for continuity. Five for trying." Her review brought an immediate agonized response from Alberto Cavalcanti, Maurice Jaubert and John Grierson, who called it "the silliest and most irresponsible criticism that has disgraced our film columns these many months." When the film eventually opened in the United States in 1947, reviewers were considerably kinder, but nonetheless critical. "A. W.," in *The New York Times* (June 23, 1947), thought the film, along with *L'Atalante*, "examples of avant garde pictures which have now become passé." *The Hollywood Reporter* (October 3, 1947) wrote, "Vigo, called a genius by some, has been said to have been much ahead of his time. Judging from *Zero for Conduct*, he still is." It was not until a major reissue of *Zéro de Conduite* by Brandon Films in 1962 that Vigo and his film at last gained major critical recognition in this country.

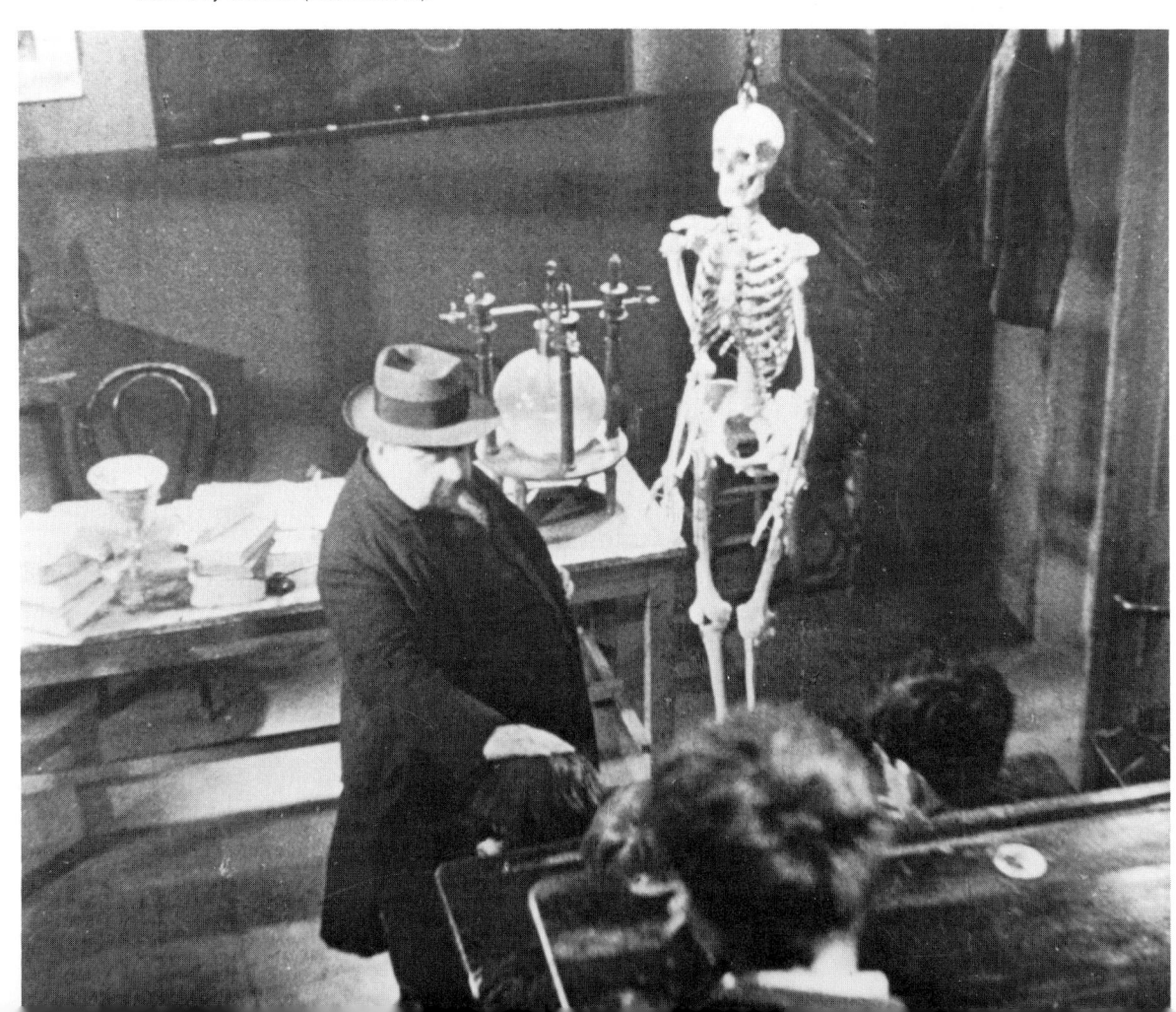

ABOVE: The two boys (Constantin Goldstein-Kehler and Louis Lefebvre) return to school. BELOW: The chemistry teacher (Léon Larive).

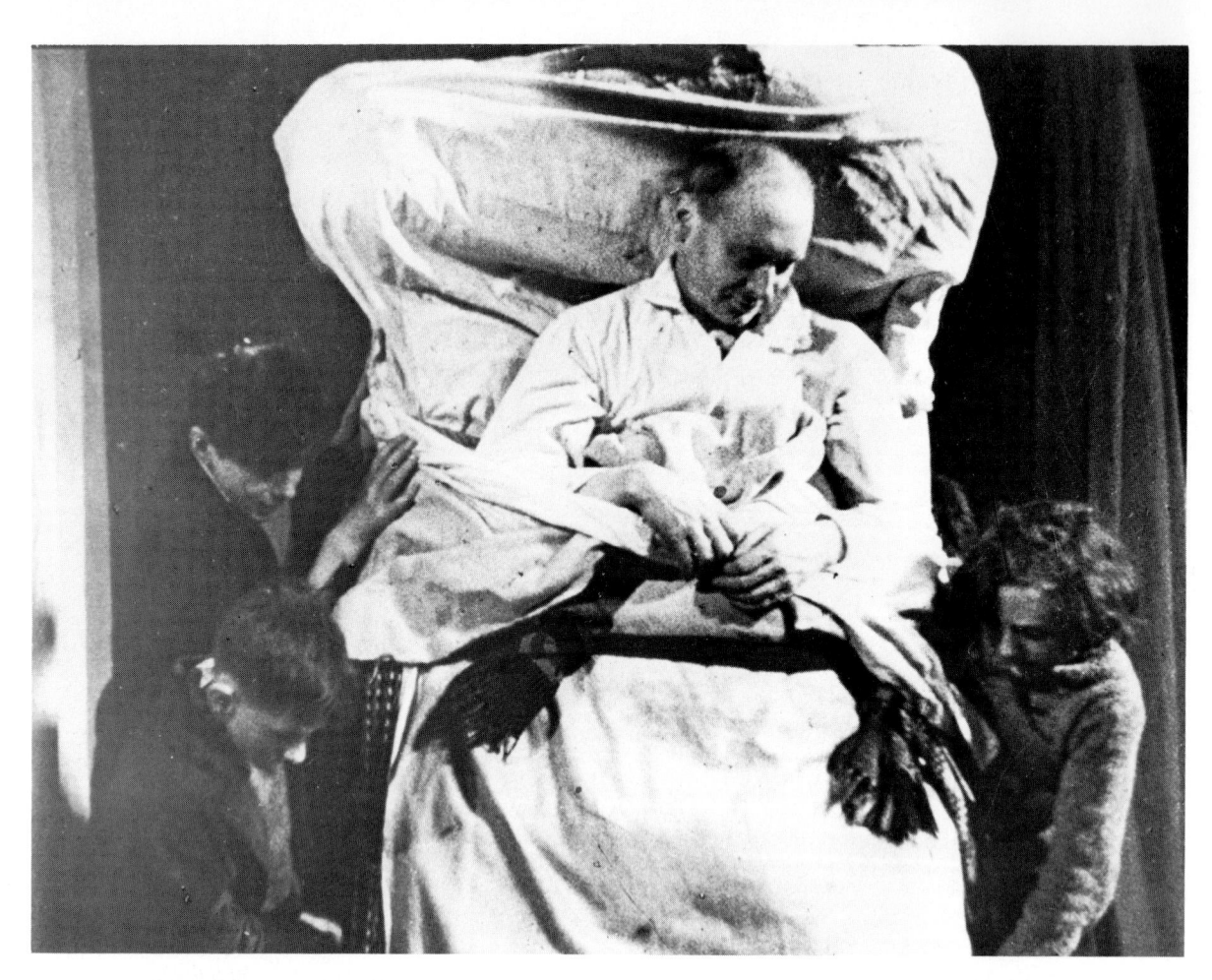

ABOVE: The revolution in the dormitory. BELOW: Commemoration Day; Delphin is the bearded principal at far left.

30

CARNIVAL IN FLANDERS
LA KERMESSE HÉROÏQUE

Producer: Films Sonores Tobis. *Released:* 1935, Tobis (France); 1936, American Tobis (U.S.). *Running Time:* 115 minutes (France); 95 minutes (U.S.).

Director: Jacques Feyder. *Screenplay:* Charles Spaak and Jacques Feyder (based on a story by Charles Spaak). *Dialogue:* Bernard Zimmer. *Photography:* Harry Stradling. *Music:* Louis Beydts. *Art Director:* Lazare Meerson. *Costumes:* G. K. Benda. *Film Editor:* Jacques Brillouin. *Sound:* Herman Storr.

CAST: Françoise Rosay (*the burgomaster's wife*); Jean Murat (*the Duke*); André Alerme (*the burgomaster*); Louis Jouvet (*the priest*); Lyne Clévers (*the fishwife*); Micheline Cheirel (*Siska*); Maryse Wendling (*the baker's wife*); Ginette Gaubert (*the innkeeper's wife*); Marguerite Ducouret (*the brewer's wife*); Bernard Lancret (*Breughel*); Alfred Adam (*the butcher*); Pierre Labry (*the innkeeper*); Arthur Devère (*the fishmonger*); Marcel Carpentier (*the baker*); Alexandre d'Arcy (*the captain*); Delphin (*the dwarf*).

SYNOPSIS: It is 1616 in the Flemish town of Boom. As the burgomaster and his council pose for an official portrait and the burgomaster rejects the request of the painter, Breughel, for his daughter Siska's hand in marriage (in favor of the butcher's request), there comes word that a troop of Spanish soldiers are approaching the town. The burgomaster hatches a scheme whereby he will pretend to be dead and the Spaniards will not harm the town or its people out of sympathy for the bereaved. However, the burgomaster's wife takes matters into her own hands. She leads the women of the town to greet the Spanish Duke and his troops and all the women strive to make the Spaniards feel comfortable. The Duke is not taken in by the burgomaster's deception, but he enjoys his visit with the burgomaster's wife, and agrees to command Siska to marry Breughel, as she wishes. In the morning the Spaniards depart, and the burgomaster's wife reads a proclamation freeing the town from taxes for a year; she also gives her husband full credit for the town's being spared.

COMMENTARY: *Carnival in Flanders* is surely one of the most ambitious French features of the Thirties, with its stunning recreation of a Flemish town, at the Epinay-sur-Seine Studios, its superb ensemble playing and the camerawork of British-born and American-trained cinematographer Harry Stradling (who also photographed Feyder's *Knight Without Armour*). It is lighthearted, even foolish, and yet *Carnival in Flanders* impresses as a brilliant piece of filmmaking, with the director apparently recreating, without fault, the look, costumes and makeup of seventeenth-century Flanders. "Its qualities are all of one piece," wrote Otis Ferguson in *The New Republic* (October 14, 1936), "it is almost a comfortable thing."

Here is a true feminist comedy-drama. Admittedly the women use feminine guiles to win the day, but in so doing they put one over on the men not only of their own Flemish town but also of Spain. The screenplay of Charles Spaak and Jacques Feyder is very subtle in its presenting the men, in the early scenes, as self-important and superior, organizing the town's annual carnival, while the women take care of their homes and children. With the threat of a Spanish "invasion," the men become unimportant cowards, and the women, led by the burgomaster's wife, take charge. "Do we not already rule our homes and our children?" she asks, adding that to rule men is a lot easier. Finally, after she has delivered the Duke's edict concerning a year's exemption from taxes, the wife steps into the background, urging the burgomaster to move into the foreground, once again taking his rightful position in the community. All would appear to have returned to male-dominated normality, but one senses from his wife's fingering of the pearls, given to her by the Duke, that she might once again step into the forefront of civil matters.

The dominant figure in *Carnival in Flanders* is Françoise Rosay (1891-1974), Jacques Feyder's wife and his leading lady in many films, who enjoyed a brief career in British films of the Forties and American features of the Fifties and Sixties. As James Shelley Hamilton wrote, in *The National Board of Review Magazine* (November 1936), here is "a hearty and illuminating piece of acting, masterly in an astonishing mass of detail that sums up into a complete, living portrait." Françoise Rosay was also starred in the German-language version, *Die klugen Frauen*, shot simultaneously. One can only ponder why the producers decided against making a simultaneous English-language version, for here is a film that obviously has universal appeal, and could have been an even greater success in the United States and British Empire with an English-language soundtrack.

As a result of his work on *Carnival in Flanders*, Jacques Feyder (1885-1948) was invited to England to film *Knight Without Armour* (1937), featuring Marlene Dietrich and Robert Donat. He had commenced his directorial career in France in the mid-'teens, and also enjoyed a brief Hollywood career, which included Garbo's last silent film, *The Kiss* (1929), a couple of Ramon Novarro vehicles, *Daybreak* and *Son of India* (both 1931), and the German-language version of Garbo's first talkie, *Anna Christie* (1930). He directed his last film, *Une Femme Disparaît/Portrait of a Woman*, starring Françoise Rosay, in Switzerland in 1941. *World Film News* (March 1937) wrote of him: "Feyder is a tall man, a trifle scholarly in appearance, with charming manners, and, like many notable film directors, an air of distinction. But he possesses a quality which many notable filmmakers seem to lack. That is enthusiasm. An honest, thoroughly temperamental enthusiasm, which he expresses, according to caprice, in either English or French. At the same time, he has a sense of humour. Not that sort of slightly overrated 'sense of humour,' which often has to compensate for uninspired creation, but one that evidently permeates his whole philosophy."

Carnival in Flanders was the opening film, on September 22, 1936, at New York's Filmarte Theatre, formerly the John Golden. The critics were almost unanimous in their praise; the one negative comment came from Meyer Levin, who wrote, in *Esquire* (January 1937), "It's just a drawn-out gag about the men of painter Breughel's time, wearing bloomers." Drawn-out gag or not, *Carnival in Flanders* is still mildly sexy, still witty, and certainly great fun—"a gallery of famous Flemish pictures comes to life for your pleasure," as the foreword to the original U.S release proclaimed.

ABOVE: The burgomaster's wife (Françoise Rosay) welcomes the Duke (Jean Murat) to her town, as the priest (Louis Jouvet) looks on. At far right is Delphin, who was the school principal in *Zero for Conduct*. LEFT: Bernard Lancret and Micheline Cheirel as the two young lovers, Breughel and Siska.

ABOVE: The fishmonger and his wife (Arthur Devère and Lyne Clévers). BELOW: The Spaniards and the women of the town enjoy a party at the inn.

A DAY IN THE COUNTRY
UNE PARTIE DE CAMPAGNE

Producer: Pierre Braunberger for Panthéon. *Released:* 1946, Films de la Pléïade (France); 1951, Joseph Burstyn (U.S.). In both releases, *A Day in the Country* formed a portion of a three-part feature, known in the United States as *Ways of Love. Running Time:* 37 minutes.

Director: Jean Renoir. *Screenplay:* Jean Renoir (based on a short story by Guy de Maupassant). *Photography:* Claude Renoir and Jean Bourgoin. *Music:* Joseph Kosma. *Film Editors:* Marguerite Renoir and Marinette Cadix. *Sound:* Joseph de Bretagne.

CAST: Sylvia Bataille (*Henriette Dufour*); Georges Saint-Saëns/Georges Darnoux (*Henri*); Jacques Borel/Jacques Brunius (*Rodolphe*); Jeanne Marken (*Mme. Dufour*); André Gabriello (*M. Dufour*); Paul Temps (*Anatole*); Gabrielle Fontan (*Grandmother Dufour*); Jean Renoir (*Poulain*); Marguerite Renoir (*servant*); Pierre Lestringuez (*priest*); Henri Cartier-Bresson (*seminary student*); Alain Renoir (*little boy fishing*).

SYNOPSIS: The period is presumably the 1890s, and Henriette Dufour, her father, mother, grandmother and her fiancé Anatole, out on an excursion from Paris on a warm summer's day, stop for a picnic lunch at an inn run by Monsieur Poulain. Henriette and her mother attract the attention of two young men, Henri and Rodolphe, and while Anatole and the father lazily fish, they are taken by the men for a boat ride. The pair happily argue as to which shall accompany Henriette, and Henri (who is not particularly interested in the "adventure") is the winner. He and Henriette leave the boat, walk to a clearing and the implication is that they make love. The years pass and Henriette and Anatole are married. On another summer's day, Henri sees the two at the same spot; briefly he and Henriette meet and she tells him that the one moment of happiness she has known was with him that day in the country.

COMMENTARY: *A Day in the Country* has had a checkered history. "I had undertaken to make a film of Maupassant's short story, 'Une Partie de Campagne,'" wrote Jean Renoir in his autobiography. "It was intended to be a 'short,' and in fact ran for fifty minutes. But the theme is so important that it could very well have been a full-length film. A tale of disappointed love, followed by a ruined life, could furnish matter for a long novel. But Maupassant gives us the essentials in a few pages, and it was the transposition to the screen of these bare bones of a big story that attracted me."

The film is very much Renoir's personal *hommage* to his father, painter Pierre-Auguste Renoir, and the filmmaker decided to shoot his story near the village of Marlotte, where his father had worked and where the young Renoir had also filmed *La Fille de l'Eau*, his first production, in the summer of 1924. Shooting was expected to take no more than a week, but because of an unseasonably wet summer filming continued into the fall. Finally, Renoir had no alternative but to call a halt to the project in order to commence work on his next feature-length film, *Les Bas-Fonds/The Lower Depths*. Producer Pierre Braunberger liked the footage that Renoir had shot, suggested turning *A Day in the Country* into a feature, and commissioned Jacques Prévert to write a screenplay. However, the Second World War temporarily halted future consideration of the project, and it was not until the cessation of hostilities that film editor Marguerite Renoir was able to re-edit the footage, Joseph Kosma was able to compose a score, some explanatory titles were added to cover missing scenes, and *A Day in the Country* was eventually released in France in 1946, some ten years after its initial production.

A Day in the Country did not receive an American release until 1951, and then as part of a trilogy, *Ways of Love*, which also included Marcel Pagnol's *Jofroi* and Roberto Rossellini's *The Miracle*. Because of the controversy over the last film, particularly its condemnation by the American Catholic Church and its banning in various locations, the critics did not pay too much attention to *A Day in the Country*. In *The New Yorker* (December 16, 1950), John McCarten found *A Day in the Country* "perhaps a trifle too long .. but the genial spoofing of the Parisian bourgeoisie is entertaining indeed." In *The Saturday Review* (January 27, 1951), Hollis Alpert wrote, "Renoir in this is by and large the craftsman who whatever his material understands it thoroughly. It is a Sunday afternoon in the country that he wishes to describe; and it is a day that has, sadly, some consequences. But he does not mean for you to shed more than a small tear." Bosley Crowther commented, in *The New York Times* (December 13, 1950), "Using assorted definitions of that multi-meaningful word to introduce each item, the assembler has opened the film with Renoir's *A Day in the Country* by Guy de Maupassant. This is a bitter-sweet vignette, playful and humorous yet passing sad, of love in its most elementary, romantic, persistent and popular respect." *Ways of Love* was selected by the New York Film Critics as the Best Foreign Film of 1950.

A Day in the Country is the most deceptively simple of all Jean Renoir's films, and it succeeds thanks to its simplicity and to the natural charm of its visual imagery. It evokes another era, an era where sorrow and joy were less subtly mingled; it brings forth remembrances of warm summer days, of picnics, fishing, boating on the river and youthful love affairs. It is charming, comical and sad. The players are young and attractive, as well as callow and ludicrous. Most ludicrous of all is Henriette's fiancé, Anatole, who looks like Stan Laurel with long hair.

One of the most impressive moments in the film occurs shortly after Henri and Rodolphe have been sitting at a table in the inn, denigrating the Dufour family as Parisian shopkeepers. They open up the shutters at the window, flooding the room with sunlight and with the image of Henriette and her mother on the swings outside. As Henriette swings, so does the camera, capturing for the viewer the girl's exuberant joy at her release from the confines of the city.

That a film as short and as simple as *A Day in the Country* can be considered a great work is a unique tribute to the artistry of Jean Renoir, and, indirectly, to a man's love for his father. For certainly it is no overstatement to describe *A Day in the Country* as a Renoir painting brought to life, a canvas by Renoir Senior recreated on film by Renoir Junior.

34

The inn in whose environs *A Day in the Country* is set.

A happy and carefree Henriette (Sylvia Bataille) on the swing.

ABOVE: Rodolphe and Madame Dufour (Jacques Brunius and Jeanne Marken). BELOW: The film's sad finale with Henriette and Anatole (Sylvia Bataille and Paul Temps).

GRAND ILLUSION
LA GRANDE ILLUSION

Producer: Frank Rollmer and Albert Pinkovitch for Les Réalisations d'Art Cinématographique. *Released:* 1937, R.A.C. (France); 1939, World Wide Pictures (U.S.). *Running Time:* 114 minutes (France); 95 minutes (U.S.).

Director: Jean Renoir. *Screenplay:* Charles Spaak and Jean Renoir. *Photography:* Christian Matras. *Set Designer:* Eugène Lourié. *Technical Advisor:* Carl Koch. *Music:* Joseph Kosma. *Film Editors:* Marguerite Renoir and Marthe Huguet. *Sound:* Joseph de Bretagne.

CAST: Jean Gabin (*Maréchal*); Pierre Fresnay (*De Bœldieu*); Erich von Stroheim (*von Rauffenstein*); Marcel Dalio (*Rosenthal*); Dita Parlo (*Elsa*); Julien Carette (*the actor*); Gaston Modot (*the engineer*); Jean Dasté (*the teacher*); Georges Péclet (*a French soldier*); Jacques Becker (*an English officer*).

SYNOPSIS: Shot down behind German lines, Lieutenant Maréchal and Captain De Bœldieu are invited to dine with their captor, Captain von Rauffenstein, before they are taken to a prisoner-of-war camp. At the camp (Hallbach) the two men are housed in the officers' quarters, along with an engineer, an actor, a teacher and a wealthy Jew, Rosenthal. The group digs a tunnel in an escape attempt and also presents a show for the camp commandant and his officers, which is interrupted by Maréchal announcing that the fortress of Douaumont, recently captured by the Germans, has been recaptured by the French. After a spell in solitary confinement, Maréchal returns when the escape tunnel is completed, but just before the group plans its escape, they are transferred to another camp. Months later, Maréchal, De Bœldieu and Rosenthal are reunited at Wintersborn, a fortress commanded by von Rauffenstein, removed from active combat, who develops a friendship with De Bœldieu out of a feeling that their social class is doomed. During a roll call, De Bœldieu is not present, is chased by the guards while he plays a flute, and is shot by von Rauffenstein after he refuses to return. Bœldieu's antics have covered the escape of Maréchal and Rosenthal, who argue after the latter hurts his ankle. They find shelter in a barn, where they are discovered by Elsa, a German peasant, whose husband and brothers have been killed in the war. She takes care of them, and on Christmas Eve she and Maréchal realize their love for each other. However, the two men must make good their escape, and they leave Elsa for the safety of Switzerland.

COMMENTARY: In his exquisitely written autobiography, *My Life and My Films,* Jean Renoir notes: "The theme of the bringing together of men through their callings and common interests has haunted me all my life." It is a theme crucial to *La Grande Illusion* and present, in a lesser fashion, in all of the films of this master of the French cinema. Jean Renoir (1894-1979) displayed the same warmth and feeling for humanity in his work as can be found in the best films of D. W. Griffith. Not that the two men are in many ways comparable—although Renoir certainly respected Griffith and Griffith admired some of Renoir's films—but both men demonstrated the same concern for the motion picture as a medium for understanding, tolerance if you will, and this is most apparent in their respective masterworks, *Intolerance* and *La Grande Illusion.*

The son of impressionist painter Auguste Renoir, Jean entered the film industry in the early Twenties, making his mark with a 1926 adaptation of Zola's *Nana* starring his first wife, Catherine Hessling. His major films date from the sound era and include *Boudu Sauvé des Eaux/Boudu Saved from Drowning* (1932), *Toni* (1935), *Le Crime de M. Lange/The Crime of Monsieur Lange* (1936), *A Day in the Country, La Marseillaise, La Bête Humaine/The Human Beast* (1938), *The Rules of the Game, Le Caporal Epinglé/The Elusive Corporal* (1962) and *Le Petit Théâtre de Jean Renoir* (1971), as well as his non-French features: *Swamp Water* (1941), *The Southerner* (1945), *Diary of a Chambermaid* (1946), *The River* (1951) and *La Carrozza d'Oro/The Golden Coach* (1953).

The idea for *La Grande Illusion* dated back to 1915 when Renoir met a Major Pinsard, a French flier, and became fascinated with his career and his exploits in escaping from German prisoner of war camps. The screenplay, conceived with Charles Spaak, was drastically changed when Erich von Stroheim was signed to play von Rauffenstein, with his character giving new impetus and meaning to the film. Despite some initial problems with his new star, Renoir appears to have kept von Stroheim under control, and there are none of the melodramatics so typical of the actor's American work.

Renoir shot his film during the winter of 1936-1937 initially on location in Alsace, at the barracks of Colmar and at the Haut-Koenigsberg château (standing in for the Wintersborn fortress). Interiors were filmed at the Billancourt and Eclair Studios.

La Grande Illusion is a model of understated filmmaking. There are only two examples of what might be termed "flashy" cinematography, at the meal in the first prisoner-of-war camp and as the prisoners sing the "Marseillaise" in the makeshift theatre. Otherwise, *La Grande Illusion* offers no irritating or obtrusive samples of screen technique, but rather relies on the heroic quality of the story to involve its audience. Unlike most war dramas, the war never openly intrudes into the story—there are no battle scenes, no moments of bravery and heroism on the front—and the film concerns itself only with the reality of the lives of the prisoners who are the central characters in Renoir's story.

"War is the grand illusion," wrote Frank S. Nugent, in *The New York Times* (September 13, 1938), "and Renoir proceeds with his disillusioning task by studying it, not in the front line, but in the prison camp, where captors and captives alike are condemned to the dry rot of inaction. War is not reality; prison camp is. Only the real may survive it." Perhaps because of this attitude, De Bœldieu does not survive, just as his class was not to survive (although it survived a lot longer than did De Bœldieu, as witness Renoir's *The Rules of the Game*). *La Grande Illusion* is also a drama of escape, literally and figuratively, as each man faces his world and makes a choice, particularly Maréchal, who is forced to choose between the woman he loves (in a romantic sequence thrown in almost as an afterthought) and the freedom that Switzerland can offer. For Rosenthal, the Jew, escape—as later events were to prove—could be only transitory.

Unlike *The Rules of the Game* and its initial critical appraisals, *La Grande Illusion* was immediately recognized as a major contribution to the motion picture. One trade paper, *Motion Picture Herald* (July 3, 1937), declared it to be "one of the best French films ever made." When the film reopened New York's Filmarte Theatre on September 12, 1938, *Variety* (September 14, 1938) hailed it as "an artistically masterful feature."

ABOVE: The French prisoners arrive at Hallbach. De Bœldieu (Pierre Fresnay) is at the left; Maréchal (Jean Gabin), at the right. BELOW: Erich von Stroheim as von Rauffenstein.

ABOVE: Maréchal interrupts the prison show with news of an Allied victory. BELOW: At Wintersborn, the French prisoners practice the whistling that will cover their escape.

THE PEARLS OF THE CROWN
LES PERLES DE LA COURONNE

Producer: Serge Sandberg for Cinéas. *Released:* 1937, Tobis (France); 1938, Lenauer International (U.S.). *Running Time:* 120 minutes (France); 105 minutes (U.S.).

Directors: Sacha Guitry and Christian-Jaque. *Screenplay:* Sacha Guitry. *Photography:* Jules Krüger and Raymond Voinquel. *Music:* Jean Françaix. *Set Designer:* Jean Perrier. *Costumes:* Georges K. Benda. *Film Editor:* William Baroche. Original English version by Stuart Gilbert.

CAST: Jacqueline Delubac (*Françoise Martin, Mary Queen of Scots and Joséphine de Beauharnais*); Sacha Guitry (*Jean Martin, Francis I, Barras and Napoleon III*); Yvette Pienne (*Queen Elizabeth I, Mary Tudor and Queen Victoria*); Lyn Harding (*Henry VIII and the King's officer*); Arletty (*Queen of Ethiopia*); Ermete Zacconi (*Clement VIII*); Simone Renant (*Madame Du Barry*); Enrico Glori (*the Papal Chamberlain*); Barbara Shaw (*Anne Boleyn*); Raimu (*a southerner*); Marguerite Moreno (*Catherine de Médicis and the old Empress Eugénie*); Aimé Simon-Girard (*Henry IV*); Colette Borelli (*Mary Queen of Scots as a child*); Catalano (*Spanelli*); Paulette Elambert (*Catherine de Médicis as a child*); Jean-Louis Barrault (*Bonaparte*); Germaine Aussey (*Gabrielle d'Estrées*); Andrews Engelmann (*James*); Raymonde Allain (*Empress Eugénie*); Emile Drain (*Napoleon I*); Lisette Lanvin (*the playgirl and the young Queen Victoria*); Marcel Dalio (*the Abyssinian*); Cécile Sorel (*the Frenchwoman of the age of Louis XIV*); Robert Seller (*a French prisoner*); Huguette Duflos (*Queen Hortense*); Claude Dauphin (*an Italian prisoner*); Laurence Atkins (*Mme. Tallien and Mme. d'Etampes*); Romuald Joubé (*Clouet*); Pauline Carton (*chambermaid*); Henri Crémieux (*auctioneer*); Damia (*woman of the people*); Jean Coquelin (*old bourgeois*); Marfa Dhervilly (*old courtesan*); Gaston Dubosc (*the Grand Duke*); Rosine Déréan (*the girl and Catherine of Aragon*); Robert Pizani (*Talleyrand*); Craven (*Hans Holbein*); Percy Marmont (*Cardinal Wolsey*).

SYNOPSIS: Sacha Guitry relates the history of seven pearls to his wife, Jacqueline Delubac. Pope Clement VIII has obtained these pearls and presents them to his niece, Catherine de Médicis, when she becomes the wife of the Dauphin of France. Catherine, in turn, gives the pearls to her daughter-in-law, Mary Stuart, but at her death they are stolen. Four are found and sealed in a casket by Queen Elizabeth I of England, and are not rediscovered until three centuries later by Queen Victoria, who adds them to the Royal Crown. Of the remaining pearls, one comes into the hands of an English family, which passes it from one generation to the next, until 1937, when it is gambled away. The second pearl is given by Henry IV of France to his favorite, Gabrielle d'Estrées. It is later owned by Louis XV's favorite, Madame Du Barry, and by Napoleon's first wife, Joséphine de Beauharnais. It disappears when given as a gift to a Madonna by the Empress Eugénie during the First World War. The third pearl is used as "a gift of love," and is lost when dropped from the liner *Normandie* en route to New York.

COMMENTARY: There is no one who epitomizes the sophistication and glamour of the popular French theatre more than Sacha Guitry (1885–1957). From 1905 until his death he dominated the theatre, except for a brief period following the Second World War when he was unfairly accused of collaboration with the Nazis. He made his initial film, *Ceux de Chez Nous*, in 1915, the first of more than twenty features. Guitry was also very much a ladies' man, the ardent lover, whose wives have included Yvonne Printemps and Jacqueline Delubac, who is prominently featured in *The Pearls of the Crown*.

Guitry was very fond of historical subjects for his features and no film gave him more scope than *The Pearls of the Crown*, which he planned as a tribute to the coronation of Britain's George VI, with the pearls of the title referring to the pearls in the British crown jewels. Guitry may well be considered the French Noël Coward, and on the whole, the British enjoyed the film. A. T. Borthwick, in *The News Chronicle*, found it "interesting and unusual." The critic for *The Times* was less impressed: "He sets out not to tell one, two, or even three stories . . . He tells them in three different languages, and ransacks the ages and spoils the climbs in the pursuit. Kings, Queens, Cardinals, and Ministers come and go, are switched on the screen only to disappear before one's eyes with the smoothness and rapidity of soup-plates at the hands of expert waiters, and, at the end, the dazed spectator has the sensation that he has been treated to a reading of *Little Arthur's History* and hustled round the Vatican, Versailles, and the Tower all in a space of an hour and a half, with an incidental trip to Abyssinia to say nothing of a final tour of the Normandie."

Certainly *The Pearls of the Crown* is little more than a series of historical tableaux, but Guitry presents them in a very modern fashion, cutting abruptly from one sequence to the next with a total lack of fades or wipes, so popular at this period. He also tells his story with the participants using the language of their respective countries. British actor Lyn Harding, as Henry VIII, speaks in English, as do the supporting players of the English sections of the story. Ermete Zacconi, as Pope Clement VIII, speaks in Italian. And so forth. The one, amusing exception is Arletty, as the Ethiopian Queen, looking quite hilarious in blackface and with an Afro hairstyle, who talks in a gibberish created by playing the soundtrack backwards.

Just about anyone who is anyone in French cinema and theatre is to be found in *The Pearls of the Crown*: Cécile Sorel, Marcel Dalio, Raimu, Jean-Louis Barrault, etc. His ninth film as a director, *The Pearls of the Crown* was Guitry's first original screenplay, but he does have a co-director here, Christian-Jaque. Completed in March of 1937, *The Pearls of the Crown* received its premiere at the Cinéma Marignan in Paris on May 12, 1937.

The Pearls of the Crown opened in the United States at the Filmarte Theatre in New York on April 11, 1938, and was apparently somewhat re-edited from the French release version. Despite Guitry's claim that subtitles were unnecessary, Stuart Gilbert provided a satisfactory amount. The New York critics all admired the feature: Eileen Creelman, in the *Sun*, hailed it as "unique"; Archer Winsten, in the *Post*, commented, "A picture like nothing offered this season or any other"; Frank S. Nugent, in the *Times*, allowed: "M. Guitry's adventurous chronicle is unusual enough to compensate for its weaknesses."

ABOVE: Pope Clement VIII (Ermete Zacconi) sends his emissary in search of five pearls to add to the two he has already given as a wedding gift to Catherine de Médicis. The Papal Chamberlain (Enrico Glori) looks on. BELOW: Anne Boleyn (Barbara Shaw) and Henry VIII (Lyn Harding).

LEFT: Napoléon Bonaparte (Jean-Louis Barrault) and Joséphine de Beauharnais (Jacqueline Delubac). BELOW: On board the *Normandie,* Sacha Guitry shows the third pearl to his wife (Jacqueline Delubac).

PÉPÉ LE MOKO

Producer: M. M. Hakim for Films Hakim. *Released:* 1937, Paris Film (France); 1941, Mayer and Burstyn (U.S.). *Running Time:* 90 minutes (France); 85 minutes (U.S.).

Director: Julien Duvivier. *Screenplay:* Julien Duvivier and Henri Jeanson (based on the novel by Detective Ashelbé). *Photography:* Jules Krüger and Marc Fossard. *Art Director:* Jacques Krauss. *Music:* Vincent Scotto and Mohammed Yguerbuchen. *Film Editor:* Marguerite Beaugé.

CAST: Jean Gabin (*Pépé le Moko*); Mireille Balin (*Gaby*); Gabriel Gabrio (*Carlos*); Lucas Gridoux (*Inspector Slimane*); Marcel Dalio (*L'Arbi*); Saturnin Fabre (*the grandfather*); Fernand Charpin (*Régis*); Line Noro (*Inès*); Gilbert Gil (*Pierrot*); Gaston Modot (*Jimmy*); Roger Legris (*Max*); Fréhel (*Tania*); Charles Granval (*Maxime*); Olga Lord (*Aïcha*); René Bergeron (*Meunier*).

SYNOPSIS: French police are unable to capture gangster Pépé le Moko, who is hiding in the Casbah district of Algiers. Escaping from a police raid, Pépé meets the beautiful Gaby, on a visit to Algiers as the mistress of the wealthy Maxime. She is being escorted through the Casbah by Inspector Slimane, with whom Pépé is friendly, but who has vowed eventually to capture the gangster. A police attempt to capture Pépé through a young member of his gang, Pierrot, betrayed by Régis, fails, but Slimane devises a plan to have Pépé come to Gaby's hotel, while he tells her that Pépé is dead. Upon learning of Pépé's supposed death, Gaby goes back to Maxime (whom she was going to leave out of love for the gangster) and sets sail with him. Pépé is captured as he boards the ship on which she is leaving, but kills himself with a knife and dies with his mistress, Inès, at his side. A final cry to Gaby on board ship had been drowned out by the ship's whistle.

COMMENTARY: It is, perhaps, not surprising that *Pépé le Moko* should have attracted a Hollywood producer and been quickly remade as *Algiers* (1938), for the French film has all the melodramatic qualities that would have appealed to Hollywood. Its central character is a vicious gangster with a romantic flair. No setting could be more romantic—at least on film—than the Casbah. The story of a gangster betrayed, albeit innocently, by his love for a mysterious and beautiful woman has all the clichés one might expect in a Hollywood feature. What *Pépé le Moko* has and what *Algiers* does not is atmosphere; the French film captures the violence and romanticism of Algiers thanks to the lighting effects, to the characterizations and to Julien Duvivier's taut direction. It starts off rather badly with a travelogue-type tour of the Casbah, and the viewer expects the worst, but then Duvivier recreates the atmosphere we have just seen and peoples it with characters every bit as fascinating as those from real life. (After shooting some exteriors in Algiers, Duvivier brought back a young native composer, Mohammed Yguerbuchen, whose contribution to the score adds another advantage to the film.)

Following *Pépé le Moko*'s Paris premiere—at the Marivaux—Erich von Stroheim, who was in the audience, cabled Eddie Mannix at M-G-M and suggested that the studio acquire the film, along with its directors and two stars—Jean Gabin and Mireille Balin—for an American remake. For a mere $38,000, M-G-M acquired the remake rights and signed both Balin and Duvivier. Gabin refused to come to Hollywood, pointing out that like some French wines, he did not "travel well." Mireille Balin remained in Hollywood for eight months without making a film, before she returned to France. Duvivier (1896-1967) made *The Great Waltz* (1938) and then returned to France—where his major films include *Poil de Carotte* (1925 and 1932), *Un Carnet de Bal/Life Dances On* (1937) and *Le Petit Monde de Don Camillo/The Little World of Don Camillo* (1951)—although he did come back to the States during the Second World War. Eventually M-G-M sold the remake rights to Walter Wanger, who produced the film as a vehicle for Hedy Lamarr (in her first American feature) and Charles Boyer, who had originally turned down the title role in the French version.

Usually once a French film is remade by Hollywood, the American producers are anxious not to have the original in circulation for fear of adverse comparison. Such was not the case with *Pépé le Moko*. Wanger waited only three years before releasing the French film, perhaps not coincidentally with Jean Gabin's arrival the day after the New York premiere—at the World Theatre on March 3, 1941—in the United States. Jean Gabin (1904-1976) was here under contract to 20th Century-Fox, but appeared in only two American features, *Moontide* (1942) and *The Imposter* (1944), with the latter directed by Julien Duvivier.

Pépé le Moko had already been widely praised on its British release. In *The Sunday Observer*, C. A. Lejeune commented, "In my first burst of enthusiasm, I would have said that *Pépé le Moko* is the most brilliant film ever produced in a French studio. Perhaps it is not quite as good as that, but it is enormously, and horribly, memorable."

American critics were no less enthusiastic in their praise. In the New York *Tribune* (March 9, 1941), Howard Barnes wrote, "It ranks with the few masterpieces of the screen, in whatever country they were made. In its taut melodramatic line and its inevitable progression to a smashing climax, it bears more kindred to John Ford's memorable *The Informer* than to most French films. In any language, in any period, it is a consummate screen work and a stunning show."

ABOVE: Pépé (Jean Gabin) and Inspector Slimane (Lucas Gridoux). In the background are Max (Roger Legris) and Jimmy (Gaston Modot). BELOW: Pépé (Jean Gabin) becomes infatuated with Gaby (Mireille Balin).

ABOVE: Pépé (Jean Gabin) with his mistress Inès (Line Noro). BELOW: The death scene.

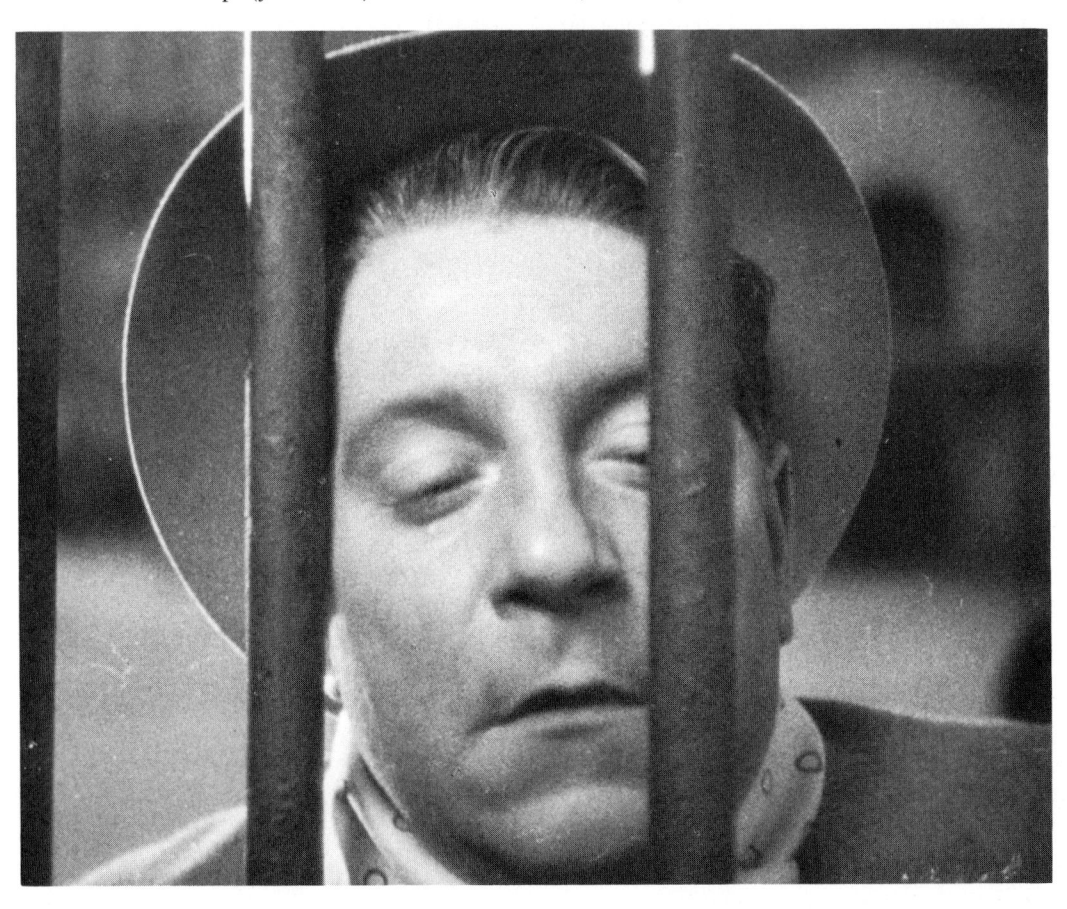

THE BAKER'S WIFE
LA FEMME DU BOULANGER

Producer: Marcel Pagnol for La Société des Films Marcel Pagnol. *Released:* 1938, Marcel Pagnol (France); 1940, The Baker's Wife Inc./Hakim Bros. (U.S.). *Running Time:* 98 minutes.

Director: Marcel Pagnol. *Screenplay:* Marcel Pagnol (based on an incident in the novel *Jean le Bleu*, by Jean Giono). *Photography:* Georges Benoit, Roger Ledru and N. Daries. *Film Editor:* Charles Jahrblum. *Music:* Vincent Scotto. *Production Manager:* Charles Pons. *English Titles:* John Erskine.

CAST: Raimu (*Aimable, the baker*); Ginette Leclerc (*Aurélie, the baker's wife*); Charles Moulin (*Dominique, the shepherd*); Fernand Charpin (*the marquis*); Robert Vattier (*the curate*); Robert Bassac (*the schoolteacher*).

SYNOPSIS: A new baker, along with his young and beautiful wife, arrives in town, and the local citizens are pleased with his bread, as is the local marquis, whose handsome shepherd, Dominique, is to collect his master's bread twice a week. The shepherd and two friends serenade the baker's wife at night, and the baker, believing their song (which is in Spanish) is in gratitude for his bread, tells his wife to give the shepherd something in thanks. The wife and shepherd agree to meet early in the morning, and because she is not there to awaken the baker at 6:00 A.M. the bread is burnt. The baker takes to drink and refuses to bake bread after he has learned his wife has gone off with the shepherd. The curate and teacher go to meet with the couple, who have taken refuge on an island in the marshes, and upon seeing the priest the shepherd realizes his sin and dives into the water. The wife returns, asks the husband for forgiveness and promises never to leave him again.

COMMENTARY: *The Baker's Wife* is a guileless film, which succeeds thanks to its unabashed simplicity. The plot is slight, although rather drawn out and longwinded, particularly in its overemphasis on the baker's depression and alcoholism—a veritable advertisement for Pernod—after his wife's desertion. Like Pagnol's previous film, *Harvest*, *The Baker's Wife* is based on a work by Jean Giono, but in this case only an incident in a book. The direction is straightforward, with the camera doing little more than record the actors' behavior, although there is one unusual shot that takes the viewer inside the baker's oven and lets him see the joy on the man's face as he removes his newly baked bread. The acting is naturalistic, with Raimu's presence dominating the film. As the baker, he is a primitive man, basically a slob, his appearance in direct counterpoint to the almost sulky beauty of his wife, played by Ginette Leclerc. The latter and Charles Moulin as the shepherd make a handsome couple, but as with many such couples one senses that theirs is an empty relationship with nothing but primal eroticism and beauty holding it together. The baker represents materialistic pleasure, the promise of a steady, enduring relationship. Here again, as in the English *The Private Life of Henry VIII*, food/bread is equated with sex.

Marcel Pagnol uses the film to depict the way of life in a small French town. It is a community where arguments are a part of the daily ritual; a local complains that his neighbor's trees cast shade over his garden and prevent the growth of his spinach, while the owner of the trees protests that the neighbor is stealing his shade; even the curate and the teacher disagree on the interpretation of the legend of Joan of Arc. Marcel Pagnol's town is a typical bucolic community, where men do the talking and women take care of the household chores, listening with apathetic shrugs to slurs on their character and looks.

It has three leaders: the baker (whose predecessor committed suicide), the curate and the marquis. The last lives with a group of women whom he describes as his nieces, and whose presence, he explains to the priest, is acceptable in that sins requiring a fixed income are not bad examples to the community. When one of these leaders, the baker, fails in his duty, all arguments in the town cease and the other two leaders work for his return to normality, the priest using a few well-chosen words from the Bible to bring the errant wife home and the marquis despatching the profligate shepherd to his house in the Camargue.

Arguably the best-known of all Pagnol and Raimu features, *The Baker's Wife* received extraordinary praise on its initial presentation. "Genet" (Janet Flanner) cabled *The New Yorker* from Paris that the film was "the most earthy, human, funny and realistic French movie ever seen here in years. Rabelais and Karl Marx would have liked this one, since it deals with adultery related in terms of economics." The professional critics were equally impressed. Frank Nugent, in *The New York Times* (February 27, 1940), considered *The Baker's Wife* "a true comedy and a delightful one," comparing Raimu to Chaplin in "his ability to recognize the harshness of the world."

ABOVE: Ginette Leclerc in the title role. BELOW: The baker (Raimu) explains his trade to one of the villagers (Edouard Delmont).

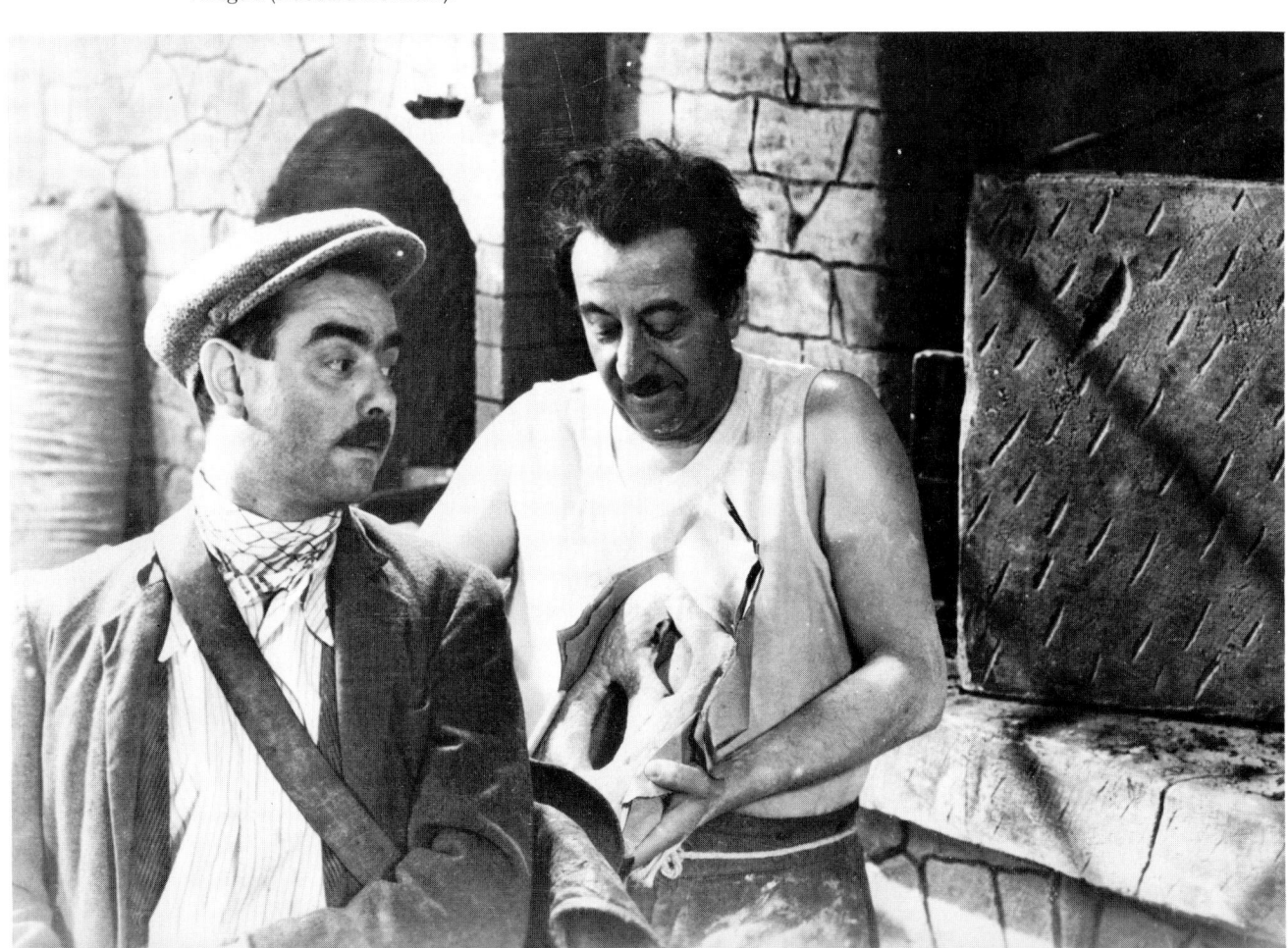

ABOVE: Edouard Delmont, Paul Dullac, Maupi, Raimu and Robert Bassac. BELOW: Fernand Charpin, Raimu, Edouard Delmont and Robert Vattier.

LA MARSEILLAISE

Producer: André Zwoboda and Marc Maurette for Société de Production et d'Exploitation du film *La Marseillaise. Released:* 1938, Réalisations d'Art Cinématographique (France); 1939, World Pictures (U.S.). *Running Time:* 135 minutes (France); 79 minutes (U.S.).

Director: Jean Renoir. *Screenplay:* Jean Renoir (historical advice by Carl Koch and Monsieur and Madame N. Martel-Dreyfus). *Photography:* Jean Bourgoin, Alain Douarinou, Jean-Marie Maillols and Jean-Paul Alphen. *Set Designers:* Léon Barsacq, Georges Wakhevitch and Jean Perrier. *Music:* Joseph Kosma (selections from compositions by Sauveplane, Lalande, Grétry, Rameau, Mozart, Bach and Rouget de Lisle). *Film Editors:* Marguerite Renoir and Marthe Huguet. *Sound:* Joseph de Bretagne, Jean-Roger Bertrand and J. Demède. Shadow theatre by Lotte Reiniger.

CAST: THE COURT: Pierre Renoir (*Louis XVI*); Lise Delamare (*Marie Antoinette*); Léon Larive (*Picard*); William Aguet (*La Rochefoucauld*); Elisa Ruis (*Mme. de Lamballe*); G. Lefébure (*Mme. Elisabeth*).

THE CIVIL AND MILITARY AUTHORITIES: Louis Jouvet (*Roederer*); Jean Aquistapace (*mayor of the village*); Georges Spanelly (*La Chesnaye*); Jaque Catelain (*Langlade*); Pierre Nay (*Dubouchage*); Edmond Castel (*Leroux*).

THE ARISTOCRATS: Aimé Clariond (*Saint-Laurent*); Maurice Escande (*lord of the village*); André Zibral (*Saint-Méry*); Jean Ayme (*Fougerolles*); Irène Joachim (*Mme. de Saint-Laurent*).

THE PEOPLE OF MARSEILLES: Andrex (*Arnaud*); Edmond Ardisson (*Bomier*); Jean-Louis Allibert (*Moissan*); Jenny Hélia (*the questioner*); Paul Dullac (*Javel*); Fernand Flament (*Ardisson*); Georges Péclet and Géo Dorliss (*leaders in Marseilles*); Géo Lastry (*Captain Massugue*); Adolphe Autran (*the drummer*); Alex Truchy (*Cuculière*).

THE PEOPLE: Nadia Sibirskaïa (*Louison*); Edouard Delmont (*Cabri*); Séverine Lerczinska (*a peasant woman*); Edmond Beauchamp (*the priest*); Gaston Modot and Julien Carette (*volunteers*); Marthe Marty (*Bomier's mother*).

SYNOPSIS: On July 14, 1789, Louis XVI is told, while breakfasting in bed at Versailles, that the Bastille has fallen and a revolution has taken place. Outside of Marseilles, a peasant is arrested for killing a pigeon, and at his trial is ordered punished; he escapes and in the mountains meets two men from Marseilles, Bomier and Arnaud, also on the run. A priest visits the men and tells them of the revolution. The date is now October 1790, and Arnaud leads the citizens of Marseilles in an attack on the city's three forts, the commander of which, Saint-Laurent, is allowed to leave for Germany, where he later lives with a group of exiled aristocrats, urging the intervention of Prussia. Back in Marseilles, a battalion is formed to march to Paris and present the views of the citizens; before leaving they hears Mireur of Montpellier sing a song that has come to be known as "The Marseillaise." In Paris, the Marseillais fight with a group of aristocrats and learn of a manifesto sent by the Prussians and Austrians. The aristocrats and the Swiss Guard defend Versailles against attack by the populace, during which Bomier is wounded and dies in the arms of his girlfriend, Louison. The final sequence shows the Marseilles battalion defending Paris and France against the invading Prussians and Austrians.

COMMENTARY: Like many historical spectacles, this is not without its faults, but it is certainly—in this writer's opinion—an infinitely superior work to Abel Gance's *Napoléon*, offering far more warmth and sympathy to its characterizations, and never allowing human emotion to be overridden by cinematic technique.

Jean Renoir has adopted a basically documentary approach to his subject, but he allows the audience to be involved in the action. At times he presents what is almost newsreel coverage of the Revolution, but coverage from both viewpoints—of the citizenry and the aristocracy. Indeed, this creates a major problem in that there are no real villains in Renoir's film. The King is a pleasant enough person as monarchs go, depicted here as fascinated with the new notion of brushing one's teeth and thrilled with the taste of tomatoes. One can feel only sympathy for the Swiss Guards whose honor demands that they must stay at the Tuileries Palace to protect the King and his court. And as for the revolutionaries, they are the cleanest, most well-dressed group of peasantry one could wish to meet.

The film's making came about in a curious way. When the Popular Government of Léon Blum came to power in 1936, its coalition of Socialists, Radical Socialists and Communists decided to subsidize a film history of the revolution, which was to feature every major French actress and actor, and was to have the collaboration of every important director, writer and composer in the film industry. However, the Blum government fell before the project got under way, and, as Jean Renoir explains in his autobiography, "A subscription was opened, the purchasers of tickets having the right to see the film for nothing. This was how the film was financed, and it proves that films can be made by subscription—always provided one does not expect to make a fortune out of them."

When the film opened in Paris in March of 1938, it ran for over two hours, but *La Marseillaise* was cut to a mere seventy-nine minutes for its American premiere—at New York's Cameo Theatre—on November 3, 1939. The American critics were only lukewarm in their response to the feature. In *Motion Picture Herald* (November 18, 1939), Paul C. Mooney, Jr. wrote, "It is an amiable film with a fair share of comedy and although it would appear as if the production was originally intended for its dramatic possibilities it never approaches dramatic intensity as did Mr. Renoir's *Grand Illusion*." Less enthusiastic was Frank S. Nugent, in *The New York Times* (November 6, 1939), who commented, "It is probably the least dramatic film ever made about one of the most dramatic events in history—the French Revolution. It has received a rich production, with huge sets, free access to the Tuileries and Versailles, and a cast (as they say) 'of thousands,' over whom director, principals, writers and editors seem constantly to have been stumbling. Rarely has a screen been so crowded and to so little purpose. Revolutionists march, muskets blaze, a Louis trembles and a kingdom falls; but it might as well be some pageant put on for a holiday show, long in costuming and fireworks, short in the stuff of drama."

LEFT: The citizens of Marseilles. BELOW: Louis XVI and Marie Antoinette (Pierre Renoir and Lise Delamare).

ABOVE: A confrontation between Roederer (Louis Jouvet) and Marie Antoinette (Lise Delamare). BELOW: Bomier (Edmond Ardisson) dies in the arms of Louison (Nadia Sibirskaïa).

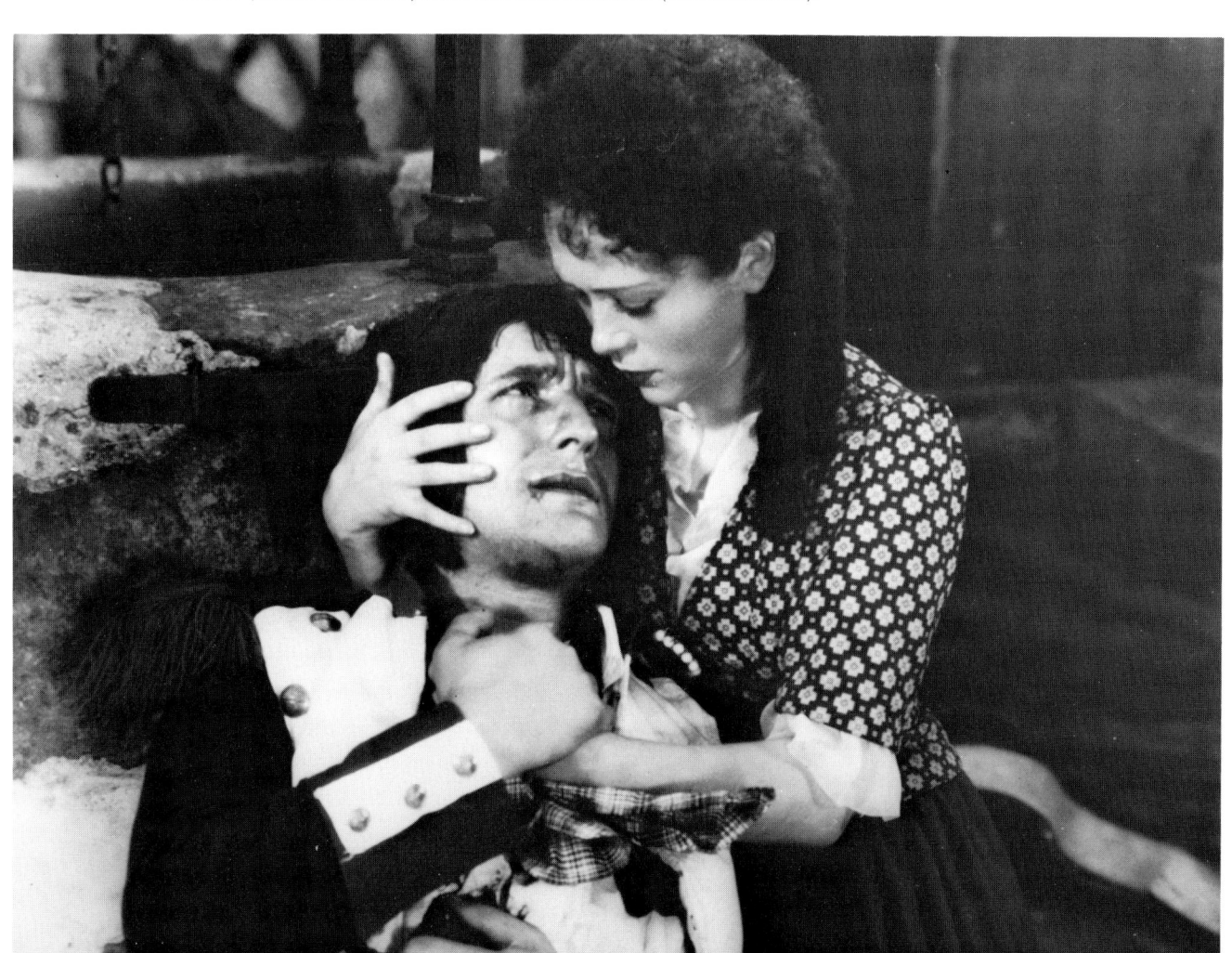

PORT OF SHADOWS
QUAI DES BRUMES

Producer: Marcel Carné for Ciné-Alliance. *Released:* 1938, Osso Films (France); 1940, Film Alliance of the United States (U.S.) *Running Time:* 90 minutes.

Director: Marcel Carné. *Screenplay:* Jacques Prévert (based on the novel by Pierre MacOrlan). *Photography:* Eugène Schüfftan. *Art Director:* Alexandre Trauner. *Music:* Maurice Jaubert. *Film Editor:* René Le Hénaff.

CAST: Jean Gabin (*Jean*); Michele Morgan (*Nelly*); Michel Simon (*Zabel*); Pierre Brasseur (*Lucien Laugardier*); Robert Le Vigan (*Michel Krauss*); Jenny Burnay (*Lucien's friend*); Marcel Pérès (*chauffeur*); René Génin (*the doctor*); Edouard Delmont (*Panama*); Raymond Aimos (*Quart-Vittel*).

SYNOPSIS: Jean, an army deserter, meets Nelly (who is wating for her boyfriend) at a dive in Le Havre, where he is looking for passage out of the country. After gangster Lucien has appeared, looking for Nelly's boyfriend, shots are heard outside and Zabel, Nelly's guardian, appears with blood on his hands, but leaves without seeing Nelly. Later, Lucien visits Zabel's shop and warns him that he will incriminate Zabel if the latter tries to harm him. When Jean enters the shop—to buy a gift for Nelly—Zabel recognizes him from Lucien's description, and tries to persuade him to kill Lucien in return for a passport and cash, but Jean refuses in disgust. Jean finds the passport, suitcase and clothes left for him by painter Michel Krauss, who, in despair, has drowned himself, and arranges to sail for Venezuela. He meets Nelly at the fair, humiliates Lucien and spends the night with the girl, promising to send for her once he has reached South America. When Jean returns to Zabel's shop, he discovers Nelly fighting with her guardian after discovering he has killed her boyfriend out of lust for her. Jean kills Zabel with a brick, but on his return to the ship is shot by Lucien and dies in Nelly's arms.

COMMENTARY: *Port of Shadows* established Marcel Carné (born 1909) as one of France's leading directors; still in his twenties, Carné was dubbed by Gavin Lambert as "the youngest of the masters." A former film critic, Marcel Carné had made his first feature, *Jenny*, in 1936, and come to the attention of American critics with his 1937 film, *Drôle de Drame/Bizarre, Bizarre*. In 1938, he directed two major films, *Port of Shadows* and *Hôtel du Nord*, the first of which has been described by French critic Raymond Borde as "the most important film of the decade."

The film is a classic of Poetic Realism, "a film of atmosphere, its characters momentarily thrown into relief and then obscuring again" (as Gavin Lambert wrote in *Sequence* [Spring 1948]). Marcel Carné has created a mood piece, with the characters mostly seen in half-shadow and with the fog used as a dramatic device, as is the atmospheric score by Maurice Jaubert. *Port of Shadows* was initially to have been a German-French co-production but the German government considered the subject matter unsuitable, and the film was eventually shot at the Pathé-Nathan Studios and on location in Le Havre.

As Georges Sadoul has written, "The film expresses clearly (though unconsciously) the pessimistic mood of France before the 1940 debacle when the Vichy government came to power." Sadoul claims that one government spokesman maintained that "if we have lost the war it is because of *Quai des Brumes*," to which Carné is supposed to have responded that a storm cannot be blamed on the barometer. It was, as Sadoul reports, a sign of the times in Europe, but in the United States, critics were perhaps unable to perceive the film as anything more than a tragic drama, a slice of life that was perhaps a little too sordid for American audiences reared on Hollywood's glossy and glamorous view of existence.

In The New York Times (October 30, 1939), Frank S. Nugent wrote, "The film is nothing more than a lament for the living expressed somberly by a camera greedy for shots of rain and fog, by a writer who has looked at life through gray-tinted glasses [the novel on which *Port of Shadows* is based was, in reality, more than a decade old and set in a much earlier period], seeing nothing but its drabness, its sordidness and the futility of those who expect anything more of it.... No, it's a thorough-going study in blacks and grays, without a free laugh in it; but it is also a remarkably beautiful motion picture from the purely pictorial standpoint and a strangely haunting drama. As a steady diet, of course, it would give us the willies; for a change it's as tonic as a raw Winter's day." *The National Board of Review Magazine* (January 1940) found *Port of Shadows* "Rich in the atmosphere and drama of the waterfront and deeply poignant in its character portrayals." In *The New Republic* (November 1939), Otis Ferguson cried, "I will take this treatment of love as the sudden hope of heaven, between a roughened man and a scared young woman, before any Romeos or Juliets, even as played in double exposure by Orson Welles."

Of course Jean Gabin dominates *Port of Shadows* but he is aided by Michèle Morgan (with, as André Bazin wrote, "the fathomless eyes") and Michel Simon in an unusually sleazy characterization as the lecherous guardian/gangster. A powerful actor, Michel Simon (1895-1975) was featured in many major French features by Jean Renoir, Jean Vigo, Marcel Carné, René Clair and Julien Duvivier. Of him, Sacha Guitry wrote, "I put you among the greatest actors: Frédérick Lemaître, Sarah Bernhardt, my father, Zacconi, Chaliapin. Like them, you stand alone, voluntarily apart—like them, you possess that valuable quality that cannot be acquired and cannot be passed on, the innate sense of theatre, in other words the ability of making other people experience emotions that you yourself do not feel."

Perhaps because of its very pessimism, its grainy and harshly beautiful quality, *Port of Shadows* has stood the test of time better than many lightweight French films of the same period. None of its characters are particularly fine—not even Jean Gabin and Michèle Morgan can evince much sympathy—but the audience is compelled to become part of the action, part of the plot—eventually to suffer and cry. It is an experience that few films before or since have created.

Michel Simon as Zabel: "a combination of grimness and pathos," Nigel Dennis in *The National Board of Review Magazine* (November 1939).

Jean (Jean Gabin) and Nelly (Michèle Morgan) after their first meeting.

ABOVE: Michèle Morgan (born 1920) as Nelly. She enjoyed a brief career in Hollywood during the Second World War, but it is for her French features that she will be remembered. BELOW: Jean (Jean Gabin) and Quart-Vittel (Raymond Aimos).

DAYBREAK
LE JOUR SE LÈVE

Producer: Marcel Carné for Sigma. *Released:* 1939, Vog (France); 1940, A.F.E. Corporation (U.S.). *Running Time:* 95 minutes (France); 88 minutes (U.S.).

Director: Marcel Carné. *Screenplay:* Jacques Viot. *Adaptation and Dialogue:* Jacques Prévert. *Photography:* Curt Courant. *Art Director:* Alexandre Trauner. *Music:* Maurice Jaubert. *Film Editor:* René Le Hénaff.

CAST: Jean Gabin (*François*); Jacqueline Laurent (*Françoise*); Arletty (*Clara*); Jules Berry (*Valentin*); Jacques Baumer (*police officer*); Mady Berry (*concierge*); Bernard Blier (*Gaston*); Germaine Lix (*singer*); Marcel Pérès (*Paolo*).

SYNOPSIS: After shooting Valentin, François barricades himself in his room and in three flashbacks relives the events leading up to the evening's tragedy. He meets Françoise when she comes to the factory where he works to deliver flowers to the manager's wife, and falls in love with her, but one night she leaves him to visit a music hall, where she meets Valentin (who has a dog act) and where François meets Clara, who has just walked out as Valentin's assistant. After François and Clara have become lovers, Valentin tells the former that he is Françoise's father—both she and François are orphans—a claim that Françoise denies. When François and Clara break up, she shows him a brooch that Valentin gives to all his conquests, and one of which Françoise also has. When Françoise refuses to see Valentin again, he goes to François's room and draws a gun, with which, after an argument, François shoots him. As the police prepare to lob a tear-gas bomb into François's room, he shoots himself. Throughout the film, there are scenes of a crowd outside the lodging house, sympathetic to François. Françoise also arrives to try and help him, but she is forced back by the police and taken by Clara to her room.

COMMENTARY: "Poetic Realism" is a phrase often used in connection with Marcel Carné's work, and there could be no better example of this directorial style than *Le Jour Se Lève*. The setting is a French industrial town—brilliantly recreated in two major sets at the Billancourt Studios by Alexandre Trauner—and the lives of the principal characters are basically sordid. Georges Sadoul has suggested that even Trauner's sets express a state of mind. François works as a sandblaster and lives in a one-room garret. Clara works on the fringes of the music hall, as an assistant to a dog trainer and previously with a seal act. She is not exactly world-weary, but she is certainly worldly wise. Valentin, the dog trainer, has branded his animals and flicks their wounds with his whip to get them to perform. As portrayed by Jules Berry, he is a wonderfully slimy individual, similar to the character portrayed by Berry in Renoir's *Le Crime de M. Lange/The Crime of Monsieur Lange* (1936). François seeks escape from his world through fantasy, such as reading the schedule for an ocean liner. Only Françoise seems able to rise above her surroundings, thanks to her innate innocent beauty and the flowers that she grows and sells (and that first bring her and François together)—although Françoise also fantasizes—about the South of France and the mimosa blossoms.

It is hard to argue with Gavin Lambert's comment—in *Sequence* (Spring 1948)—that "There is, perhaps, no other film which has conveyed so intensely the drama, irony and nostalgias of urban life." Marcel Carné has created a working-class music hall, hotel rooms and a lodging house, all of which personify the working-class milieu. There is the realism. The poetry is to be found in his characterizations and his players' responses to life and death, particularly in Jean Gabin's portrayal of the haunted and obsessed man whose life is suddenly torn apart by love. The audience relives the last weeks of his existence as he chain-smokes through one long night; with the end of the cigarette comes the daybreak. When his alarm clock rings that it is time for the day to begin, his life is over.

Gabin and the viewer relive the past through three long flashbacks—Gavin Lambert claims this is "the only great French film to make use of the flash-back"—each of which begins and ends with a long dissolve, and each of which is seen without musical accompaniment (except for the beautifully photographed love scene in the hothouse, as the camera slowly follows Jean Gabin and Jacqueline Laurent as they almost glide along through the flowers). The only music is the haunting—very modernistic at the time—score by Maurice Jaubert, heard as Gabin agonizes through the night. *Le Jour Se Lève* marks Jaubert's last major work for the cinema; he died in 1940. Jean Gabin, of course, is as superb as always—with "one laughing eye and one sad eye," as Françoise tells him, just like her teddy bear, Bolop.

Le Jour Se Lève may be, as Bosley Crowther wrote in *The New York Times* (July 30, 1940), "a drab, moody and depressing picture," which demonstrates "the morbid pre-occupation of certain French producers . . . with characters who live in cold-water walk-ups and go crazy and do violent things." But it is also, as *Time* (August 19, 1940) commented—in a reference to the film's being the last feature to reach the United States from free France—"perhaps the last major product of a cinema industry that was as long on brains as it was short on budget. . . . It has the same distinguishing Gallic qualities of artistic shrewdness and spiritual disenchantment that make most Hollywood pictures by comparison seem, for better or worse, not quite grown-up."

If there are faults with *Le Jour Se Lève*, it is the difficulty in understanding Françoise's falling for Valentin, and for François's becoming so suddenly angry with the latter's behavior. After all, all the people in the drama are adults, and can presumably make their own decisions as to their lives. Françoise may have a juvenile infatuation for Valentin, but her looks and her body belie her supposed innocence.

Le Jour Se Lève was remade in 1947 by Anatole Litvak under the title of *The Long Night*, with Henry Fonda in the Gabin role, and with a happy ending. Georges Sadoul also claims that the 1958 British film, *The Man Upstairs*, has a similar plot.

ABOVE: François cycles to visit Françoise: an example of Alexandre Trauner's brilliant sets for *Le Jour Se Lève*. LEFT: François and Françoise (Jean Gabin and Jacqueline Laurent).

A crowd gathers in the square outside the lodging house where François is barricaded. Another superb set by Alexandre Trauner.

François (Jean Gabin) looks out from his last refuge.

VOLPONE

Producer: Ile de France. *Released:* 1939, Ile de France (France); 1947, Siritzky International (U.S.). *Running Time:* 98 minutes.

Director: Maurice Tourneur. *Screenplay:* Jules Romains and Stefan Zweig (based on the play by Ben Jonson). *Art Director:* André Barsacq. *Music:* Marcel Delannoy.

CAST: Harry Baur (*Volpone*); Louis Jouvet (*Mosca*); Fernand Ledoux (*Corvino*); Marlon Dorian (*Canina*); Jean Temerson (*Voltore*); Alexandre Rignault (*Leone*); Charles Dullin (*Corbaccio*); Jacqueline Delubac (*Colomba*).

SYNOPSIS: When Volpone, a Levantine shipowner, is cast in jail after one of his ships is erroneously reported sunk, he meets the rascally Mosca, whom he engages, after his release, as his steward. Volpone plans revenge on his "friends" by pretending to be dying in order to watch their actions and reactions as they jockey for positions as his heirs. Each is told privately that he is to be the sole beneficiary of Volpone's will, and is anxious to please his benefactor. Silk merchant Corvino sends his attractive wife Colomba to "nurse" his ailing friend, while Corbaccio disinherits his own son and names Volpone beneficiary of his estate. However, during a final and riotous carnival sequence, Mosca tricks Volpone, becomes his legal heir and throws the old man out of his home.

COMMENTARY: No listing of classic French films could be complete without the inclusion of at least one feature directed by Maurice Tourneur. Despite his best work having been created in the United States, Maurice Tourneur (1876-1961) is generally considered one of France's more important directors, and certainly one of its best known. Beginning his professional life as a magazine illustrator, Tourneur worked in the theatre from 1900 to 1912 before entering the film industry at the invitation of Emile Chautard. From Chautard, Tourneur learned the rudiments of filmmaking, and in 1914 came to the United States as a director, with his first American film being *Mother*, featuring Emma Dunn.

Maurice Tourneur was noted for the visual quality in his films, the care in composition and lighting; indeed he claimed in the September 1918 issue of *Motion Picture Magazine* to have "brought stylization to the screen." Films such as *The Wishing Ring* (1914), *Trilby* (1915), *The Pride of the Clan* (1917), *The Poor Little Rich Girl* (1917), *Prunella* (1918) and *The Blue Bird* (1918) are considered some of the best American features of the 'teens and all were directed by Maurice Tourneur. He continued to make American films through 1926, but somehow features such as *Lorna Doone* (1922), *The Christian* (1923) and *Aloma of the South Seas* (1926) lacked the quality of Tourneur's earlier work. He was always very critical of the types of films he was expected to direct, and once wrote to a friend, "I consider bootlegging as being a much more elevating business." This concern with the quality of projects he was offered, together with M-G-M's insistence on having a producer supervise his direction of *The Mysterious Island*, led to Tourneur's abrupt decision to return to France.

His first French film, after an absence of thirteen years, was *L'Equipage*, produced in 1927, but not released in the U.S. until 1929 under the title of *Last Flight*. Tourneur's first sound feature was *Accusée, Levez-Vous* (1930), featuring Gaby Morlay and Charles Vanel. It was followed by *Partir!* (1931), *Les Deux Orphelines* (1933, featuring Yvette Guilbert in a story based on the same material as D. W. Griffith's *Orphans of the Storm*), *Koenigsmark* (1936, shot in both French and English and featuring Elissa Landi and Pierre Fresnay) and *Samson* (1936).

Shortly before the Nazi occupation of northern France, Tourneur filmed what is arguably his best French sound feature and the only one readily available for viewing in the United States, *Volpone*, based on Ben Jonson's 1606 comedy, which has been filmed a couple of times since and has also seen life as the Broadway play *Sly Fox*, starring George C. Scott. Tourneur remains faithful to Ben Jonson, but adds a touch of Gallic wit, and moves the film along at an exhilarating pace, with the humor occasionally bordering on the slapstick.

Volpone is a delight thanks in no small part to the performances of Harry Baur and Louis Jouvet. A classic actor of the French stage and screen, Harry Baur (1880-1943) is outstanding in *Les Misérables* (1934), *Le Golem* (1936), *Un Grand Amour de Beethoven/The Life and Loves of Beethoven* (1936) and *Un Carnet de Bal/Life Dances on* (1937). He and his Jewish wife were arrested during the occupation and Baur died under mysterious circumstances. Louis Jouvet (1887-1951) was lucky in that he stayed away from France during the Second World War; it is Jouvet who made the memorable remark that the cinema "is an American industry, but a French art."

It took eight years for *Volpone* to reach the United States, and then with major censorship cuts. The critics liked it, with Bosley Crowther, in *The New York Times*, describing the film as "a rollickingly naughty motion picture. . . . it has a gusto that is to be admired."

Maurice Tourneur worked, innocuously, throughout the German occupation, directing five features. His last two films were *Après l'Amour* (1947) and *L'Impasse des Deux Anges* (1948). His French features may not have quite the style and panache of Tourneur's early American films, but nonetheless they have a deserved and prominent place in the history of the motion picture.

LEFT: Louis Jouvet as Mosca. BELOW: Mosca (Louis Jouvet) and Volpone (Harry Baur) plot.

ABOVE: Volpone (Harry Baur) shows one of his jeweled rings to Corbaccio (Charles Dullin). BELOW: Corvino (Fernand Ledoux) sends his wife Colomba (Jacqueline Delubac) to nurse Volpone.

THE RULES OF THE GAME
LA RÈGLE DU JEU

Producer: Jean Renoir for La Nouvelle Edition Française. *Released:* 1939, Gaumont (France); 1950, Cine-Classics (U.S.). *Running Time:* 113 minutes (restored French version), 85 minutes (original French release); 80 minutes (U.S.).

Director: Jean Renoir. *Screenplay:* Jean Renoir and Carl Koch. *Photography:* Jean Bachelet. *Set Designers:* Eugène Lourié and Max Douy. *Costumes:* Coco Chanel. *Music:* Joseph Kosma and Robert Desormières, based on works by Mozart, Monsigny, Saint-Saëns and Johann Strauss. *Film Editors:* Marguerite Renoir and Marthe Huguet. *Sound:* Joseph de Bretagne.

CAST: Marcel Dalio (*Robert de La Chesnaye*); Nora Gregor (*Christine de La Chesnaye*); Roland Toutain (*André Jurieu*); Jean Renoir (*Octave*); Mila Parély (*Geneviève de Marrast*); Paulette Dubost (*Lisette*); Gaston Modot (*Schumacher*); Julien Carette (*Marceau*); Odette Talazac (*Charlotte de La Plante*); Pierre Magnier (*the general*); Pierre Nay (*Saint-Aubin*); Richard Francœur (*La Bruyère*); Eddy Debray (*Corneille*); Léon Larive (*the cook*); Claire Gérard (*Mme. de La Bruyère*); Anne Mayen (*Jackie*); Lise Elina (*radio reporter*); Roger Forster (*the homosexual*); Tony Corteggiani (*Berthelin*); Nicolas Amato (*the South American*); Camille François (*the radio announcer*); André Zwoboda (*engineer at Caudron*); Henri Cartier-Bresson (*English servant*); Jenny Hélia (*kitchen servant*).

SYNOPSIS: To his château, La Colinière, Robert de La Chesnaye invites his wife, Christine, her former and would-be lover André Jurieu (who has just achieved a new record for flying the Atlantic), his mistress Geneviève de Marrast, André's friend Octave and assorted other members of the French upper class. Also accompanying the group is Lisette, Christine's maid, who is married to La Colinière's gamekeeper Schumacher, but prefers life with Christine to living in the country with her husband. When Schumacher catches a poacher, Marceau, de La Chesnaye hires him as a servant, and Lisette is immediately attracted to the man. After seeing Geneviève and Robert together at a pheasant shoot, Christine learns of their relationship. Events reach their climax at a big party, complete with entertainment by the guests. Christine tells André that she loves him and a fight ensues between the latter and Robert. At the same time, Schumacher catches Lisette and Marceau together and chases them, armed with a gun. The head servant, Corneille, disarms Schumacher, and he and Marceau are fired by Robert, but Lisette says she will stay with Christine. Octave and Christine go for a walk in the garden, with the latter wearing Lisette's cloak, and in the greenhouse Octave tells Christine that he loves her. Octave returns to the château for Christine's coat, and there Lisette tells him that Christine will not be happy with him. Octave gives André both his and Christine's coats and tells him to join Christine, but Schumacher, who believes Christine to be Lisette, mistakes André for Octave and shoots and kills him. Octave and Marceau leave, as Robert tells his guests there has been an unfortunate shooting accident.

COMMENTARY: "Society has some stiff rules," says Jean Renoir in the character of Octave, and it is these rules of conduct and behavior that the director examines on both a serious and a comic level in *The Rules of the Game*. Everything about *The Rules of the Game* is overtly silly, but, at the same time, it is covertly tragic. It is silly and amusing in that here is a game of love, but it is also as pathetic as Robert de La Chesnaye with his painted eyebrows and his mechanical toys, in that it is ultimately a game of death.

Because of problems he had experienced with his previous film, *La Bête Humaine/The Human Beast* (1938), Renoir had decided to form his own production company, La Nouvelle Edition Française, to make *The Rules of the Game* at a budget of 2,500,000 francs. Some casting problems arose when Simone Simon, Renoir's original choice for the role of Christine, demanded too much money, and with Fernand Ledoux unavailable for the part of Schumacher. To replace Simone Simon, Renoir selected Nora Gregor, the Princess Starhemberg, an Austrian (who is quite magnificent in the role), and with whom, apparently, Renoir was considerably taken, to the extent that he replaced his brother Pierre in the role of Octave. The entire production was filmed between the historic Munich meeting, from which Neville Chamberlain returned with the promise of "peace in our time," and the outbreak of the Second World War.

At its Paris premiere on July 7, 1939, *The Rules of the Game* was greeted with ridicule, shortly cut by ten minutes or more and, within three months, banned by the French government as "demoralizing." The film did not reach the United States until 1950—and then in a severely truncated version—and did not fare well with the American critics. "H. H. T.," in *The New York Times* (April 10, 1950), described it as "a baffling mixture of stale sophistication, coy symbolism and galloping slapstick that almost defies analysis."

Indeed *The Rules of the Game* does contain many of those elements of which the *Times*'s critic complained, but it delights and impresses in Renoir's *use* of such elements. It is a film like no other before or since. It can be viewed as a comedy in the style of Beaumarchais's *The Marriage of Figaro—The Rules of the Game* opens with a quote from Beaumarchais—or as a magnificent dramatic work, with important historical and social content.

It was not until 1959 that *The Rules of the Game* was restored to its original length thanks to the efforts of Jean Gaborit and Jacques Durand. However, it was six years until the film again received an official French opening, and gained a permanent, and long awaited, place as a masterpiece of world cinema.

Following *The Rules of the Game*, Jean Renoir, accompanied by his beloved wife-to-be Dido Freire, left France, and was not to return, as a filmmaker, until 1954. With his departure the golden age of French filmmaking came to a close.

ABOVE: Octave (Jean Renoir) says goodnight to Christine (Nora Gregor). BELOW: André and Robert (Roland Toutain and Marcel Dalio).

ABOVE: Christine (Nora Gregor) meets Marceau (Julien Carette) as he collects the guests' shoes for cleaning. BELOW: Robert and André (Marcel Dalio and Roland Toutain) fight over Christine.

CHILDREN OF PARADISE
LES ENFANTS DU PARADIS

Producers: Fred Orain and Raymond Borderie for Pathé. *Released:* 1945, Pathé (France); 1947, Tricolore Films (U.S.). *Running Time:* 195 minutes (France); 161 minutes (U.S.).

Director: Marcel Carné. *Screenplay:* Jacques Prévert. *Photography:* Roger Hubert. *Art Directors:* Léon Barsacq, Raymond Gabutti and Alexandre Trauner. *Costumes:* Mayo. *Music:* Maurice Thiriet, Joseph Kosma and Georges Mouque. *Film Editors:* Henri Rust and Madeleine Bonin. *Sound:* R. Teysserre.

CAST: Arletty (*Garance*); Jean-Louis Barrault (*Baptiste Debureau*); Pierre Brasseur (*Frédérick Lemaitre*); Maria Casarès (*Nathalie*); Marcel Herrand (*Lacenaire*); Louis Salou (*Count Edouard de Montray*); Pierre Renoir (*Jéricho*); Jeanne Marken (*Madame Hermine*); Fabien Loris (*Avril*); Etienne Decroux (*Anselme Debureau*); Marcel Pérès (*director of the Funambules*); Pierre Palau (*stage manager of the Funambules*); Gaston Modot (*Fil-de-Soie*); Jacques Castelot (*Georges*); Robert Dhéry (*Célestin*); Florencie (*the policeman*); Paul Frankeur (*the inspector*); Rognoni (*director of the Grand-Théâtre*); Albert Rémy (*Scarpia Barigni*); Auguste Boverio (*first actor*); Paul Demange (*second actor*); Diener (*third actor*); and F. Favières, Marcelle Monthil, G. Quero, Lucette Vigier, Habib-Benglia, Raphaël Patorni, Léon Larive, Léon Walter, Jean Lanier and Melrac.

SYNOPSIS: *Part One:* In Paris of the the 1830s, on the Boulevard of Crime, Baptiste saves a girl, Garance, from being falsely accused of theft when he mimes what actually happened. Baptiste and his friend, Frédérick Lemaître, who dreams of becoming a Shakespearian actor, get their opportunity to appear at the Funambules, where the stage manager's daughter, Nathalie, falls in love with the former. But Baptiste thinks only of Garance, whom he meets again at a low dive, Le Rouge-Gorge (to which he is taken by Fil-de-Soie). He dances with her and for her sake he confronts the bullying Lacenaire. Baptiste takes Garance back to his rooms, where he does not press his affection on her; instead she has an affair with Lemaître. Baptiste presents a mime drama of his love for Garance, with himself as Pierrot, Garance as Phoebe and Lemaître as Harlequin. Because of her friendship with Lacenaire, Garance is accused of being an accomplice in a robbery, and to protect herself produces a card left by the Count Edouard de Montray, who has fallen in love with her.

Part Two: Several years later, Garance is the Count's mistress, Baptiste is married to Nathalie, and both Baptiste and Lemaître have gained fame. When Nathalie learns that Garance is trying to see Baptiste again, she sends their son to warn Garance off. The Count, believing that Lemaître is Garance's lover, challenges him to a duel, but he himself is killed by Lacenaire seeking revenge for insults. In the meantime, Garance and Baptiste have spent the night together, forcing Nathalie to confront Garance, who leaves, pursued by Baptiste. He cannot reach her because of the carnival crowd, among whom are mocking figures dressed as Pierrot.

COMMENTARY: Just as Charles Dickens made nineteenth-century London come to life for his readers, so did Marcel Carné and Jacques Prévert bring Paris of the Romantic era to life for filmgoers. The *Children of Paradise* are the theatregoers of the cheapest seats—"the gods"—the seats nearest to heaven, those who see life and the theatre from a humble vantage point.

Children of Paradise is a stunning achievement in terms of acting, costumes, sets and a complex plot that never fails to hold one's attention. It is romantic cinema at its most lush and intelligent, a costume picture at its most spectacular, and a theatrical experience unsurpassed in the history of the French motion picture. Marcel Carné handles mob scenes as effectively as he handles quiet and intimate moments. What is particularly remarkable is that the entire film was shot between 1943 and 1944 while France was still occupied by the Nazis, partially at the Victorine Studios in Nice and partially at Joinville. The budget for the film was a staggering—particularly in view of when *Children of Paradise* was shot—sixty million francs, with the gigantic Boulevard of Crime set costing five million francs and 67,500 hours of labor to create.

The feature was the first to be shown in France after the liberation. Despite his not particularly liking the film, André Bazin—writing in *Le Parisien Libéré* (March 30, 1945)—had to admit that "Marcel Carne's film is undoubtedly the most important cinematographic event that French film production has known in the last two years" and that "Marcel Carné is incontestably our best director."

The American critics were very mixed in their reactions to the production. In *The New York Times* (March 2, 1947), Bosley Crowther wrote, "For many material reasons, this picture will not impress the average American audience as forcibly as it has hit those in France—or even the audiences in London, which have gone for it equally big. For, despite its elaborate production and its performance in magnificent style, it seems long-drawn and heavily burdened with emotional contrivances. Likewise, its antique symbolism and vague philosophy are a bit hard to grasp."

Of course, all the critics were unanimous in their praise for the film's performers, notably Jean-Louis Barrault as the white-robed mime Baptiste. Barrault (born 1910) has been a major force in French theatre, as a member of the Comédie Française and as director of the Théâtre de France, but he has also contributed much to films over the past fifty years. Whereas Barrault has continued to impress, Marcel Carné appears to have reached the peak of his form with *Children of Paradise*, perhaps because shortly thereafter Carné ended his working relationship with Jacques Prévert.

ABOVE: Nathalie and Jéricho (Maria Casarès and Pierre Renoir). BELOW: As Garance (Arletty) watches, Avril (Fabien Louis) threatens Baptiste (Jean-Louis Barrault).

ABOVE: Jean-Louis Barrault as Harlequin. BELOW: Garance and Count Edouard de Montray (Arletty and Louis Salou).

BEAUTY AND THE BEAST
LA BELLE ET LA BÊTE

Producer: André Paulvé for Discina. *Released:* 1946, Discina (France); 1947, Lopert (U.S.). *Running Time:* 96 minutes (France); 87 minutes (U.S.).

Director: Jean Cocteau. *Screenplay:* Jean Cocteau (based on the story by Madame LePrince de Beaumont). *Photography:* Henri Alekan. *Music:* Georges Auric. *Set Designer and Costumes:* Christian Bérard. *Film Editor:* Claude Ibéria.

CAST: Jean Marais (*the Beast, Avenant and the prince*); Josette Day (*Beauty*); Marcel André (*the merchant*); Mila Parély (*Adélaïde*); Nane Germon (*Félicie*); Michel Auclair (*Ludovic*).

SYNOPSIS: It is the seventeenth century and an impoverished merchant has four children: Beauty, Ludovic (interested only in drinking and gambling), Félicie and Adélaïde. Avenant, Ludovic's best friend, asks Beauty to marry him, but she refuses because of her father's need of her. Returning from a trip, the merchant rides through a mysterious forest and comes upon a castle in which doors open by themselves and human hands hold candles. The merchant eats a meal, apparently prepared for him, and remembering a promise to Beauty to bring her back a rose, picks a magnificent one in the castle garden. In so doing he unleashes the Beast, who accuses the merchant of stealing, and agrees to let him go only with the promise that his daughter will come to the castle. Beauty agrees to do as the Beast requested, but on first seeing him faints. Each night at seven o'clock, the Beast visits Beauty as she eats supper and asks her to marry him; each evening she refuses. Gradually Beauty comes to lose her fear of the Beast, who gives her permission to return home on the understanding she will return, otherwise he will die. As a token of his faith, the Beast gives Beauty the golden key to the Pavilion of Diana, which he tells her holds priceless treasures. At home strange things happen; Beauty's tears become diamonds, and when her sister Félicie grabs Beauty's necklace it becomes simply a piece of rope. Beauty learns that the Beast is dying and hastens to return, but not before the golden key has been stolen and given to Avenant. The latter and Ludovic break into the Pavilion of Diana, but the statue comes to life and shoots an arrow through Avenant, who is transformed into the dead Beast, while the Beast becomes a handsome prince who flies through the air with Beauty to his kingdom.

COMMENTARY: Jean Cocteau once wrote that "Anglo-Saxons manage the horror story, the weird tale, better than anybody else." That may be so. But no one has more triumphantly captured the poetry and the lyricism of the Beauty and the Beast theme than this extraordinary French intellectual and man of letters. Cocteau did not seek to aim for poetry; that, he considered, came of its own accord. His plan was merely to create a film which would please himself "and a few people I like. More than that, I can't promise." He sought to create "the reality of childhood. The fairyland without fairies. Fairyland in the kitchen."

Cocteau's *Beauty and the Beast* opens with a foreword in which its maker writes, "I am appealing to what remains of the child within you. The child listens to fairy tales without questioning one word. The child believes that the picking of a single rose can result in dire consequences. The child believes that the hands of a beast that has just killed may burst into smoke, that a beautiful maiden may teach him shame. The child believes a thousand things as artless as these. I ask you to recapture what you may of that simple faith. Let me begin with four magic words, the true Open Sesame to childhood: Once upon a time . . ."

The time here is the seventeenth century, and the setting is very real; the house of a poverty-stricken merchant with four children, three girls and one boy. There is a Cinderella quality to the spiteful way in which Félicie and Adélaïde treat the third daughter, "Beauty," but there is nothing grotesque about the two women's makeup, and the only artistic "trick" that Cocteau plays is in comparing their voices to that of cackling hens.

This is a simple fable of good versus evil, of the struggle of hard work against easy living (as represented by the son's drinking and gambling). Roger Manvell has perceptively written, in the British Film Institute publication, *Records of the Film* (No. 10), that Beauty and the Beast "is the story of a victorious test of a girl's faith and love assailed by the powerful adverse forces of selfishness, pride, fear, weakness, diffidence, poverty and ugliness. . . . Belle alone in her devotion for her father and service to her kinfolk represents true faith and love."

Yet it is Beauty's request of her father—that he bring her back a rose—which leads to his meeting the Beast. The request at first brings tragedy and fear, as the Beast demands the father have his daughter return to live with the Beast. But, in the ultimate conclusion, that one simple request brings happiness for all, the transformation of the Beast into a handsome prince and the realization that fear can be controlled. In the final scenes, as Beauty and her prince are transported through the clouds to fly to his kingdom, Beauty tells her hero, "I don't mind being afraid with you."

Beauty and the Beast rejects reality and takes on a surrealistic cloak with the story's move to the Beast's castle. Doors mysteriously open and close. Corridors are lighted by candles held by human hands and arms outstretched from the walls. Carvings beside the fireplace boast human faces and eyes that watch the visitor. If there is any criticism to be leveled at these sequences—and at the film as a whole—it is that there is a certain coldness to the characters. When the Beast asks Beauty, "Forgive me for being a beast," there is a lack of warmth to his request and to Beauty's response. Beauty is a little too dignified, to the point of being almost prissy in her dealings with the Beast.

Although contemporary critics were a little uneasy with Cocteau's fantasy world, their response was immediately enthusiastic. Bosley Crowther wrote, in *The New York Times* (January 4, 1948), "Studied or not for philosophy, this is a sensuously fascinating film, a fanciful poem in movement given full articulation on the screen." Even *The Hollywood Reporter* (December 5, 1947) announced that Cocteau had "created a rare and abiding work of film art that must take its rank with the few masterpieces of the screen."

Jean Cocteau with his leading lady, Josette Day.

Jean Marais as Avenant.

ABOVE: Beauty (Josette Day) makes her first entrance into the Beast's castle. RIGHT: Jean Marais as the Beast. "It is as it should be that in the fierce and dolorous make-up of the Beast he displays a warmth and tenderness that are absent in the man [Avenant]"— Hermine Rich Isaacs in *Theatre Arts* (January 1948).

MONSIEUR VINCENT

Producer: Léon Carré for Edition et Diffusion Cinématographique and Union Générale Cinématographique under the patronage and with the cooperation of L'Office Familial de Documentation Artistique. *Released:* 1947, A.G.D.C. (France); 1949, Lopert Films (U.S.). *Running Time:* 122 minutes (France); 104 minutes (U.S.).

Director: Maurice Cloche. *Screenplay:* Jean Bernard-Luc and Jean Anouilh. *Photography:* Claude Renoir. *Music:* Jean-Jacques Grunewald. *Settings and Design:* René Renoux. *Film Editor:* Jean Feyte. *Original English Titles:* Herman Weinberg.

CAST: Pierre Fresnay (*Vincent de Paul*); Aimé Clariond (*Cardinal de Richelieu*); Jean Debucourt (*Count Philippe de Gondi*); Lise Delamare (*Countess de Gondi*); Germaine Dermoz (*Anne of Austria*); Gabrielle Dorziat (*Mme. Groussault*); Yvonne Gaudeau (*Louise de Marillac*); Jean Carmet (*Abbé Portail*); Pierre Dux (*Chancellor Seguier*); Georges Vitray (*M. de Rougemont*); Marcel Vallée (*administrator of the Hôtel-Dieu*).

SYNOPSIS: The story of St. Vincent de Paul (1581–1660), ordained in 1600 and canonized in 1737. He leaves a life of comparative luxury and ease in Paris to fight disease, hunger and cruelty as a priest. Arriving as a young priest at Châtillon, Vincent de Paul finds the village decimated by fear of the plague, and fights the terror and bigotry of the villagers, who have left the victims to die of starvation while they enjoy drunken revelry behind locked doors. Cardinal Richelieu learns of his work and appoints him as chaplain of the French Navy, where he witnesses the cruel way in which the galley slaves are treated, and takes the place of an ailing one at the oars. He enlists the aid of wealthy patrons, persuading the rich to work for and with the poor, founding the Ladies of Charity and the Sisters of Charity. He dies as humbly as he had lived as he is eulogized by Anne of Austria, Queen of France.

COMMENTARY: *Monsieur Vincent*'s primary claim to fame is as the first film to receive an Honorary Oscar for Best Foreign Language Film from the Academy of Motion Picture Arts and Sciences, some eight years before such an award was given on a regular basis. It is also of interest because it has remained permanently in distribution in the United States, a popular film with religious groups—Catholic and non-Catholic—and one that was paid for (rather like Renoir's *La Marseillaise*) outside of the mainstream of film financing. The thirty-five-year-old Vicomte Georges de la Grandière raised the money for *Monsieur Vincent*'s $210,000 budget by going directly to the French people. As he explained, "I gave speeches all over France asking for funds. I wrote thousands of letters. I told the people they were contributing to a celluloid monument to St. Vincent. And now 50,000 Frenchmen are in the movie industry."

An obviously genuine and sincere tribute to the work of St. Vincent de Paul, *Monsieur Vincent* is an episodic, somewhat slow and rambling film, which is, surprisingly, unmoving and lacking in emotion. Certainly it has an honesty lacking, for example, in a Hollywood religious epic of the same year, *The Miracle of the Bells*, but the film does not live up totally to its lofty ideals. As Bosley Crowther wrote, in *The New York Times* (December 21, 1948), "Unfortunately, these individual episodes are not effectively combined to do more than give a general impression of wretchedness in seventeenth-century France. And the painful disorder of the story, either by origin or from cutting on this side, despoil it of dramatic compulsion—or or even of coherence at times. The career of de Paul is made indefinite, and characters appear and disappear in provoking multiplicity and confusion."

The faults in *Monsieur Vincent* lie in the script by Jean Bernard-Luc and Jean Anouilh and in the direction by Maurice Cloche. Cloche (born 1907) never amounted to much as a director. *Monsieur Vincent* is his best-known work and one of his few features to gain an American release, although he did co-direct a touching 1951 drama, *Never Take No for an Answer*, based on a story by Paul Gallico, which has a young boy fighting for the right to bring his ailing donkey into the crypt of St. Francis of Assisi in order that the Saint might cure the animal. *Never Take No for an Answer* is a far more emotionally satisfying film than *Monsieur Vincent*.

Monsieur Vincent's one good point is the performance of Pierre Fresnay. "His acting is so exceptional," wrote *Newsweek* (January 17, 1949), "that his exposition of the film's difficult theme—that it is 'for your love alone that the poor will forgive you the bread you give them'—becomes as moving and as genuinely important as it should be." Pierre Fresnay (1897–1975) was one of the best and most diversified of twentieth-century French actors, equally at ease in the Marius trilogy or *La Grande Illusion*. An eleven-year member of the Comédie Française, Fresnay gained international fame as the Duc de Chancigny-Varennes in Noel Coward's *Conversation Piece*, in which he starred on both the West End and Broadway stages. He delighted Parisian audiences with his work on stage opposite his wife Yvonne Printemps. "Change personalities as often as possible," he once said. "Those actors who continually typify a single character, however varied it may be, are usually capitalizing on an initial success. . . . I feel that the true personality of the actor should have to be divined from the several different characters he portrays."

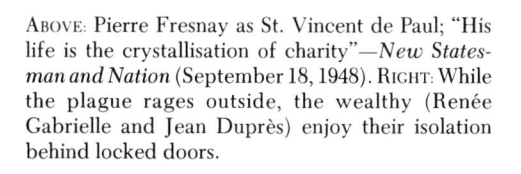

ABOVE: Pierre Fresnay as St. Vincent de Paul; "His life is the crystallisation of charity"—*New Statesman and Nation* (September 18, 1948). RIGHT: While the plague rages outside, the wealthy (Renée Gabrielle and Jean Duprès) enjoy their isolation behind locked doors.

LEFT: M. de Rougemont and Vincent de Paul (Georges Vitray and Pierre Fresnay). BELOW: The Abbé Portail and Vincent de Paul (Jean Carmet and Pierre Fresnay).

ORPHEUS
ORPHÉE

Producer: André Paulvé for Les Films du Palais Royal. *Released:* 1950, Discina (France); 1950, Discina International (U.S.). *Running Time:* 95 minutes.

Director: Jean Cocteau. *Screenplay:* Jean Cocteau. *Photography:* Nicolas Hayer. *Art Director:* Jean d'Eaubonne. *Costumes:* Escoffier. *Music:* Georges Auric. *Film Editor:* Jacqueline Sadoul. *Sound:* J. Calvet.

CAST: Jean Marais (*Orphée*); François Périer (*Heurtebise*); Maria Casarès (*the Princess*); Marie Déa (*Eurydice*); Henri Crémieux (*the man*); Jacques Varennes (*the first judge*); Pierre Bertin (*the commissioner*); Juliette Gréco (*Aglaonice*); Roger Blin (*the writer*); Edouard Dermithe (*Cégeste*).

SYNOPSIS: Orpheus, a highly successful poet, is a witness when alcoholic, young and upcoming poet Cégeste is injured in a hit-and-run accident involving two mysterious motorcyclists outside the Café des Poètes. Cégeste's patron, the Princess, asks Orpheus to accompany her and Cégeste in her car as she takes Cégeste to the hospital. En route, Orpheus realizes Cégeste is dead, and is surprised to see the two motorcyclists join the procession to a château, where Cégeste is apparently restored to life and joins the Princess as she walks through a mirror. After passing out, Orpheus comes to next to the Princess' car, and her chauffeur, Heurtebise, takes him home. Eurydice, Orpheus' wife, is delighted that he has returned but upset that he is unwilling to hear the news that she is pregnant, but instead wishes to spend his time in the car listening to mysterious messages. Eurydice is killed by the motorcyclists, and Orpheus accompanies her, the Princess and Heurtebise through the mirror into the realm of death. At a trial before three judges, the Princess is accused of having acted precipitously in the matter of Eurydice's death, and Orpheus is permitted to take his wife back to the living on condition he does not look at her face. Heurtebise tries to help the pair, but Orpheus sees Eurydice's face in the mirror of the Princess' car. Eurydice dies again, and Orpheus is attacked and accidentally killed by gunshot by a group of jealous poets and writers. Again Orpheus and Heurtebise journey into the land of the dead, and the latter and the Princess sacrifice themselves in order to restore Orpheus and Eurydice once more to life.

COMMENTARY: Jean Cocteau based his feature on his first play, dating back to 1926, and on the Greek mythological legend of Orpheus, the Thracian bard whose beautiful music on the lyre was said to charm even the rocks and the trees. The legend also forms the basis for the 1960 Brazilian film, *Black Orpheus,* and, of course, has been popular with opera librettists. In modernizing the story, Cocteau took a number of liberties, notably in that the trial judges (representing the Greek gods) are not charmed by Orpheus' words, but are concerned that the Princess, as the emissary of death, has acted hastily; and that the legend requires Orpheus not to look at Eurydice *only* until the couple has returned to earth.

Orpheus is a difficult film to appreciate. It has a somewhat dated quality, in that the leading men (Jean Marais and Edouard Dermithe) are very much in the late Forties/early Fifties mould. The land of the dead resembles a bombed-out landscape from the Second World War, and the messages heard on the car radio must be reminiscent of the coded messages broadcast by the French resistance movement. The camera tricks are all rather ordinary; Cocteau shows the landscape in negative form as Orpheus takes that first, fateful car ride with the Princess, and he is overly fond of reversing the film in order to have the participants suddenly arise from the dead or clothe themselves in the gloves of death in a poetically unreal fashion. Perhaps the most impressive of Cocteau's tricks involves the principals walking through mirrors—liquid mirrors made of mercury—and the duplication of the settings in a room on both sides of the mirror's frame with doubles walking away from the viewer. Heurtebise says that mirrors are the doors through which death comes and goes, but unlike the illusions of old, in a Cocteau film it is not done with mirrors.

Pauline Kael has hailed the film as a "masterpiece of magical film-making," likening the motorcyclists to the mythology of our time, black heroes and secret police. But Orpheus is not filled with contemporary mythology, and in perceiving it as such, the viewer may well lose touch with Cocteau's poetry. "To seek to understand, this is the strange mania of men," wrote Cocteau. Perhaps the viewer should take the advice of the Princess—"a dreamer must accept his dreams"—and not seek clarification in Cocteau's dream world. Or to quote Heurtebise, "It is not necessary to understand . . . only to believe."

"If your strange mania for seeking to understand is so powerful that you have to figure out every symbol and meaning in a movie, you probably won't have a very good time at *Orpheus,*" wrote Philip T. Hartung, in *The Commonweal* (December 15, 1950), "but if you're willing to let Jean Cocteau guide you into a dream world of sleep and death that is populated by a handsome cast and motivated by a mysterious hand, you'll find *Orpheus* a stimulating adventure."

Hartung was in the minority as far as American critics were concerned. Most were unwilling to give *Orpheus* very much time at all. Typical is Bosley Crowther's comment, in *The New York Times* (December 3, 1950), "The decor is fine, the acting solemn and the artfulness is intense. . . . Okay, if you like that sort of thing."

Jean Cocteau returned to the Orpheus theme in 1959 with his last film, *Le Testament d'Orphée/Testament of Orpheus,* which also featured Edouard Dermithe, Maria Casarès, François Périer and Jean Marais. As Georges Sadoul has written (translated by Peter Morris), "It forms the third part, with *le Sang d'un Poète* and *Orphée,* of a private diary whose allegory and metaphorical obsessions are confessions and whose esotericism is an expression of his sincerity."

ABOVE: Maria Casarès as the emissary of death. BELOW: Aglaonice, the commissioner and Eurydice (Juliette Gréco, Pierre Bertin and Marie Déa) await word of Orpheus.

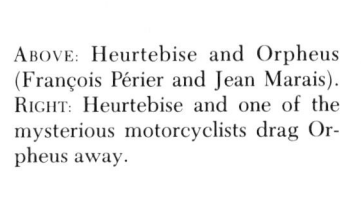

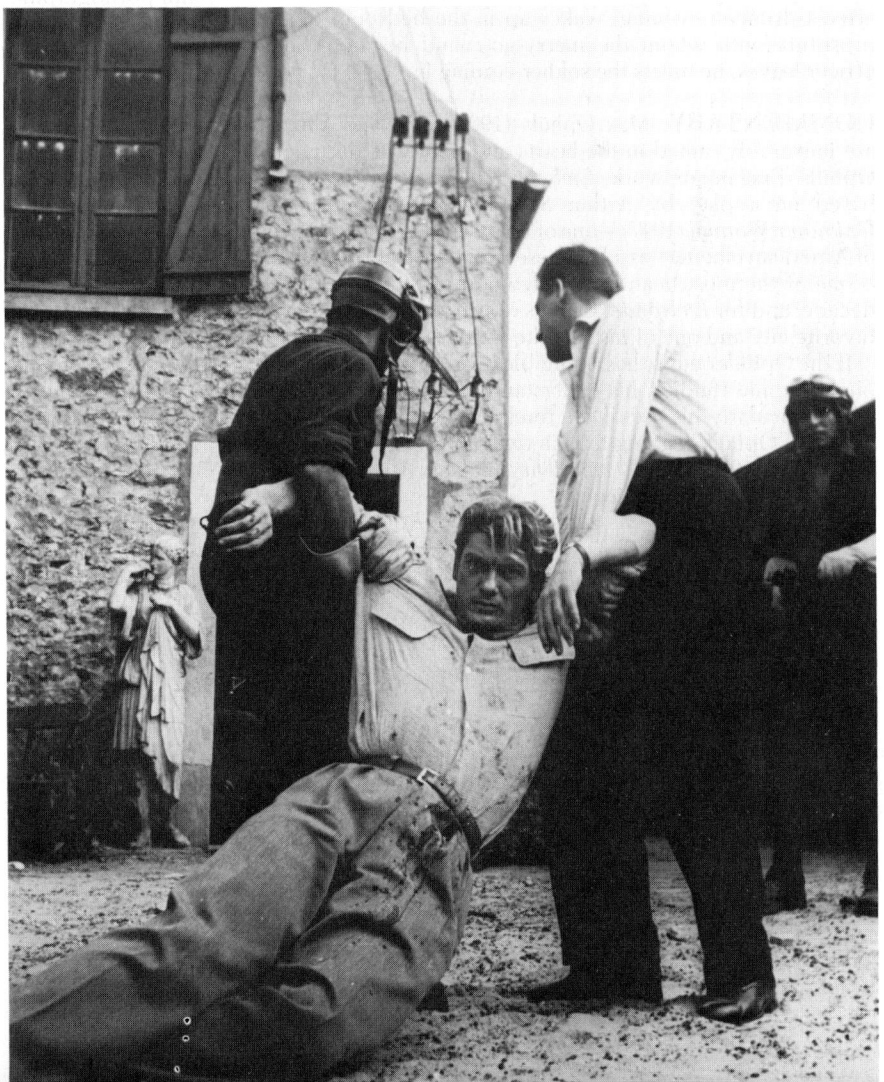

ABOVE: Heurtebise and Orpheus (François Périer and Jean Marais). RIGHT: Heurtebise and one of the mysterious motorcyclists drag Orpheus away.

LA RONDE

Producer: Sacha Gordine. *Released:* 1950, Sacha Gordine (France); 1951, Commercial Pictures (U.S.). *Running Time:* 109 minutes (France); 84 minutes (U.S.).

Director: Max Ophüls. *Screenplay:* Jacques Natanson and Max Ophüls. *Dialogue:* Jacques Natanson (based on the play *Der Reigen*, by Arthur Schnitzler). *Photography:* Christian Matras. *Music:* Oscar Straus. *Art Directors:* Jean d'Eaubonne, Marpaux and M. Frederix. *Costumes:* Georges Annenkov. *Film Editor:* Léonide Azar. *Sound:* Pierre Calvet.

CAST: Anton Walbrook (*the master of ceremonies*); Simone Signoret (*the street girl*); Serge Reggiani (*the soldier*); Simone Simon (*the maid*); Daniel Gélin (*the student*); Danielle Darrieux (*the lady*); Fernand Gravet (Gravey) (*the lady's husband*); Odette Joyeux (*the model*); Jean-Louis Barrault (*the poet*); Isa Miranda (*the actress*); Gérard Philipe (*the count*); Charles Vissière (*the concierge*).

SYNOPSIS: The merry-go-round or carousel of love, as presented by a master of ceremonies in Vienna of the late 1800s. A prostitute meets a soldier, who, after a brief romantic interlude under a bridge, rudely leaves her. A few days later, at a dance at the Prater, the soldier seduces a young housemaid, who is, in turn, abandoned, only to be seduced by her employer's son. He is attracted to an older, married woman, who breaks off the affair out of concern for her husband, not knowing that he is having an affair with a model. A poet is attracted to the model, but leaves her for a middle-aged actress, who leaves him for a young noble officer, who, after a drunken evening, wakes up in the bedroom of the prostitute with whom the merry-go-round began. As the officer leaves, he meets the soldier coming in.

COMMENTARY: Max Ophüls (1902–1957) and Vienna are inexorably linked in the hearts and minds of filmgoers. Ophüls' first major work, *Liebelei* (1932), is set there and based on a play by Arthur Schnitzler; *Letter from an Unknown Woman* (1947)—one of the forgotten masterpieces of American cinema—is a Viennese romantic tragedy, which is one of the most beautiful Hollywood productions of the decade; and for *La Ronde*, Ophüls returned once more to his favorite city and one of his favorite writers, Schnitzler.

If the Ophüls oeuvre has a tangible link it is in the director's photographic fluidity, his understanding of lighting effects and particularly his use of the tracking shot. James Mason, who was Ophüls' leading man in two Hollywood-produced features of 1947, *Caught* and *The Reckless Moment*, even wrote a jingle on the subject:

> I think I know the reason why
> Producers tend to make him cry.
> Inevitably they demand
> Some stationary set-ups, and
> A shot that does not call for tracks
> Is agony for poor dear Max,
> Who, separated from his dolly,
> Is wrapped in deepest melancholy.
> Once, when they took away his crane,
> I thought he'd never smile again.

La Ronde was Ophüls' first European feature in more than a decade, and is a delightful, light-hearted affair—far more so than the work on which it is based. The film is featherweight in plot and impact. Its message, as suggested by Bosley Crowther, in *The New York Times* (March 21, 1954), is that "Life is a merry-go-round for those who would seek excitement in wanton and clandestine amours; pleasure is flimsy and fleeting on this spinning carousel, and the mental build up of expectation is pure illusion and nothing more." Sex is what *La Ronde* is all about—sex in all its illicit heterosexual permutations. It may be, as *Variety* (September 21, 1951) commented, "one of the sexiest [films] ever to be brought to this country," but it is also one of the most tasteful. Ophüls is the master of good taste. Today, *La Ronde* is more quaint than shocking, carrying the viewer with it thanks to a lilting score (which utilizes the waltz theme from Straus's *The Chocolate Soldier*), impeccable sets, fine acting by a cast that includes Anton Walbrook, Simone Signoret, Danielle Darrieux, Jean-Louis Barrault, Fernand Gravet and Gérard Philipe and, above all, lighting that is subtle and shadowy, used without undue emphasis to create what is the epitome of romantic cinema.

Newsweek (October 22, 1951) hailed *La Ronde* as "subtle, lovely and frequently uproarious." *Time* (October 22, 1951) found it "a wry ode to love. . . . It is neither prurient, smirking nor pornographic . . . it spoofs sex rather than exploits it." On the negative side, John McCarten, in *The New Yorker* (March 27, 1954), noted that sex can become, after a while, rather tedious, adding: "While the characters are varied, their proclivities are not, and before all the affairs are over and done with, you'll probably be longing to get out of the bedroom and into a cold shower."

As far as the New York Censorship Board was concerned, a cold shower was not the remedy for dealing with *La Ronde*, and it promptly banned the film outright. The Board's action was upheld on appeal to the New York Court of Appeals, which noted, with a certain amount of smug satisfaction, that the books and stories of Arthur Schnitzler had been banned in New York State in the early Thirties. Finally, the rights and wrongs of the case were argued before the U.S. Supreme Court, which decided in January of 1954 that the censors had no right to bar the film's screening, a decision that marked the beginning of the end of film censorship in the United States on a local level.

Despite, or probably because of, the censorship campaign, *La Ronde* was a huge popular success in the United States. It was nominated for Academy Awards for Best Art Direction and Best Writing, and, in Britain, was voted Best Film of the Year by the British Film Academy.

ABOVE: The prostitute (Simone Signoret) and the soldier (Serge Reggiani). LEFT: The maid (Simone Simon) and the student (Daniel Gélin).

77

LEFT: Simone Simon (born 1911) was the quintessential French child-woman actress, who gave memorable performances in two American films, *7th Heaven* (1937) and *Cat People* (1942). BELOW: The married woman (Danielle Darrieux) and her husband (Fernand Gravet).

DIARY OF A COUNTRY PRIEST
JOURNAL D'UN CURÉ DE CAMPAGNE

Producer: Union Générale Cinématographique. *Released:* 1951, A.G.D.C. (France); 1954, Brandon Films (U.S.). *Running Time:* 120 minutes (France); 95 minutes (U.S.).

Director: Robert Bresson. *Screenplay:* Robert Bresson (based on the novel by Georges Bernanos). *Photography:* Léonce-Henry Burel. *Art Director:* Pierre Charbonnier. *Music:* Jean-Jacques Grunenwald. *Film Editor:* Paulette Robert.

CAST: Claude Laydu (*the priest of Ambricourt*); Jean Riveyre (*the count*); André Guibert (*the priest of Torcy*); Nicole Ladmiral (*Chantal*); Martine Lemaire (*Séraphita*); Nicole Maurey (*Mademoiselle Louis*); Madame Arkell (*the countess*); Jean Danet (*Olivier*); Antoine Balpêtré (*Dr. Delbende*).

SYNOPSIS: The young priest of Ambricourt finds his parishioners sullen and unresponsive. He suffers from severe stomach pains, can eat little more than stale bread soaked in wine, and is continually made aware of his own shortcomings as a priest. The children in his First Communion class poke fun at him, and he does not have the courage to speak up to the deputy mayor or to Old Fabregars arguing over the cost of his wife's funeral. At the suggestion of his mentor, the priest of Torcy, he visits the elderly, agnostic Dr. Delbende, who suggests the priest is an alcoholic; later the priest is disturbed by rumors that Delbende has committed suicide. He attempts to interest the local count in a boys' club and learns that the count is having an affair with his daughter's governess, while his wife remains in permanent mourning for her dead son. The priest is able to restore the countess' faith, but she dies that same night and the priest is accused of indirectly causing her death. He refuses to produce a letter from the countess in his defense when the count threatens to take the matter up with the local Catholic hierarchy. Desperately ill, the priest collapses while walking round the parish and is found and cared for by Séraphita, one of the girls who had teased him in the Communion class. Meanwhile the count's daughter (Chantal) has taken over control of the manor and forced her father to fire the governess. En route to consult a doctor in Lille, the count's son, Olivier, gives the priest a ride on his motorbike, tells him of the Foreign Legion, of which he is a member, and gives the priest his first glimpse of the pleasures of youth. In Lille, the priest discovers he has cancer of the stomach, and he dies at the home of Dufrety, whom he had known at the seminary, and who is now living with his mistress.

COMMENTARY: François Truffaut has said that Robert Bresson's cinema is closer to painting than to photography, and that viewpoint is very apparent in Bresson's best-known and second major feature, *Diary of a Country Priest*. Watching the film, one is very much aware that here is a film whose maker perceives it as a work of art. There is a harsh, almost grainy quality to much of the cinematography, but there is also evidence of careful composition—the touch of a painter—particularly in the shots of the lonely priest walking across a stark, unyielding landscape. The music by Jean-Jacques Grunenwald is reminiscent of Mahler's work. Bresson's continual utilization of natural sounds in the background—birds singing, dogs barking—is very pleasing. The acting is, at least to a non-French eye, very naturalistic, and the director insisted on unknowns or nonprofessionals for all of the roles, except those of Dr. Delbende and the Countess. As Raymond Durgnat has noted, Bresson, like Dreyer, casts for character rather than "acting ability."

Diary of a Country Priest presents one with the essence of the unhappy life of a young priest, physically and emotionally unsuited for such a life. The priest's isolation is immediately made apparent in the first scene, when he sees a couple kissing—the count and his daughter's governess—and immediately his presence ends the emotion of the moment; the two stop and stare coldly at him. He finds "the simple tasks are not the easiest," and that makes doubly hard the major tasks he must face in his parish. When he does succeed in restoring the countess' faith, the priest must then face the censure of his superiors.

He is "a prisoner of the Holy Agony," and that feeling is always apparent in the manner and acting of Claude Laydu as the priest. Wearing the genuine clothing of a priest, Laydu apparently fasted in order to obtain the appearance of a dying man. But it is not the body that first draws one's attention, but rather the priest's soulful, innocent eyes. They are beautiful eyes, as Séraphita says, but they are also—as the doctor remarks—the eyes of a dog. They are the eyes of a follower, not a leader of men.

When the feature was released in the United States a further twenty-five minutes were deleted from the French release version (which had already been cut by forty minutes), including one whole scene—that between the priest and the foreign legionnaire. Such cuts were made at the instigation of the Fifth Avenue Cinema (formerly the Fifth Avenue Playhouse) in New York, where *Diary of a Country Priest* was the opening presentation on April 5, 1954. *New York Times* critic Bosley Crowther was not overly enthusiastic about the film. A subsequent letter from Bresson—published in the *Times* on May 2, 1954—blamed Crowther's view on the American cutting of the film. However, Crowther responded that "more material of the sort that is in it might well only complicate it more—that is, for one to whom its contents and its reckonings are essentially abstruse."

Because *Diary of a Country Priest* is such a difficult film to understand, because it is such a bleak, unswervingly moral tale, because it is cinema in one of its purest forms—André Bazin has suggested it is basically a silent film—audiences will continue to debate its value and its place in the history of French cinema. One thing is very certain: *Diary of a Country Priest* is a unique work, outside of both traditional French cinema and the New Wave which it just preceded.

ABOVE: Claude Laydu as the insecure priest of Ambricourt.
LEFT: The priest and Chantal (Claude Laydu and Nicole Ladmiral).

ABOVE: The priest (Claude Laydu) visits Dr. Delbende (Antoine Balpêtré) for medical advice. BELOW: Séraphita (Martine Lemaire) helps the ailing priest.

LE PLAISIR

Producer: Max Ophüls for Stera Films—CCFC. *Released:* 1952, Columbia (France); 1954, Mayer-Kingsley (U.S.). *Running Time:* 97 minutes.

Director: Max Ophüls. *Screenplay:* Jacques Natanson and Max Ophüls (based on three short stories, "Le Masque," "La Maison Tellier" and "Le Modèle," by Guy de Maupassant). *Photography:* Christian Matras and Philippe Agostini. *Art Directors:* Jean d'Eaubonne and Jacques Guth. *Costumes:* Georges Annenkov. *Film Editor:* Léonide Azar. *Music:* Joe Hajos and Maurice Yvain (from themes of Offenbach). *Sound:* Jean Rieul and Pierre Calvet. *Narrators:* Peter Ustinov (English version), Jean Servais (French version), Anton Walbrook (German version).

CAST: LE MASQUE: Claude Dauphin (*the doctor*); Janine Viénot (*his friend*); Jean Galland (*Ambroise*); Gaby Morlay (*Denise*); Paul Azaïs (*the owner of the Palais de Danse*); Emile Genevois (*the groom*); Gaby Bruyère (*Frimousse*); Huguette Montréal (*dancer*); Liliane Yvernault (*dancer*).
LA MAISON TELLIER: Madeleine Renaud (*Madame Tellier*); Danielle Darrieux (*Rosa*); Ginette Leclerc (*Flora*); Paulette Dubost (*Fernande*); Mila Parély (*Raphaële*) Mathilde Casadesus (*Louise*); Amédée (*Frédéric*); Michel Vadet (*a sailor*); Jo Dest (*a German*); Claire Olivier (*Madame Tourneveau*); Georges Vitray (*the captain*); Charles Vissière (*the old man*); Zélie Yzelle (*his wife*); Pierre Brasseur (*Julien Ledentu*); Jean Gabin (*Joseph Rivet*); Helena Manson (*Marie*); Joëlle Jany (*Constance*); René Blancard (*the mayor*).
LE MODÈLE: Daniel Gélin (*Jean*); Simone Simon (*Joséphine*); Michel Vadet (*the journalist*); Jean Servais (*Guy*).

SYNOPSIS: LE MASQUE: A strangely masked figure arrives at a large and elegant dance hall; he is a substitute for one of the dancers, but passes out on the floor and, when a doctor is called and the mask removed, proves to be an elderly gentleman. The doctor takes him home, where the man's wife explains that he was a former barber, a ladies' man, who has never been able to accept his growing old.
LA MAISON TELLIER: The Maison Tellier, otherwise known as No. 3, is a well-known brothel in a Normandy town. One evening, its regular customers find the place closed because Madame Tellier has taken her girls to attend the first Communion of her brother's daughter in a small village. En route, the girls share a railway compartment with two elderly peasants and a traveling salesman. They are met at the station by Madame Tellier's brother, Joseph Rivet, who is obviously attracted to one of the girls, Madame Rosa. They present a Communion dress to Rivet's daughter Constance, have problems in falling asleep because of the quiet of the countryside, and are treated as honored guests at the church ceremony. After lunch, the women return to town and the brothel reopens that evening.
LE MODÈLE: A young and promising artist (Jean) falls in love with a model (Joséphine), but soon tires of her. When she threatens to commit suicide after he has left her, Jean tells her to go ahead. She does attempt suicide by throwing herself from the window, but succeeds only in becoming paralyzed, a condition that forces Jean to marry her and take care of her for the rest of their days.

COMMENTARY: *Le Plaisir* may be, as Bosley Crowther described it in *The New York Times* (May 30, 1956), a "frilled and fluffy trifle," but it is one of the best and most pleasantly satisfying of all Max Ophüls' films. Indeed, the viewer probably derives more pleasure from the film than do the antagonists in this triple tale of pleasure, as it relates to old age, to the sacrifice of self and the simple joy of sex. Based on three stories by Guy de Maupassant, who is heard from in the film—in the English-language version—through the voice of Peter Ustinov (a not entirely satisfying experience), *Le Plaisir* contains two extremely short episodes, which are little more than sketches, and one major tale, which could well stand release as a feature in its own right.

The short episodes, *Le Masque* and *Le Modèle*, are chiefly notable for the expensive sets of the first, and for the abrupt camera change from objective to subjective as Joséphine, the model, walks up the stairs and throws herself out of the window. There is also an air of spontaneous excitement apparent in both episodes, particularly the first as the viewer enters the expensive dance hall and as the doorman rushes to find first a doctor and then a pair of scissors. That same excitement reappears in *Le Modèle* as Joséphine and Jean realize their incompatibility after three months together, and the camera literally chases the arguing couple through the house.

Those two episodes are, perhaps, neither particularly sweet nor substantive. The *Maison Tellier* episode also has little substance, but it does not, "like most weekends in the country . . . drag a little on Sunday afternoon," as *Time* (June 14, 1954) has suggested. Here is to be found a wealth of minute and entrancing detail, a fascinating study of characters. Ophüls shows us the townspeople arguing out of the frustrated emotion occasioned by the abrupt closure of the brothel, and compares this sequence with the end of the episode as the brothel is reopened and joy and tranquility return once more to the town.

If there is a fault in *Le Plaisir*, it is in the unrealistic exterior sets of the Maison Tellier episode, although the artificiality of these sets is more than countered by the natural realism of the country scenes. In *The Monthly Film Bulletin* (March 1953), Gavin Lambert complained that Guy de Maupassant was not the best of authors for Ophüls' style of filmmaking, but this is certainly debatable. For the American release of *Le Plaisir*, the Maison Tellier story was shown as the final episode in the film, which unfortunately means the episode loses the sense of being a major attraction, showcased by two vignettes.

ABOVE: The exterior of the Palais de Danse. BELOW: The mysterious masked dancer is carried from the floor after his collapse.

Above: Joseph Rivet (Jean Gabin) collects the visiting prostitutes. Below: Joseph Rivet with his wife Marie (Héléna Manson).

MR. HULOT'S HOLIDAY
LES VACANCES DE MONSIEUR HULOT

Producer: Fred Orain for Cady Film-Discina-Éclair Journal. *Released:* 1953, Discina (France); 1954, G-B-D International (U.S.). *Running Time:* 90 minutes (France); 85 minutes (U.S.).

Director: Jacques Tati. *Screenplay:* Jacques Tati and Henri Marquet. *Photography:* Jacques Mercanton and Jean Mousselle. *Art Director:* Henri Schmitt. *Music:* Alain Romans. *Film Editors:* Jacques Grassi, Suzanne Baron and Charles Bretoneiche.

CAST: Jacques Tati (*M. Hulot*); Nathalie Pascaud (*Martine*); Louis Perrault (*Fred*); Michèle Rolla (*the aunt*); André Dubois (*the commandant*); Valentine Camax (*the Englishwoman*); Lucien Frégis (*the hotelkeeper*); Marguerite Gérard (*the strolling woman*); René Lacourt (*the strolling man*); Suzy Willy (*the commandant's wife*); Raymond Carl (*the boy*); Michèle Brabo (*a vacationer*).

SYNOPSIS: Monsieur Hulot arrives, in his 1924 car, for his annual vacation at the Hotel de la Plage, located in a small seaside resort. Anxious to please, but accident-prone, M. Hulot leaves doors open at the hotel with disastrous results, tracks mud through the hotel, upsets an exercise class, is trapped in his canoe, and has his car drive off without him. On Hulot's final evening at the hotel, he enters a building where fireworks are stored, and the resulting pyrotechnic display is a fitting conclusion to his holiday.

COMMENTARY: Jacques Tati (1908–1982) has been compared to the greatest of film clowns. Penelope Gilliatt has described him as "the one film comedian of today who is Keaton's equal." Tati himself has discussed his work in comparison to Chaplin's and, perhaps more correctly, to that of Max Linder. In fact, with his gift of mime, Jacques Tati can be more aptly compared to Marcel Marceau, although Tati's comedy is broader, aiming more for the belly laugh than the restrained smile. (Indeed, Tati is superior to Marceau in that he can get a laugh by not even being seen, but having his character, Monsieur Hulot, merely suggested—as in *Monsieur Hulot's Holiday* with the sound of his age-worn automobile.) However, like Marcel Marceau, Jacques Tati's humor can become more than a little tedious; at times one feels obligated to sit through his films, not from a sense of enjoyment, but a sense of duty. I tend to agree with Andrew Sarris that it is sufficient to view Tati's films once. There is no point in going back to see them a second time. Unlike Chaplin, or Keaton, or Lloyd, or even Langdon, Jacques Tati's humor does not improve through repeated screenings.

Despite my own lack of enthusiasm, there can be no question that Jacques Tati belongs in a book such as this. The choice of film is almost immaterial. It might be *Jour de Fête* (1949), *Mon Oncle* (1958) or *Playtime* (1967). However, it must be admitted that his last two features—*Traffic* (1971) and *Parade* (1973)—do not deserve the classic status of his earlier work.

Jacques Tati was an individualist, as is his creation, Monsieur Hulot. He is not a particularly funny person, but, rather, his actions create comic situations, as does the behavior of those around him. As Tati has explained, "It is for us in the picture to be serious, for the audience to laugh."

Monsieur Hulot's Holiday is a film for all those who take their vacations seriously, and are willing to work at enjoying themselves. Filming commenced in the summer of 1951 at St. Marc-sur-Mer in Brittany, and the production was not completed until fall of the following year. The setting is French, but the characterizations are almost universal; the plot could have been as easily set in a small seaside resort in America or England. There is no real story, simply a series of episodes involving the middle class at play. "To me," said Tati, "a simple man spending a fortnight at a lovely beach, a vacation for which he has saved his money all year, and to which he goes with his mind set on having a good time—his is a great adventure to him annd to all people who can understand his desires."

Monsieur Hulot is the central character in the film, but the comedy does not rely solely on his antics. His activities are, at times, peripheral to the humorous situations. There is humor in the hotel's radio announcer pontificating, emphasizing—at times overemphasizing—the comic situation. The running gag concerning Hulot's playing a jazz recording in his room much too loudly is typical of Tati's humor not involving the leading player. When, as the audience has been continually expecting, angry guests burst into the room in anger, they find there not Hulot, but a small girl.

In France, reported *The New Yorker*'s Genet (Janet Flanner), Parisians thought the film either droll or merely silly. Genet also noted that during the general strike that hit Paris in the summer of 1953, "the speechless, invincible, unlucky, and unappreciated Hulot . . . generously showed French vacations as something Parisians should be glad they have to miss." *Life* (July 5, 1954) called the production "the year's funniest film and a modern masterpiece of slapstick, a throwback to the days of Keaton and the Keystone shorts when a comedian made you laugh by what he did, not by what he said."

If there is a link to the golden age of screen comedy, as *Life* suggested, it is in the film's lack of dialogue. Monsieur Hulot does not speak—he doesn't need to. In his study of *The Films of Jacques Tati*, Brent Maddock has written, quite rightly, that "Tati finds, in the natural sounds of the world, a music of his own. He is a master of the expressive sound effect." In that sense, Tati is slightly better off than the silent clowns who had no sound upon which to rely.

Monsieur Hulot's Holiday has continued to appeal to Americans. It was first reissued, in a re-edited (by Tati) form in 1966, and all of the Tati features were reissued for a major Jacques Tati revival in 1983.

ABOVE: Jacques Tati as M. Hulot dominates every scene in the film. BELOW: M. Hulot demonstrates his skills as a tennis player.

ABOVE: Both hotel guests and employees are outraged by M. Hulot's antics. BELOW: At the masked ball, M. Hulot dances with Martine (Nathalie Pascaud).

THE WAGES OF FEAR
LE SALAIRE DE LA PEUR

Producer: H-G. Clouzot for CICC-Silver Films-Vera Films-Fono Roma. *Released:* 1953, Filmsonor-CICC (France); 1955, Distributors Corporation of America (U.S.). *Running Time:* 155 minutes (France); 104 minutes (U.S.).

Director: H-G. Clouzot. *Screenplay:* H-G. Clouzot (based on the novel by Georges Arnaud). *Photography:* Armand Thirard. *Music:* Georges Auric. *Art Director:* René Renoux. *Film Editors:* Madeleine Gug and Henri Rust. *Sound:* William-Robert Sivel.

CAST: Yves Montand (*Mario*); Charles Vanel (*Jo*); Véra Clouzot (*Linda*); Peter Van Eyck (*Bimba*); William Tubbs (*O'Brien*); Dario Moreno (*Hernandez*); Jo Dest (*Smerloff*); Folco Lulli (*Luigi*).

SYNOPSIS: A group of down-and-outs are living in a small Central American town near an American-controlled oil field. When a fire breaks out at a well three hundred miles up country, the company manager offers $2,000 to any volunteers who will drive two truckloads of nitroglycerin, which is highly volatile, over bad roads, to the site. A young Corsican, Mario; an Italian bricklayer, Luigi; a silent German, Bimba; and a gangster, Jo (who kills off another volunteer in order to take his place), are selected for the assignment. The journey is slow and perilous, with Luigi and Bimba driving one truck, and Jo and Mario the other, and there is the additional problem of Jo's losing his nerve and Mario's coming to despise him. On the final leg of the trip, Luigi's and Bimba's truck explodes, killing them both and opening up an oil pipe that spills into the crater caused by the blast. Jo stands in the pool of oily mud, guiding the truck, but he slips and Mario drives over him, crushing his leg. Mario drags Jo out and drives with him to the oil field, but by the time they arrive Jo is dead. Mario returns the following day, in high spirits, but because of his reckless driving sends the truck over a cliff, resulting in his own death.

COMMENTARY: *The Wages of Fear* must have come as quite a surprise to most filmgoers, who did not expect a French film to resemble a Hitchcockian thriller with violent overtones. Those familiar with the work of director Henri-Georges Clouzot (1907-1977) knew exactly what to expect. He was very much the French equivalent of Alfred Hitchcock—but without the humor and with a decidedly cruel and violent streak—as indicated by *L'Assassin Habite au 21/The Murderer Lives at No. 21* (1942), *Le Corbeau/The Raven* (1943), *Quai des Orfèvres/Jenny Lamour* (1947) and *Les Diaboliques/Diabolique* (1955). Bosley Crowther called Clouzot a sadist with a camera.

"The director is always his own spectator and when I am a spectator I must have suspense," said Clouzot in a January 23, 1955 interview with *The New York Times*. "Art for me is a provocation. I do not always know why I do what I do. I cannot say why there is a cruel side to my films, although the problems interest me. But I do know it is necessary for me to show the black side of men as well as the white. I do not like the gay police film. To play with death is to cheat and that is indecent."

In fact, the suspense and tensive aspects of *The Wages of Fear* do not appear until well into the film. Clouzot uses the first third of the production to set the scene and to develop the characterizations of the four protagonists—the outcasts making the deadly trip to the oil fields. But in showing these men and their sordid existence, Clouzot does not disappoint those expecting him to display a cold and cruel streak. "At the outset," complained Bosley Crowther, in *The New York Times* (February 17, 1955), "this lethally laden thriller looks as though it is taking off to be a squalid and mordant contemplation of the psychological problems of a group of men stuck without hope of salvation in a fetid South American oil town." However, Genet, in *The New Yorker* (May 16, 1953), described the first half as "like a remarkably photographed novel, showing the barflies' sordid, greedy quarrels as a guide to what is coming."

Much of the early section was cut from the initial American release version because it was perceived as anti-American in its implied criticism of exploitation of the country by the American oil company. Certainly there can be no question, as Clouzot has admitted, that *The Wages of Fear* is an anti-trust film. Clouzot was no stranger to controversy—*Le Corbeau* had been criticized as pro-German and resulted in a brief exile from filmmaking for its director; the Communists attacked *Manon* (1949); and when *The Wages of Fear* won the Grand Prix at the Cannes Film Festival, both Clouzot and his star Yves Montand were accused of being card-carrying Communists.

Clouzot was attracted to Georges Arnaud's thriller after spending some time in Brazil. He cast his Brazilian wife Véra in the small role of the barmaid. *The Wages of Fear* was filmed on location in and around Nîmes, and the shooting was marred by extreme bad weather and financial difficulties which forced the filming to stretch from 1951 through 1952.

One of the most interesting contemporary aspects of the production was the casting of Yves Montand in his first straight role. Up to this time, Montand was France's most popular ballad singer, a Gallic version of Bing Crosby, but to Clouzot, Montand *looked* like a truck driver, and, of course, gives a superb performance. His moods range from admiration, through hatred and fear, to exaltation as he drunkenly drives his truck, to the music of a remembered juke-box waltz, off the road and to his death. As John McCarten wrote in *The New Yorker* (February 26, 1955), he "makes a believable transition from sycophancy to raw courage."

The Wages of Fear was severely cut—mutilated is a better word—for its American release, but nevertheless it became an immediate popular success. In Britain, it was the first foreign-language film to receive a national release (through the J. Arthur Rank Organization). A 1977 American remake by William Friedkin, under the title of *Sorcerer*, was a disaster.

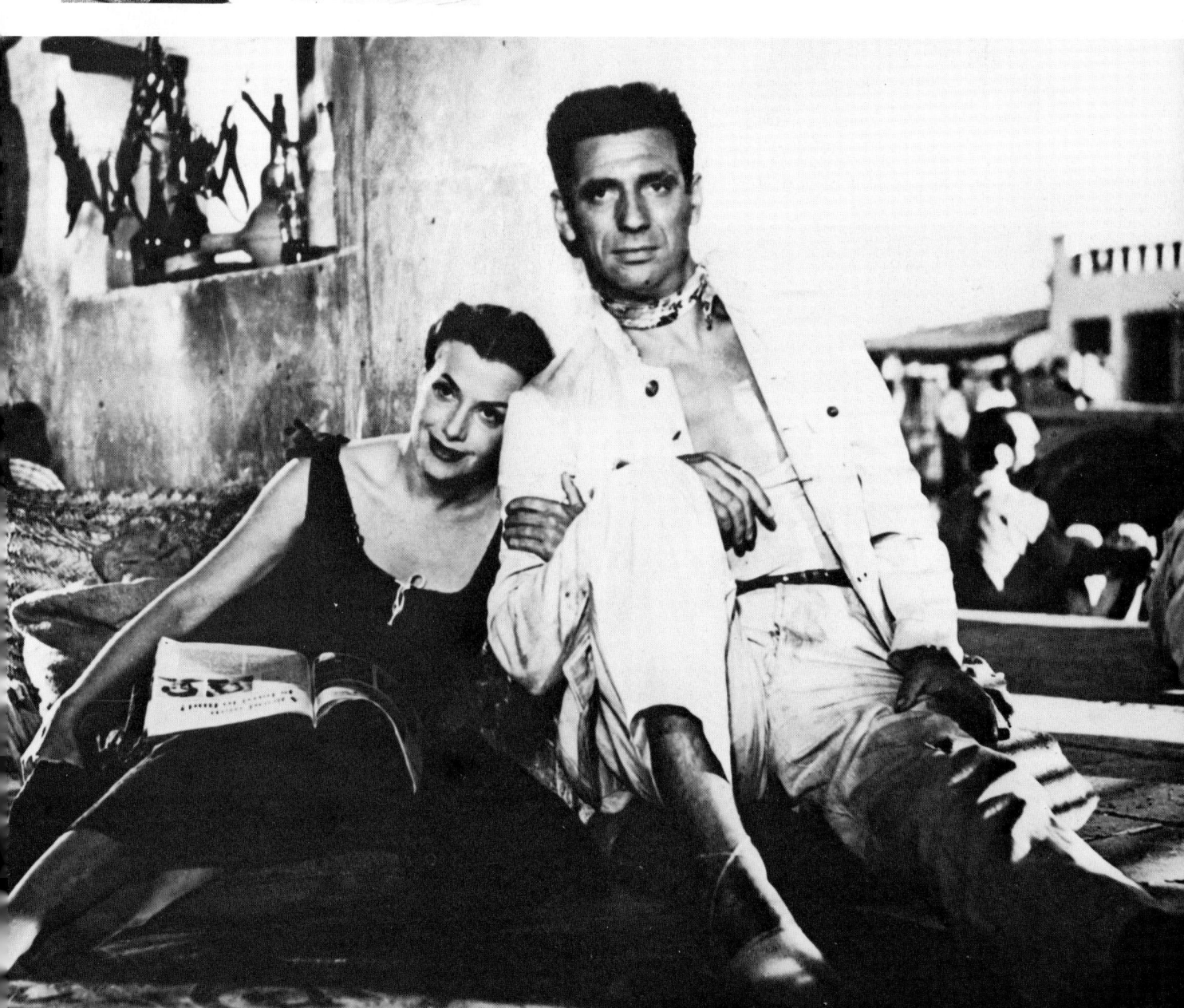

LEFT: Henri-Georges Clouzot. BELOW: Linda and Mario (Véra Clouzot and Yves Montand).

ABOVE: Mario and Jo (Yves Montand and Charles Vanel) at the start of their perilous journey. BELOW: Mario pulls Jo from the pool of oily mud after the latter's leg has been crushed by the truck.

THE SHEEP HAS FIVE LEGS
LE MOUTON A CINQ PATTES

Producer: Raoul Ploquin for Cocinex. *Released:* 1954, Cocinor (France); 1955, United Motion Picture Organization (U.S.). *Running Time:* 100 minutes (France); 93 minutes (U.S.).

Director: Henri Verneuil. *Screenplay:* Albert Valentin. *Adaptation:* René Barjavel (based on stories by Jean Marsan, Henry Troyat, Jacques Perret, Henri Verneuil and Raoul Ploquin). *Photography:* Armand Thirard. *Film Editor:* Christian Gaudin.

CAST: Fernandel (*Edouard, Alain, Bernard, Etienne, Charles, Désiré*); Françoise Arnoul (*Marianne*); Edouard Delmont (*Dr. Bolène*); Louis de Funès (*Pilate*); Noël Roquevert (*Brissard*); Lina Lopez (*the native girl*); René Génin (*the mayor*).

SYNOPSIS: Forty years after the birth of quintuplet sons, Papa Saint-Forget feels only bitterness toward his children and refuses to cooperate with Dr. Bolène's plans for a major celebration to put the village of Trézignan back on the map. Dr. Bolène finds that one son, Alain, is now the wealthy owner of a beauty salon, disparaging another brother, Désiré, who, in revenge, lets white mice loose in his brother's salon. Désiré, a poor yet honest character, is persuaded by Pilate the undertaker to sign an agreement, whereby his dying wish is that his brother Alain provide an expensive funeral for him. Immediately after signing the agreement, Désiré imagines himself ill, but it is Pilate who dies, and Désiré initiates a scheme whereby he signs similar agreements for cash payments with all the Paris undertakers. In the South Seas, another brother, Etienne, is involved in a game of chance as to whether a fly will land first on his lump of sugar or his opponent's; Etienne wins. In Paris, Bernard writes an advice-for-the-lovelorn column, and helps a young girl forced into an engagement with an older man by her parents. In Morvan, Charles is a pastor, a figure of ridicule because he bears such a striking resemblance to a movie star named Fernandel, who appears as the priest Don Camillo. Back in Trézignan, celebrations are under way, but the police come to arrest Désiré for his fraudulent agreements. However, he is saved by his wife's giving birth to sextuplets (all girls). A reconciliation takes place between Papa Saint-Forget and his children, and the proud father declares to the president of France that his generation delivered five, the newer generation has produced six, and the family has not finished yet.

COMMENTARY: One's immediate reaction to *The Sheep Has Five Legs*, in which Fernandel plays six roles, is that it is a Gallic version of *Kind Hearts and Coronets*, without the satiric humor of the latter, and with Fernandel not quite measuring up to the artistry of Alec Guinness' performance. "Less pointed but almost as funny," commented *Newsweek* (August 29, 1955). The performance of Delmont, as the village doctor who links the various stories together, also recalls Jean Hersholt's characterization of the country doctor in the series of American features concerning the Dionne quintuplets. Certainly *The Sheep Has Five Legs* is not a major film in the history of French cinema, but it is interesting as an example of popular filmmaking—its director Henri Verneuil has always proudly described himself as a commercial director—and as a feature that offers Fernandel varied characterizations, a chance to prove he is as much an actor as a comedian. Coincidentally, the film provides the viewer with an opportunity to study the sly and witty performance of Louis de Funès as the undertaker urging Fernandel to sign a pact with him as to his funeral arrangements, an almost Faustian concept, which is assuredly the funniest sequence in the film.

Fernandel (1903-1971) was born Fernand Contandin, and selected his stage name after his engagement to Henriette Manse, when his family started calling him "le Fernand d'elle." His career began in the music halls, but he became an international star with his film career, which began in the early Thirties and included only one serious feature. With his horselike features and toothy grin, Fernandel was a natural comedian. He had his biggest success as the priest in *Le Petit Monde de Don Camillo/The Little World of Don Camillo* (1952), which led to a series of features, and comic reference to which is made in *The Sheep Has Five Legs*.

In an article in *Films and Filming* (October 1960), Fernandel wrote, "Probably the director that I prefer to work with is Henri Verneuil. I appeared in the first film that he made and also in his most recent, *The Cow and the Prisoner* [*La Vache et le Prisonnier*]. I like working with him because I know him from A to Z. By that I don't mean to imply that I gave him his talent, because he had talent to start with. But I know several people who have worked with me who have said to me, 'You are not doing for me what you did for Henri Verneuil. You're not making me famous.' You just can't 'start' anybody, if he has talent this will appear in the films he makes, and this was the case with Henri Verneuil. . . . In my opinion Verneuil, not a member of the 'New Wave' because he is forty but of the generation that came just before the 'new wave,' is one of the best directors that I know. On top of his technical knowledge, he listens to what people think. And he knows how to listen."

The Sheep Has Five Legs was well received in the United States, providing Fernandel with national attention as the film played some thirty-three cities. (Ten years later the comedian was to make a personal appearance tour through America, something which, say, Jacques Tati, whose films were reaching the States at the same time as Fernandel's, could not have done.) In *The New Yorker* (August 20, 1955), John McCarten found Fernandel "droll," adding, "*The Sheep Has Five Legs* flags a trifle toward the end, but such a lot of satisfactory stuff has gone before that it would be carping to complain very much." Jesse Zunser, in *Cue* (August 13, 1955), found Fernandel "wondrously comical." Similarly, *Time* (September 5, 1955) hailed the film as "a rollicking demonstration of his [Fernandel's] virtuosity. . . . With the slightest nuances of his elastic face—a leer, a bucktoothed grin, a cocker-spaniel look of sadness—he proves that he is one of the most versatile comedians alive." Bosley Crowther was the most enthusiastic of all; in *The New York Times* (August 10, 1955), he hailed *The Sheep Has Five Legs* as "not only . . . the best Fernandel in years, but it is probably the cleverest and most hilarious French comedy we've seen since the war."

It was claimed at the time that *The Sheep Has Five Legs* marked Fernandel's 150th screen role. In fact, it could be argued it provided the comedian with his 150th through 155th. Whatever the number—and there seems little question that Fernandel had made around 150 films at the time of his death—*The Sheep Has Five Legs*, in its own simple way is one of Fernandel's greatest comedy achievements, beating out those brilliant early films for Marcel Pagnol, and the credit, of course, goes not to director Verneuil, but to the star, a true "auteur" of the cinema.

ABOVE: Pilate (Louis de Funès) offers Désiré (Fernandel) instant cash if he will sign an agreement asking his wealthy brother to accept responsibility for payment of an expensive funeral. BELOW: Désiré (Fernandel) with the employees of Pilate's funeral parlor; Louis de Funès at left.

ABOVE: Bernard (Fernandel) with a grateful Marianne (Françoise Arnoul). BELOW: The sight of Désiré's children helps Papa Saint-Forget (Fernandel) forget his animosity toward his sons; Dr. Bolène (Edouard Delmont), center, looks on.

ONLY THE FRENCH CAN
FRENCH CANCAN

Producer: Louis Wipf for Franco-London Film-Jolly Film. *Released:* 1955, Gaumont (France); 1956, United Motion Picture Organization (U.S.). *Running Time:* 100 minutes (France); 93 minutes (U.S.).

Director: Jean Renoir. *Screenplay:* Jean Renoir (based on an idea by André-Paul Antoine). *Photography:* Michel Kelber. *Art Director:* Max Douy. *Costumes:* Rosine Delamare. *Music:* George Van Parys. *Song Lyrics:* Jean Renoir. *Film Editor:* Boris Lewin. *Sound:* Antoine Petit-Jean.

CAST: Jean Gabin (*Danglard*); Françoise Arnoul (*Nini*); Maria Félix (*La Belle Abbesse*); Jean-Roger Caussimon (*Baron Walter*); Max Dalban (*patron of the White Queen*); Dora Doll (*La Génisse*); Gaston Modot (*servant*); Gianni Esposito (*the prince*); Annick Morice (*laundress*); Jean Parédès (*Coudrier*); Franco Pastorino (*Paulo*); Valentine Tessier (*Madame Olympe*); Michèle Philippe (*Eléonore*).

SYNOPSIS: In the Paris of the 1880s, music-hall entrepreneur Danglard is a success thanks to his dancing star, La Belle Abbesse, who is also his mistress. When he sees Nini, a laundress, at a cheap dance hall, he decides, with the help of his backer Baron Walter, to build a new music hall, the Moulin Rouge, with Nini as its star. When La Belle Abbesse becomes jealous, the Baron withdraws his support, but Danglard finds a new backer in a prince who is in love with Nini. In the meantime, Nini has fallen in love with Danglard, and, upon discovering he is now in love with a new singing discovery, refuses to perform on opening night. However, Danglard tells her that she must choose between the theatre and her private life, that she will not enjoy happiness in both, and Nini goes on stage to perform the cancan for the first time.

COMMENTARY: For those who view Jean Renoir's films as works that entertain only after the audience has been given pause to ponder and consider, *French Cancan* comes as a delightful surprise. Here is pure escapist fare, impeccably directed, "an act of homage to our calling, by which I mean show business," as Renoir has described it. The director's first French film since *The Rules of the Game*, *French Cancan* is comparable in its subtle, easy mix of gaiety, charm and artistry with Renoir's previous film, *Le Carrosse d'Or / The Golden Coach* (1953). The film also shows us Renoir's almost casual skill in the use of color, already demonstrated in the aforementioned production and *The River* (1951).

French Cancan is a backstage musical ostensibly like any Hollywood backstage musical, but with an honesty in its depiction of relationships and an exuberant final twenty minutes, culminating in the cancan, which puts any of Busby Berkeley's climaxes to shame. "His plot," wrote *Newsweek* (May 7, 1956), "is as pat as a Hollywood hand-me-down. But the music, the color, and the excitement are a starry-eyed dream of Paris of the 1890s." *French Cancan* is a comedy with no serious undertones; there is no great tragedy here, no political implication, no social commentary, no ending with a deeper, disturbing meaning. Renoir has turned nostalgic, and returned to the world of his father. He has also demonstrated a nostalgia for one of his greatest leading men, Jean Gabin, by casting him as the impresario Danglard (modeled after Ziegler, who created the Moulin Rouge on the site of the earlier Cabaret de la Reine Blanche). Renoir has written, in his autobiography, of *French Cancan*'s offering "a chance to work again with Jean Gabin," an opportunity that Gabin, apparently, faced with some reluctance after so many years away from the director, but both men's work shows that their working relationship had not diminished through the years.

Playing opposite Jean Gabin is Mexican actress Maria Félix as an Arabian belly dancer who raises cooch dancing to a new level of artistry. "As the impresario, Jean Gabin is full of tired charm," reported John McCarten, in *The New Yorker* (April 28, 1956); "as the young lady who takes his fancy, Françoise Arnoul is toothsome; and as the Algerian, Maria Félix is sinuous as all get out." Appearing all too briefly are Patachou and Edith Piaf, "impersonating" two famous entertainers from the end of the last century, Yvette Guilbert and Eugénie Buffet.

On the whole American critics liked *French Cancan*. Jesse Zunser, in *Cue* (April 21, 1956), called it "The most elaborate and entertaining musical yet to come from France." But there were minor complaints. John McCarten, in *The New Yorker*, considered the film as "another example of excellent photography coupled to a porous plot." In *The New York Times* (April 17, 1956), Bosley Crowther wrote, "It appears that the French can be as maudlin about their Montmartre and Moulin Rouge as we can be about the old Bowery, Wabash Avenue or the Barbary Coast. . . . In a gay splurge of fin-de-siècle costumes, feminine décolletage, swirling and leaping can-can dancers and a routine story of how the show must go on, M. Renoir is treating us to a big rush of Gallic sentiment. It is colorful and atmospheric, but it could do with a little more Gallic wit."

Jean Renoir was to direct five more features: *Eléna et les Hommes/Paris Does Strange Things* (1956), *Le Testament du Docteur Cordelier/The Testament of Dr. Cordelier* (1959), *Le Déjeuner sur l'Herbe/Picnic on the Grass* (1959), *Le Caporal Epinglé/The Elusive Corporal* (1962) and *Le Petit Théâtre de Jean Renoir* (1970). All the films are major achievements, but only the last—made for French television—has the charm of *French Cancan*. Jacques Rivette has suggested that *French Cancan* is a film for dilettantes rather than Renoir purists. Perhaps. But *French Cancan* is an easy—decidedly pleasant—introduction to the work of France's greatest director. It entertains, but it also offers promise of the delights to be found in Renoir's more classicist features. The film also leaves one with the impression that Renoir is, at last, at peace with the world. He seems more relaxed, in a reflective mood, no longer anxious to warn his audiences of the dangers of political and social unrest. He was back in his beloved France, reunited with one of his favorite actors, and, for Renoir at least, all was right with the world.

ABOVE: Danglard (Jean Gabin) with his star and mistress, La Belle Abbesse (Maria Félix). (The solemn servant is played by veteran Gaston Modot.) BELOW: Nini and Paulo (Françoise Arnoul and Franco Pastorino).

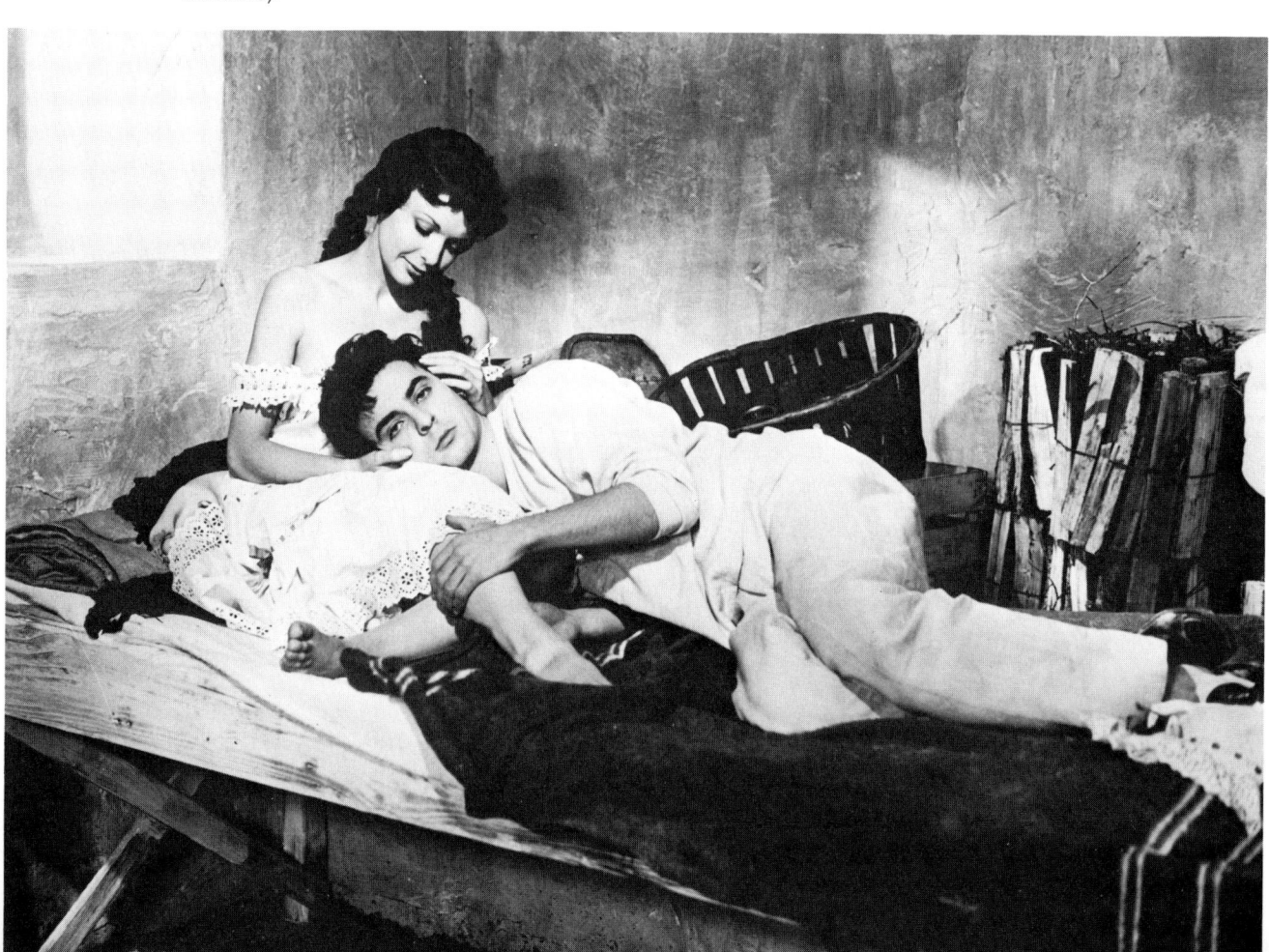

ABOVE: "The universe of our picture is like the universe composed of different small worlds"—Jean Renoir. BELOW: "I think with our film we succeeded in giving an idea what the Cancan was at the creation of the Moulin Rouge"—Jean Renoir.

AND GOD CREATED WOMAN
ET DIEU . . . CRÉA LA FEMME

Producer: Raoul J. Lévy for Iëna-Hodu Productions-Cocinor; *Released:* 1957, Cocinor (France); 1957, Kingsley International (U.S.). *Running Time:* 90 minutes (France); 90 minutes, but generally cut by censorship boards (U.S.).

Director: Roger Vadim. *Screenplay:* Roger Vadim and Raoul J. Lévy. *Photography:* Armand Thirard. *Music:* Paul Misraki. *Art Director:* Jean André. *Film Editor:* Victorian Mercanton.

CAST: Brigitte Bardot (*Juliette*); Curd Jurgens (*Eric*); Jean-Louis Trintignant (*Michel*); Christian Marquand (*Antoine*); Georges Poujouly (*Christian*); Jean Tissier (*M. Vigier-Lefranc*); Jane Marken (*Mme. Morin*); Marie Glory (*Mme. Tardieu*); Isabelle Corey (*Lucienne*); Jean Lefebvre (*René*); Philippe Grenier (*Perri*); Jacqueline Ventura (*Mme. Vigier-Lefranc*).

SYNOPSIS: An eighteen-year-old orphan, Juliette is uncontrollably attracted toward men; she has an affair with a wealthy shipyard owner, Eric Carradine, is infatuated with the masculine and domineering Antoine, and marries the kind and gentle younger brother, Michel. Juliette renews her relationship with Antoine, which leads to a fight between him and Michel. At a club where Juliette is dancing the mambo, Michel meets Eric, who decides to hide his desire for Juliette, and Michel takes his wife back home, after she has assured him she will remain faithful.

COMMENTARY: "And God created woman," proclaimed the publicity, "But the Devil created Brigitte Bardot." It was one of the more tantalizing publicity slogans invented by the motion-picture industry. As he indicates in his autobiography, Roger Vadim, the film's director, views himself as the Devil. However, it might well be argued that the Devil in this case, the Devil that brought fame and fortune to Brigitte Bardot, was none other than the religious and moral groups that sought to ban Bardot's films in general, and *And God Created Woman* in particular.

And God Created Woman created the same controversy as that engendered by the 1956 American feature *Baby Doll*. It was condemned by the Legion of Decency, a condemnation brought on in part, one suspects, by the fact that the film's dubbed version outgrossed *The Ten Commandments* in at least one community, Fitchburg, Massachusetts. In Philadelphia, police went so far as to confiscate prints of the film; local police banned the feature in Providence, Rhode Island. The censorship board of Fort Worth, Texas, banned the film outright, and in Lake Placid, New York, Monsignor James T. Lyng forbade his congregation to attend the Palace Theatre for a six-month period as a punishment for the theatre's booking of *And God Created Woman*.

Roger Vadim has described the plot of *And God Created Woman* as simply: "Three brothers, a village, a beautiful woman, a crime." The plot is certainly simplistic, and *And God Created Woman* is no major film achievement. It *is* well made, and makes intelligent use of modern music—chiefly the mambo—with its score by Paul Misraki. For Louis Marcorelles, writing in *Sight and Sound* (Winter 1959), *And God Created Woman* "remains one of the most genuine, youthful and original works produced in France since 1945." But Marcorelles is in the minority, in terms of critical reaction both in his native country and in the United States.

There are two major reasons for the importance of *And God Created Woman* in the history of French cinema. The first is that it is the initial feature to be directed by Roger Vadim (born 1928), who had worked for many years as an assistant to Marc Allégret and as a journalist for *Paris Match*. It led to an extraordinary number of competently directed features and one or two major ones, such as *Les Liaisons Dangereuses* (1959), *Barbarella* (1968) and *Night Games* (1979).

It was Vadim who recognized Brigitte Bardot's potential more as a sex symbol—France's answer to Marilyn Monroe—than as an actress, and brought her to the attention of Marc Allégret. Brigitte Bardot (born 1934) made her screen debut with *Le Trou Normand/Crazy for Love* (1952), but it was *And God Created Woman* that made her an international sex symbol, although certainly *Helen of Troy* and *Doctor at Sea*, both released in 1955, did not hurt Bardot's reputation. She was never really taken seriously until the Sixties and *Vie Privée* (1961), *Le Mépris* (1963) and *Viva Maria!* (1965).

Roger Vadim and Brigitte Bardot were married from 1952 to 1957, during which time the Bardot image became firmly established. Without question, Vadim deserves much of the credit for making his wife a star; she had few attributes that, on the surface, could appeal to the French male. She had a tiny waist, her hair was anything but chic, and she resembled a street urchin rather than an elegant Parisienne. Vadim knew exactly what image he had to capture on film; as Bosley Crowther described it, in *The New York Times* (October 22, 1957), "She is looked at in slacks and sweaters, in shorts and Bikini bathing suits. She wears a bedsheet on two or three occasions, and, once, she shows behind a thin screen in the nude. What's more, she moves herself in a fashion that fully accentuates her charms. She is undeniably a creature of superlative craftsmanship. . . . A phenomenon you have to see to believe."

If the world came to appreciate the charms of Miss Bardot, there were those Frenchmen who failed to see the attraction. One was Jean Gabin, who remarked, "That little woman has done what 30 years of getting along with people couldn't do to me: Finally disgust me with movies."

ABOVE: Juliette and Eric (Brigitte Bardot and Curd Jurgens). BELOW: The marriage of Juliette and Michel (Brigitte Bardot and Jean-Louis Trintignant).

ABOVE: Juliette and Antoine (Brigitte Bardot and Christian Marquand). BELOW: Brigitte Bardot; to every boy growing up in the Fifties she was the ultimate sex fantasy; to the French Jehovah's Witnesses she was eternally damned.

THE LOVERS
LES AMANTS

Producer: Louis Malle for Nouvelles Editions de Films. *Released:* 1958, Lux (France); 1959, Zenith International (U.S.). *Running Time:* 90 minutes.

Director: Louis Malle. *Screenplay:* Louis Malle and Louise de Vilmorin (based on the novel *Point de Lendemain*, by Dominique Vivant). *Photography:* Henri Decaë. *Art Directors:* Jacques Saulnier and Bernard Evein. *Music:* Brahms Sextet No. 1 in B-flat, Opus 18. *Additional Music:* Alain de Rosnay. *Film Editor:* Léonide Azar. *Sound:* Pierre Bertrand.

CAST: Jeanne Moreau (*Jeanne Tournier*); Alain Cuny (*Henri Tournier*); Jean-Marc Bory (*Bernard Dubois-Lambert*); Judith Magre (*Maggy Thiébaut-Leroy*); José-Luis de Villalonga (*Raoul Florès*); Gaston Modot (*Coudray*); Patricia Garcin (*Catherine Tournier*); Claude Mansard (*Marcelot*); Georgette Lobbe (*Marthe*).

SYNOPSIS: Jeanne has found her eight-year marriage to newspaper publisher Henri and her life in Dijon boring, and has taken a lover, Raoul, in Paris. To cover her liaison, Jeanne has implied to Henri that her friend, Maggy, with whom she stays in Paris, is Raoul's mistress, and Henri insists that the two be invited for a visit. Returning from Paris, after delivering the invitation, Jeanne meets a boorish young man, Bernard, whom she persuades to drive her home after her car breaks down. Discovering Bernard is an archaeologist and a man of some social standing, Henri invites him to stay the night. After the family has retired, Bernard stays in the study playing a recording of Brahms, which awakens Jeanne. The two walk through the fields and over a small waterfall and eventually make love in a boat. Their lovemaking continues on the couple's return to the house. Awakened at four o'clock in the morning by a fishing party organized by Henri, Jeanne and Bernard dress, get into the latter's car and drive away. After stopping for breakfast, they agree to move on together, and a voice on the soundtrack—which throughout the film has explained Jeanne's thoughts and behavior—comments, "She was afraid but she regretted nothing."

COMMENTARY: With *The Lovers*, Louis Malle heralded the French New Wave, became an internationally renowned director and made a star of Jeanne Moreau. Born in 1932, Louis Malle had entered the film industry in the early Fifties, and prior to making *The Lovers* had co-directed the 1956 Jacques Cousteau feature, *Le Monde du Silence/The Silent World* and also solo directed one other feature, *Ascenseur pour l'Echafaud/Elevator to the Gallows*, for which he received the 1957 Louis Delluc Prize. He followed *The Lovers* with *Zazie dans le Métro* (1960), *Vie Privée* (1961), *Le Feu Follet* (1963), *Viva Maria!* (1965), *Le Souffle au Cœur/Murmur of the Heart* (1971), *Lacombe Lucien* (1973), *Pretty Baby* (1978) and *Atlantic City* (1981), among others. For the last, Malle received an Academy Award nomination for Best Directing, an indication, perhaps, that the director's work has become far more commercially oriented in recent years. As a documentary filmmaker, Malle has received much praise—notably for his 1968 television series on India.

Although a landmark film in Louis Malle's career, *The Lovers* has not fared well with the passing of time. Much of it is dull and tedious, the use of natural sound is over-obtrusive and CinemaScope appears an unfortunate choice with most of the shots poorly framed (with the exception of one major scene at the dinner table). There is a pretentious quality to much of the film, heightened by the self-conscious pauses in the storyline and the woman's voice on the soundtrack explaining Jeanne's thoughts and actions.

The Lovers still contains elements of sophistication, but only in the love scenes between Jeanne and Bernard, exquisitely filmed and orchestrated, with the nudity more hinted at than shown. Jean-Marc Bory (whose one film of note this is) possesses a body as beautiful as that of any woman, while Jeanne Moreau is almost physically transformed in the love scenes. Not a beautiful woman, Jeanne Moreau has a cold, hard face, yet Henri Decaë here photographs her to advantage.

"These extraordinary, almost wordless scenes," wrote *The New Yorker*'s "Genet" (Janet Flanner), "possess that modesty often observed in the great incomplete sketches of nudes drawn by Matisse, in which the human figures become mere aesthetic physical compositions, without details." Awakened by music, Jeanne wanders from her room to meet Bernard outside the house. It is as if—as Louis Malle has said—she "is led out of a spiritual desert by love." The two agree that "love can be born with a single look," as they walk, hand in hand, across fields, through meadows and over a small waterfall, and release some netted salmon. Their first lovemaking occurs in the boat, and is followed by more passionate embraces first on the bed and later in the bath. Of course, these unprecedented scenes created a major stir in the United States, resulting in the film being banned in Chicago, Cleveland, Portland (Oregon) and Milwaukee. When *The Lovers* was judged obscene in Ohio, the matter was taken as far as the Supreme Court, which overturned the lower court decision.

One American critic noted that the music used in the film was from a Brahms *sex*tet, of course, and this comment was typical of the juvenile response to *The Lovers* by most U.S. reviewers. More kind was Hollis Alpert, in *Saturday Review* (August 9, 1959), who saw a similarity between Malle's work and that of Robert Bresson, noting: "There is the same ring of truth, a similar poetic realism."

The Lovers was a major success in Paris, grossing more than $360,000 on its initial engagement. Perhaps for the wrong reasons, the film was also a major box-office triumph on the American art-film circuit, breaking box-office records on its premier U.S. engagement at the Plaza Theatre in Washington, D.C., and later at the Paris Theatre in New York and the Beverly Canon Theatre in Los Angeles. Louis Malle and *The Lovers* also received the Special Jury Award at the 1958 Venice Film Festival.

ABOVE: Jeanne and Henri Tournier (Jeanne Moreau and Alain Cuny). BELOW: Jeanne (Jeanne Moreau) arrives home with a stranger (Jean-Marc Bory), to be greeted by her husband (Alain Cuny), her lover (José-Luis de Villalonga) and her friend (Judith Magre).

ABOVE: The lovers: Jeanne Moreau and Jean-Marc Bory. BELOW: In a sequence of great sensual beauty, the lovers wander through an idyllic countryside, stopping for moments of passionate lovemaking.

THE COUSINS
LES COUSINS

Producer: Claude Chabrol for AJYM Films. *Released:* 1959, Marceau (France); 1960, Films around the World (U.S.). *Running Time:* 110 minutes (France); 105 minutes (U.S.).

Director: Claude Chabrol. *Screenplay:* Claude Chabrol. *Dialogue:* Paul Gégauff. *Photography:* Henri Decaë. *Art Directors:* Jacques Saulnier and Bernard Evein. *Music:* Paul Misraki, Mozart and Wagner. *Film Editor:* Jacques Gaillard. *First Assistant Director:* Philippe de Broca.

CAST: Gérard Blain (*Charles*); Jean-Claude Brialy (*Paul*); Juliette Mayniel (*Florence*); Claude Cerval (*Clovis*); Guy Decomble (*bookseller*); Corrado Guarducci (*Italian count*); Geneviève Cluny (*Geneviève*); Michèle Meritz (*Vonvon*); Stéphane Audran (*Françoise*); Françoise Vatel (*Ernestine*); Paul Bisciglia (*Marc*).

SYNOPSIS: Charles Thomas, a somewhat maladjusted young man, comes to Paris to study law at the Sorbonne and to stay with his cousin, Paul, a cynical, bullying individual, who indulges in wild parties and surrounds himself with synthetic friends. Charles falls in love with Florence, but she allows herself to be seduced by Paul, and Charles is forced to accept his position as the odd man out in his cousin's circle. When Paul passes his exams and Charles fails, the latter loads a gun and is about to shoot his cousin as he sleeps, but the gun fails to fire. In the morning, Paul is playing with the gun and it accidentally goes off, killing Charles.

COMMENTARY: Of all the directors of the French New Wave, none have suffered such a lack of critical recognition in the United States as Claude Chabrol (born 1930), despite the immense popularity of his films in France. A critic with *Cahiers du Cinéma,* Chabrol authored a 1957 critical book-length study of Alfred Hitchcock, and entered the film industry thanks to an inheritance by his first wife, which helped to finance the setting up of his own company, AJYM. (Chabrol's second wife, whom he married in 1964, is Stéphane Audran, who has been starred in many of his features.)

Chabrol conceived of *Les Cousins* as his first feature, but the heavy cost of the production ($160,000) prevented it from being filmed until after *Le Beau Serge/Handsome Serge* (1958). Both films share the same leading men, Jean-Claude Brialy and Gérard Blain, but with their roles almost reversed—Brialy is the dominant "inside" character in *Les Cousins* and the outsider (returning to his native village) in *Le Beau Serge;* in the latter, Blain is the alcoholic and in *Les Cousins* the shy, introverted provincial cousin. Both actors give superlative performances, their characterizations fascinating (almost spine-chillingly so in Brialy's case), and with more than a passing hint of sado-masochistic homosexual urges, particularly in Paul's (Brialy's) taking the woman whom Charles (Blain) loves and making her his mistress. One senses Paul's desire to "unman" his cousin, if not physically through a homosexual relationship, then at least psychologically.

Little more than a series of scenes without much narrative flow, *Les Cousins* appeals as a view of French youth in the late Fifties, of Parisian bohemia. Abortions are commonplace, as are one-night stands. The "beatnik generation" is viewed close up, enjoying surprise parties, at the climax of one of which Paul dons a Nazi officer's hat and recites a German poem to the accompaniment of Wagner on the hi-fi. It was decadence uncontrolled, and enough to upset the conservative American critics. In *The New York Times* (November 24, 1959), Bosley Crowther wrote, "The concept of the youth of the nation corrupted by the Nazi image is profound. And the progress of the film, from this point on, while not so forceful, conveys the hopeless thought that this cousin, who is obviously a leader among the students, is an inevitable influence for ruin." Jesse Zunser, in *Cue* (November 28, 1959), concluded, "The film is a frankly horrifying shocker, particularly in its sex orgy sequences; the dialogue bristles with depravity and evil." "A fairly clever, mildly depressing study of France's I-got-it-beat generation," wrote *Time* (January 25, 1960), noting that from the final casual shooting of Charles by Paul, "the moral would seem to be, one way to keep 'em down on the farm after they've seen Paree."

Claude Chabrol might be—in the words of Stanley Kauffmann in *The New Republic* (June 15, 1974)—"one of the most talented filmmakers alive," but as the first member of the New Wave on the filmmaking scene, he was too early to enjoy the critical success achieved immediately by his colleagues. He was, as one critic noted, a symbol of the New Wave who became old hat—who went on to direct highly commercial ventures, such as *Les Biches* (1968) and the series of murder thrillers, which indicated the influence of Alfred Hitchcock and Fritz Lang (just as *Les Cousins* hints at the influence of Hitchcock, Jean Cocteau and F. W. Murnau): *Le Scandale/The Champagne Murders* (1966), *Infidèle* (1968), *Que la Bête Meure/This Man Must Die* (1970) and *Le Boucher* (1971). A prolific director, Claude Chabrol may still surprise as he becomes the grand old man of French New Wave.

ABOVE: The cousins: Paul (Jean-Claude Brialy) and Charles (Gérard Blain). BELOW: The seduction of Florence: Florence (Juliette Mayniel), Clovis (Claude Cerval) and Paul (Jean-Claude Brialy).

ABOVE: The party; Paul in the foreground. BELOW: Ménage à trois, with director Claude Chabrol sitting in the background.

THE 400 BLOWS
LES QUATRE CENTS COUPS

Producer: François Truffaut for les Films du Carrosse-SEDIF. *Released:* 1959, Cocinor (France); 1959, Zenith International (U.S.). *Running Time:* 98 minutes.

Director: François Truffaut. *Screenplay:* François Truffaut. *Dialogue:* Marcel Moussy. *Adaptation:* François Truffaut and Marcel Moussy. *Photography:* Henri Decaë. *Art Director:* Bernard Evein. *Music:* Jean Constantin. *Film Editor:* Marie-Josèphe Yoyotte. *Sound:* Jean Labussière. *English Titles:* Herman G. Weinberg.

CAST: Jean-Pierre Léaud (*Antoine Doinel*); Albert Rémy (*M. Doinel*); Claire Maurier (*Mme. Doinel*); Patrick Auffay (*René*); Georges Flamant (*M. Bigey*); Yvonne Claudie (*Mme. Bigey*); Robert Beauvais (*director of school*); Pierre Repp (*Bécassine*); Guy Decomble (*the teacher*); Luc Andrieux (*gym teacher*); Claude Mansard (*judge*); Jacques Monod (*commissioner*); Marius Laurey (*police clerk*); Henri Virloguex (*night watchman*); Daniel Couturier, François Nocher, Richard Kanayan (*children*); Jeanne Moreau (*woman with dog*); Jean-Claude Brialy (*man in street*); Jacques Demy (*policeman*); François Truffaut (*man at fun fair*).

SYNOPSIS: Twelve-year-old Antoine Doinel leads a life without purpose, experiencing indifference both at home and at school. His parents have married merely to give him legitimacy, and the boy sees his mother kissing her lover in the street. In order to excuse one of his frequent acts of truancy, Antoine pretends that his mother has died, but she appears at the school. Antoine and his friend René decide to steal a typewriter, sell it and use the money for a trip to the seaside, which they have never seen. However, Antoine is caught returning the typewriter—after having failed to sell it—and is sent by his father to the police station and from there to a juvenile detention center (where he is visited by his mother with the news that his father has no further interest in him). The following day, Antoine escapes from the center and keeps running until he reaches the sea.

COMMENTARY: Despite the disappointing quality of many of his later films, there will be few to dispute the argument that François Truffaut (1932-1984) was, after Jean Renoir, France's greatest director. He shared his mentor Renoir's love for the cinema, and that affection shone through in all his features. His first involvement with film on a professional level came about when he was invited by André Bazin to write for *Cahiers du Cinéma*. With his criticism, and with his films—from his first short, *Les Mistons* (1958), through the early features, *The 400 Blows, Shoot the Piano Player* (1960) and *Jules and Jim*—Truffaut did more than merely revitalize the French film industry: he totally reconstructed it. Truffaut loved the American cinema, and he tried to bring what he considered the best from America into French films. He created a new reality. With Jean-Luc Godard, Claude Chabrol, Eric Rohmer and Jacques Rivette, he established what has become known as the Nouvelle Vague or New Wave. As Annette Insdorf writes, in her definitive 1978 critical study of Truffaut, "The critics in what was to become the French New Wave noticed thematic and stylistic consistencies among the films of individual directors and elevated identifiable personal signature to a standard of value. They championed the director as the 'auteur,' the creator of a personal vision of the world which progresses from film to film."

In the January 1954 issue of *Cahiers du Cinéma*, Truffaut had attacked the traditional values of French cinema. With *The 400 Blows*, Truffaut gained recognition among his young peers; Jean-Luc Godard hailed the feature—in *Cahiers du Cinéma*—as "A film signed Candor, Fast Pace, Art, Novelty, Cinematography, Originality, Impertinence, Seriousness, Tragedy, Ubu-Roi, Fantasy, Ferocity, Friendship, Universality, Tenderness."

The 400 Blows is a highly personal production, based in part on Truffaut's own childhood, although unlike his hero, the director did, in reality, have a safe refuge—the cinema. The film deals with the confusion a young boy faces in standing up to and dealing with an adult world. One critic compared it to Vittorio De Sica's *Bicycle Thief*, but *The 400 Blows* possesses a realism not found in De Sica's work. The film works on two distinct levels, as a study of the tragedy of youth and as a criticism of *petit bourgeois* society. *The 400 Blows* is a cruel film at times, and yet no one in the feature is wantonly unjust.

Truffaut advertised in *France Soir* for a boy to play the character of Antoine Doinel, and he found the brilliant Jean-Pierre Léaud. "In real life I'm not interchangeable with Antoine Doinel, but I don't resent living in his shadow," said Léaud in an interview with *Sight and Sound* (Winter 1973/74). "He was the person who taught me to become an actor. It's between the ages of fourteen and thirty that a man's character is fully formed. There's a passage in Cocteau's writing where he talks about the camera's power to 'capture death at work.' I think there's a documentary side to Truffaut's Doinel films that's often overlooked: the character's physical and moral transformation." Léaud has portrayed Doinel in three other Truffaut features: in the "Antoine and Colette" episode from *L'Amour à Vingt Ans/Love at 20* (1962), *Baisers Volés/Stolen Kisses* (1968) and *Domicile Conjugal/Bed and Board* (1970).

The 400 Blows was shot on location in Paris and Honfleur between November 1958 and January 1959, with Truffaut's relatives and friends providing much of the financing. It was an immediate critical and popular success, winning the prize for Best Direction at the Cannes Festival, being screened at the London Film Festival, being named Best Foreign Film by the New York Film Critics and being named Best Foreign Language Film by the Independent Film Importers and Distributors of America. It was even nominated for an Academy Award—for Best Original Screenplay.

ABOVE: François Truffaut. BELOW: Antoine (Jean-Pierre Léaud) and his friend (René Bigey) steal a film still from a display at a local theatre—surely an image from Truffaut's own childhood.

ABOVE: Antoine steals a typewriter from his father's office. BELOW: Antoine's father (Albert Rémy) tells the police commissioner (Jacques Monod) that he and his wife can no longer handle their son.

HIROSHIMA, MON AMOUR (also known in the U.S. as HIROSHIMA, MY LOVE)

Producer: Alain Resnais and Samy Halfon for Argos Films- Como Films- Daïeï Pictures. *Released:* 1959, Pathé (France); 1960, Zenith International Films (U.S.). *Running Time:* 95 minutes (France); 88 minutes (U.S.).

Director: Alain Resnais. *Screenplay:* Marguerite Duras. *Literary Advisor:* Gerard Jarlot. *Photography:* Sacha Vierni and Michio Takahashi. *Art Directors:* Mayo, Petri and Esaka. *Music:* Giovanni Fusco and Georges Delerue. *Costumes:* Gerard Collery. *Film Editors:* Henri Colpi, Jasmine Chasney and Anne Sarraute. *Sound:* Pierre Calvet, Yamamoto and René Renault.

CAST: Emmanuelle Riva (*Elle/She*); Eiji Okada (*Lui/He*); Stella Dassas (*the mother*); Pierre Barbaud (*the father*); Bernard Fresson (*the German lover*).

SYNOPSIS: A French actress meets a young Japanese architect while she is making an anti-war film in Hiroshima, and the two spend the night together. Their lovemaking recalls for the woman an earlier affair with a German soldier during the Second World War, an affair for which she was punished by having her head shaved and being locked in the cellar by her parents. She shares the horror of the atomic bomb having fallen on Hiroshima with her Japanese lover and, in the process of remembering, each tries to forget. He asks her to stay, but the actress must return to Paris and forget him.

COMMENTARY: *Hiroshima, Mon Amour* established both Alain Resnais and Marguerite Duras as leading figures in the French film industry. The film received awards from both the Cannes Film Festival and the New York Film Critics. In stark black-and-white, *Hiroshima, Mon Amour* uneasily mixes documentary and fictional footage, disturbing the viewer with both the images seen on the screen and the two narratives—by the French actress and the Japanese architect. The opening scene sets the style for the rest of the film, as we watch a naked man and woman making love and hear a voice, later to be identified as that of the man, saying, "You know nothing of Hiroshima." That voice is followed by the woman's telling what she has seen in documentary footage of Hiroshima following the dropping of the atomic bomb. As Duras' story unfolds, we learn more of the couple and of their respective pasts.

"It is not simply a love story, it is not a document, or a plea for peace," wrote Hollis Alpert in *Saturday Review* (May 21, 1960). "It is a creative work, lovingly, poetically written by the French novelist Marguerite Duras, conceived cinematically by Alain Resnais, acted with purity by a French actress and a Japanese actor. It is, of course, a work of enormous dignity, a landmark in motion pictures."

Alain Resnais's 1955 short, *Nuit et Brouillard/Night and Fog* had documented the horrors of the Nazi concentration camps; as early as 1948, Resnais had made a travel film, shot in part at Nevers, a city that figures prominently in the past of the woman in *Hiroshima, Mon Amour*. The director initially sought to adapt his approach in *Night and Fog* to a film about Hiroshima's destruction by the atomic bomb. He discovered several months into shooting that a documentary approach was impossible. What he wanted, and what he succeeded in doing with *Hiroshima, Mon Amour*, was to juxtapose poetry with cruel reality—to have his audience understand the reality of Hiroshima's sorrow through a contemporary viewpoint.

Producer Samy Halfon originally wanted Françoise Sagan to write a screenplay, but when she decided against the project, Alain Resnais persuaded the producer to have Marguerite Duras prepare the script. (Resnais was an admirer of Duras' novel *Moderato Cantabile*.) In a 1959 interview with Richard Roud, Duras explained, "Resnais and I both agreed that we could not imagine a film about Japan which did not deal with Hiroshima, and we also felt that all that could be done along the lines of showing the horror of Hiroshima *by* horror had been done—and very well done—by the Japanese themselves in *Children of Hiroshima*. So I tried to do something different. I had nine weeks in which to write the script. All Resnais said was, 'Write literature, write as if you were doing a novel. Don't worry about me, forget the camera.' His idea was to film my scenario just as a composer would set a play to music—as Debussy did with Maeterlinck's *Pelléas et Mélisande*."

In order to give a distinct look to both the French and Japanese footage, Resnais deliberately denied French cinematographer Sacha Vierny access to the film shot in Japan by Michio Takahashi. When shooting was completed in January of 1959, Resnais worked closely with his editor, Henri Colpi (who has written in detail of his work in the Winter 1959-60 issue of *Sight and Sound*), and finally the score was composed by Italian Giovanni Fusco.

The director kept close to the shooting script at all times, considering the most important aspect of the production to be the editing. Critic Louis Marcorelles has written that "Resnais's ambition is for a cinema as disciplined in its laws as are the other arts of music, poetry or painting," and certainly *Hiroshima, Mon Amour* demonstrates the rigidty of Resnais's style, which was to reach its apotheosis with *Last Year at Marienbad*.

When *Hiroshima, Mon Amour* opened in New York at the Fine Arts Theatre on May 16, 1960, the American critics were lavish in their praise. In *The New York Times* (May 17, 1960), A. H. Weiler hailed the film as "a complex yet compelling tour de force—as a patent plea for peace and the abolition of atomic warfare; as a poetic evocation of love lost and momentarily found, and as a curiously intricate but intriguing montage of thinking on several planes in Proustian style." "With *Hiroshima, Mon Amour*," wrote John McCarten in *The New Yorker* (May 28, 1960), "Alain Resnais . . . emerges as one of the best moviemakers of our time." A year later, Resnais was to consolidate that position of fame—albeit short-lived—with *Last Year at Marienbad*.

ABOVE: Emmanuelle Riva and Eiji Okada: "partners in mysteries and miracles"—Hollis Alpert in *Saturday Review* (May 21, 1960). BELOW: Emmanuelle Riva as a French film actress in Hiroshima.

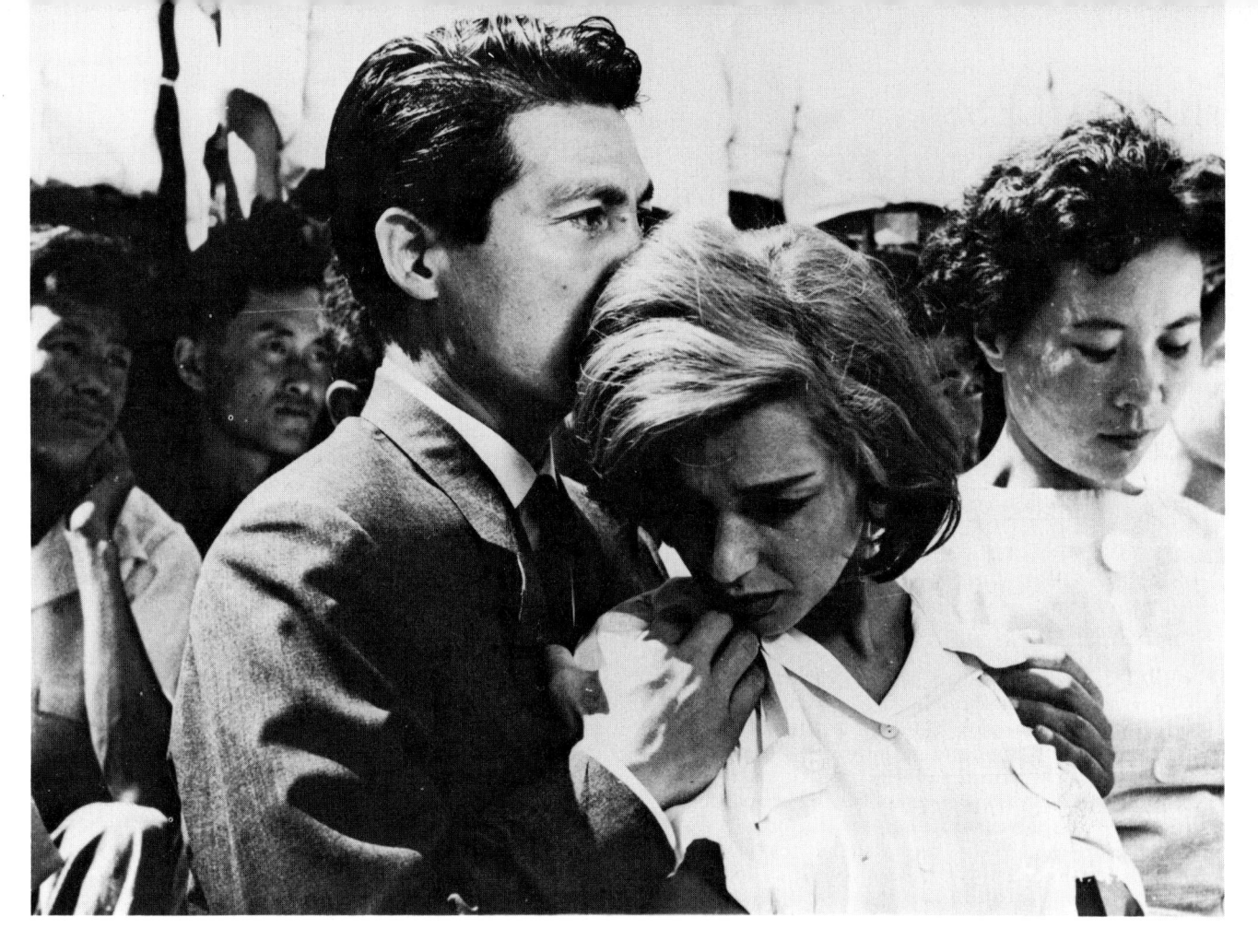

ABOVE: Eiji comforts Emmanuelle Riva as she learns of the horrors of the nuclear bombing of Hiroshima.
BELOW: New France and Old Japan.

BREATHLESS
À BOUT DE SOUFFLE

Producer: Georges de Beauregard for S.N.C. *Released:* 1960, Imperia (France); 1961, Films Around the World (U.S.). *Running Time:* 90 minutes.

Director: Jean-Luc Godard. *Screenplay:* Jean-Luc Godard (based on an unpublished story by François Truffaut). *Photography:* Raoul Coutard. *Film Editor:* Cécile Decugis. *Music:* Martial Solal. *Sound:* Jacques Maumont. *Supervisor:* Claude Chabrol.

CAST: Jean Seberg (*Patricia*); Jean-Paul Belmondo (*Michel*); Liliane David (*Liliane*); Daniel Boulanger (*the inspector*); Jean-Pierre Melville (*Parvulesco*); Henri-Jacques Huet (*Berrouti*); Claude Mansard (*used-car dealer*); Van Doude (*editor*); Jean-Luc Godard (*informer*); François Moreuil (*newsreel cameraman*).

SYNOPSIS: Michel Poiccard, a young Frenchman who models himself on Humphrey Bogart, steals a car in Marseilles, finds a gun in the glove compartment and, on his way to Paris, uses it to kill a policeman. In Paris he meets Patricia Franchini, a young American, and after mugging and robbing a man in a restaurant restroom, goes back to her apartment, where the two make love. She is threatened by the police; she leaves the house where the two are hiding, and telephones the police with details of Michel's whereabouts. In so doing, she hopes that he will go away and that she will retain her independence and will not have to travel with him to Italy, as Michel wishes. Michel is shot by the police as he runs down the street, and as he dies Michel looks up at Patricia, makes a face and then curses her.

COMMENTARY: Richard Roud sums up the critical reaction to Jean-Luc Godard when he writes of him as "of all contemporary directors, the most controversial. For many, he is the most important film-maker of his generation; for others, he is, if not the worst, then the most unbearable." Born in 1930, Godard met his fellow Nouvelle Vague filmmakers, Jacques Rivette, Eric Rohmer and François Truffaut, in the late Forties. His involvement with the French film industry began in 1950, but it was not until the release of *Breathless* in 1959 that Godard made his impact. He strengthened his position as a controversial filmmaker with *Le Petit Soldat* (1960), *Vivre Sa Vie* (1962), *Les Carabiniers* (1963), *Le Mépris* (1963), *Alphaville* (1965), *Made in USA* (1966), *La Chinoise* (1967) and *Weekend* (1967), and then his career peaked, and, quite frankly, it might well be argued—despite *Pierrot Le Fou* (1965) being voted as late as 1979 as one of the top ten French sound films of all time—that Godard has become "old wave" and passé.

His working methods were unique, and yet Godard's films are often *hommages* to other styles of filmmaking. Never is this more true than with *Breathless,* which illustrates the influence of American *film noir* moviemaking on the French filmmaking school of the late Fifties and early Sixties. He might be a revolutionary filmmaker, but Godard is—or was—a filmmaker with a popular appeal equal, in some quarters, to that of the Rolling Stones or the Beatles. He is perhaps especially unique in that he has been a radical filmmaker working within the confines of the film industry establishment.

Breathless contains more than a passing suggestion of the cinema of James Dean, Marlon Brando, Joseph H. Lewis and Nicholas Ray. Godard both admires and satirizes his heroes. *Breathless* is both brutally realistic and incredibly far-fetched. In its dedication to Monogram Pictures, *Breathless* stands as a "little picture" seeking a larger audience and, as the summation of the "New Wave," it did attract an audience out of all proportion to its contemporary importance and its historical relativity.

Breathless had its origins in a few lines conceived by François Truffaut. It was shot, without sound, in four weeks, from August 17 to September 15, 1959, on location in Paris and Marseilles, at a cost of $90,000. An often-concealed hand-held camera was utilized for much of the shooting. Much of the plot was the result of ad-libbing.

In an April 1960 article from Paris, Art Buchwald tried to explain what he described as the latest French rave, the New Wave: "No one is quite sure what the nouvelle vague is, except that it is a school of movie-making done by very young directors (preferably between the ages of 22 and 26), preferably in black-and-white, and preferably on a shoestring. The subject matter can be very good, as in the case of *Quatre Cents Coups,* and very bad, as in *A Bout de Souffle.*"

American critical reaction to *Breathless* seemed to be on the basis of the popularity or intellectual appeal of the reviewer's journal. Popular magazines were uniform in their mistrust of the film and its creators. Not so the intelligentsia. Most enthusiastic was Roger Angell, in *The New Yorker* (February 11, 1961): "It is far and away the most brilliant, most intelligent, and most exciting movie I have encountered this season. Its virtues are so numerous and so manifest that I am confident not only that it will survive the small burden of my superlatives but that it will be revisited almost instantly by many of its viewers, that it will be imitated endlessly, and probably ineptly, by dozens of film-makers, and that it may even threaten the Kennedys as the warmest topic of local conversation for weeks to come."

Has *Breathless* survived along with Godard's reputation? The answer is neither a resounding yes nor a resounding no, but rather that, like the Monogram thrillers it emulates, *Breathless* has gained a small and lasting cult appeal. Unlike the Monogram productions, it did influence contemporary filmmakers, but its imitators either stagnated or moved forward. As for Godard, he has moved forward as well, but in his rejection of filmmaking with even the slightest sense of popular appeal, he has rejected and lost much of his audience.

ABOVE: Jean-Luc Godard. BELOW: Patricia and Michel (Jean Seberg and Jean-Paul Belmondo).

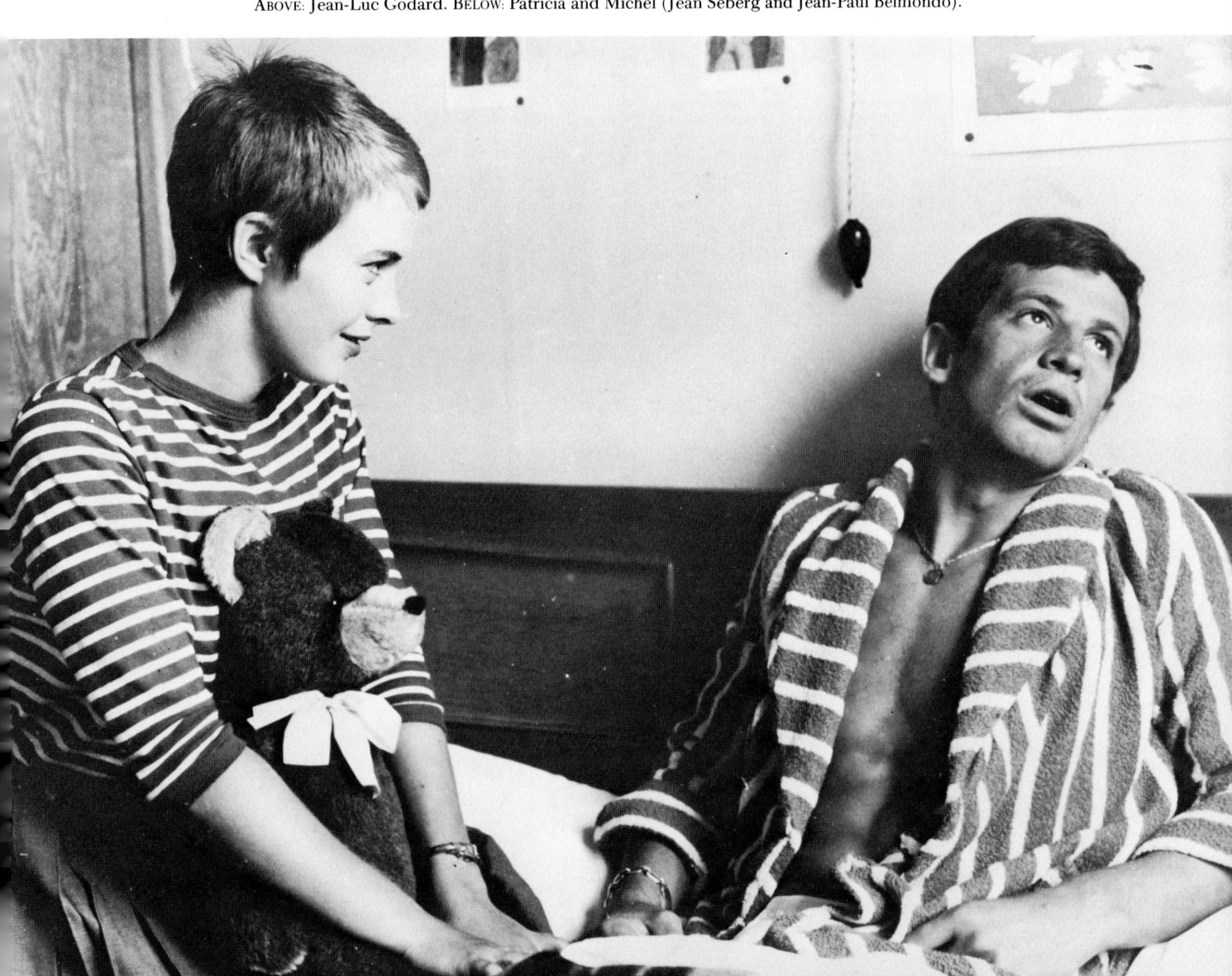

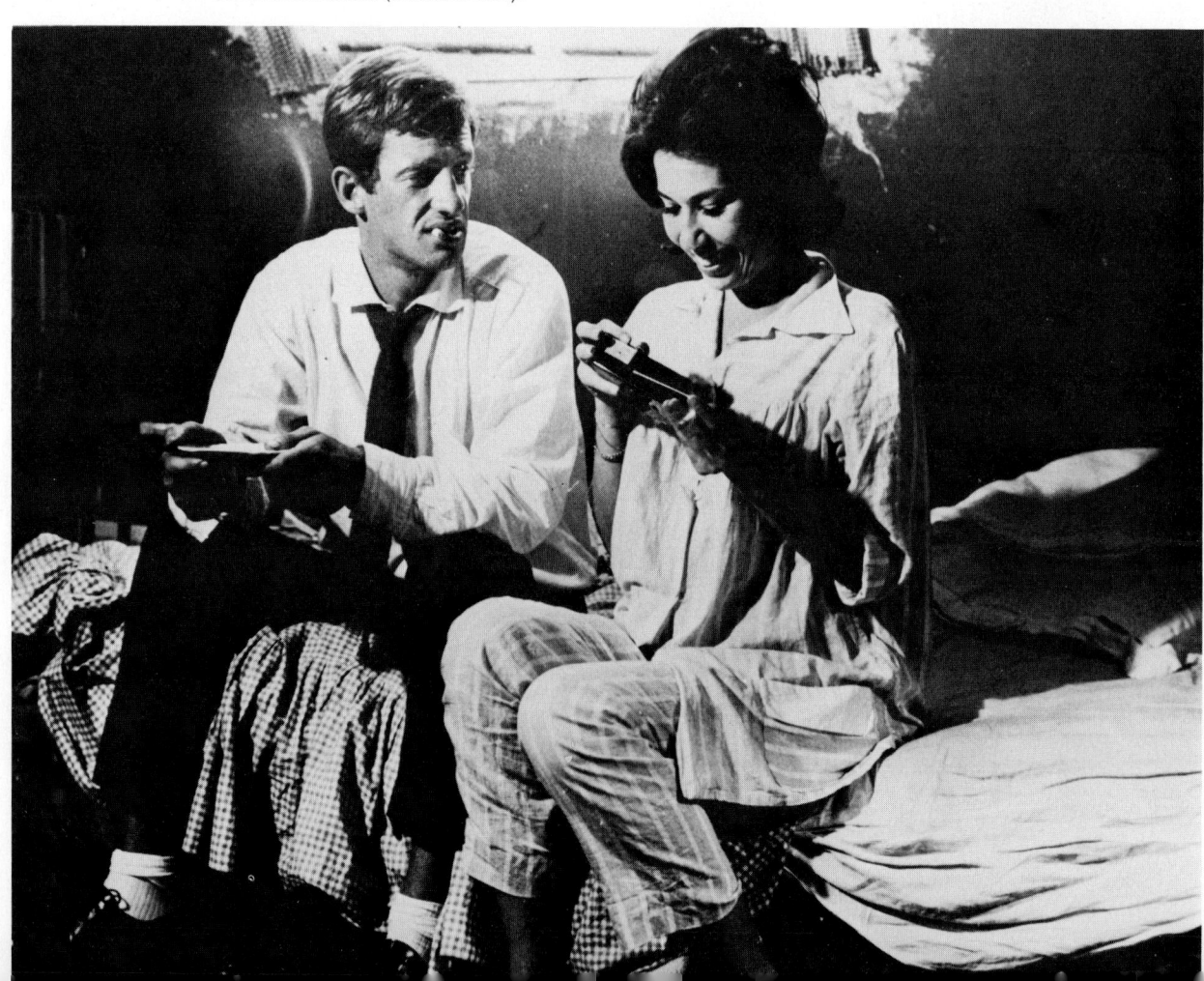

ABOVE: A pensive Patricia considers her relationship with Michel. BELOW: Michel (Jean-Paul Belmondo) with his former mistress (Liliane David).

LAST YEAR AT MARIENBAD
L'ANNÉE DERNIÈRE À MARIENBAD

Producers: Pierre Courau and Raymond Froment for Terra Films, Société Nouvelle des Films Cormoran, Préceitel, Como-Films, Argos-Films, Les Films Tamara, Cinétel, Silver-Films, Cineriz. *Released:* 1961, Cocinor (France); 1962, Astor Pictures (U.S.). *Running Time:* 94 minutes.

Director: Alain Resnais. *Screenplay:* Alain Robbe-Grillet. *Photography:* Sache Vierny and Philippe Brun. *Stage Settings:* Jacques Saulnier. *Sound Effects:* Guy Villette. *Film Editors:* Henri Colpi and Jasmine Chasney. *Music:* Francis Seyrig. *Costumes:* Bernard Evein. *Gowns for Mlle. Seyrig:* Chanel. *Assistant Director:* Jean Léon.

CAST: Delphine Seyrig (A); Giorgio Albertazzi (X); Sacha Pitoëff (M); and Françoise Bertin, Jean Lanier, Françoise Spira, Gilles Quéant, Wilhelm von Deek, Héléna Kornel, Davide Montemuri, Pierre Barbaud, Luce Garcia-Ville, Gérard Lorin, Karin Toeche-Mittler, Gabriel Werner.

SYNOPSIS: At a large, anonymous hotel, peopled by rich, anonymous guests, are X, a man; A, a woman; and M, another man who may be A's husband or lover. X reminds A that they had met the previous year at Frederiksbad or perhaps Marienbad. A has no recollection of this, but X insists that they have had an affair and that they had arranged to meet in this hotel. Slowly X persuades A that what he says is true, and eventually the two leave together.

COMMENTARY: There have been few films that have created as much intellectual controversy as Alain Resnais's *Last Year at Marienbad*. Here is a film in which past and present become one, in which fantasy becomes reality. There is beauty, but it is a disciplined, rigid beauty—as if the play had been created by a physicist. Resnais has said that, as with *Hiroshima, Mon Amour*, "it is again a question of a love story or, rather, a film about the uncertainties of love. *Marienbad* is addressed less to the intelligence than to the feelings."

That may be what Resnais believes, but, as with his film, the reality is far different from what it initially appears. If anything, *Last Year at Marienbad* shows Resnais as a cold—one might argue, even unfeeling—director, who finds difficulty in communication and in the expression of love. The film is beautifully shot—black-and-white cinematography and the CinemaScope screen have never been used to better advantage—but the production is emotionless to many people. Its characters move against a baroque background, playing out what might appear to be a simple, surrealistic drama, but there is no humanity, no warmth, no feeling to their actions.

Dwight MacDonald, writing in *Esquire* (June 1962), was one of the few American critics who succinctly summed up the film's best points and its failings: "It is a charade, a masque, beautiful to the eyes—I can't remember a film of more sustained visual delight—and interesting to the mind, or at least to a crossword-puzzle-solving part of the mind, but curiously lacking in emotional effect."

In fact, *Last Year at Marienbad* may be less a film by Alain Resnais than a film by Alain Robbe-Grillet, the screenwriter, who prepared a detailed shooting script, approved by Resnais with few alterations, which the director shot exactly as written on location in Bavaria and at the Paris studio. The editing was undertaken by Henri Colpi, who also edited *Hiroshima, Mon Amour*, under the direct supervision of Resnais during a five-month period between December 1960 and April 1961, with the film being completed almost a year and a half after producers Pierre Courau and Raymond Froment had first brought Alain Robbe-Grillet and Alain Resnais together.

"We have chosen not to make the kind of reproduction of an emotional experience that one would find in Madame Tussaud's waxworks, but rather the kind that a contemporary sculptor might fashion—not a literal truth, but a whole truth," explained Robbe-Grillet. Certainly, *Last Year at Marienbad* is not a film for those who believe two and two equal four, but rather an exercise for those willing to accept that $A + X = ?$ It demands a great deal, perhaps too much, of its audience, rather as a physics professor might seek an exorbitantly large degree of understanding from a class comprised of students of medieval history. The result is much the same in both instances—confusion and a lack of understanding.

The ambiguities of the film may be—as Jacques Brunius has argued—the ambiguities of life itself, but there are many who prefer a simpler outlook on existence. There are many who would demand: if something did indeed happen last year in Marienbad, why didn't Alain Resnais and Alain Robbe-Grillet tell us what it was! The reactionary viewpoint was admirably expressed by Louise Corbin, in *Films in Review* (April 1962), who wrote, "The simple truth about *Last Year at Marienbad* is that a not untalented young filmmaker has forsworn the hard work artistic creation entails, and has allowed his immature and meaningless fumbling to be promoted by those who wish to convert Western culture into an irrational confusion."

Last Year at Marienbad was, as one critic noted, the prophet of the New Dehumanism, a fashionable ideology among French intellectuals of the early Sixties. *Last Year at Marienbad* was a fashionable film. It was the movie that New York society discussed at cocktail parties; even Delphine Seyrig's hairdo—cut straight and short with a diagonal bang on the forehead—became fashionable, known as the Marienbad look. And like most fashionable things, *Last Year at Marienbad* was eventually forgotten by the intellectual majority, assigned to the past, an interesting byroad in the history of the cinema, but one that few directors who came later were willing to follow.

ABOVE: The classic shot of the formal gardens at Frederiksbad. BELOW: A and X (Delphine Seyrig and Giorgio Albertazzi).

ABOVE: The game of dominoes between M (Sacha Pitoëff) and X (Giorgio Albertazzi). BELOW: Delphine Seyrig: Is the film (as *Time*, March 16, 1962, asked) "like the image in a child's kaleidoscope, just an immensely intricate refraction of—a bit of fluff?"

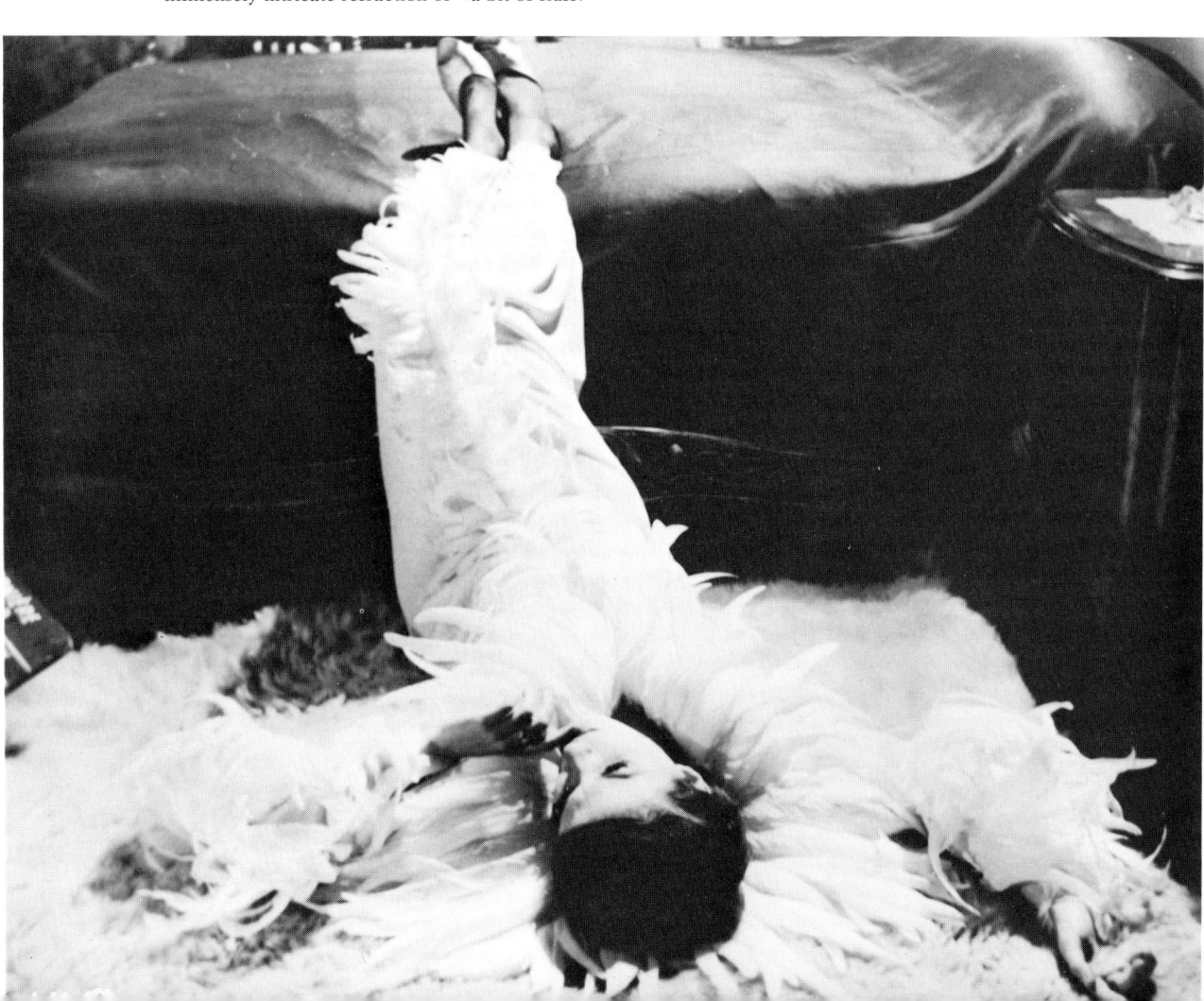

JULES AND JIM
JULES ET JIM

Producer: Marcel Berbert for Les Films du Carrosse-SEDIF. *Released:* 1962, Cinédis (France); 1962, Janus Films (U.S.). *Running Time:* 105 minutes.

Director: François Truffaut. *Screenplay:* François Truffaut and Jean Gruault (based on the novel by Henri-Pierre Roché). *Photography:* Raoul Coutard. *Music:* Georges Delerue. *Film Editor:* Claudine Bouché.

CAST: Jeanne Moreau (*Catherine*); Oskar Werner (*Jules*); Henri Serre (*Jim*); Marie Dubois (*Thérèse*); Vanna Urbino (*Gilberte*); Sabine Haudepin (*Sabine*); Boris Bassiak (*Albert*); Kate Noëlle (*Birgitta*); Anny Nielsen (*Lucy*); Christianne Wagner (*Helga*); Jean-Louis Richard, Michel Varesano (*customers in café*); Pierre Fabre (*drunk in café*); Danielle Bassiak (*Albert's friend*); Bernard Largemains (*Merlin*); Elen Bober (*Mathilde*); Dominique Lacarrière (*woman*).

SYNOPSIS: In the Montparnasse of the early 1900s, Jules, a German, and Jim, a Frenchman, develop a close friendship through their mutual interest in women, sports and the arts. They meet and fall in love with Catherine, whose smile reminds them of a statue they had admired during a visit to a Greek island. It is Jules whom Catherine marries and returns with to Germany. After the First World War, during which the two men had worried they might be shooting at each other, Jim goes to Germany, where he is encouraged by Jules to have an affair with Catherine, who has been unfaithful. Jules is willing to divorce Catherine but she has become dissatisfied with Jim, and he returns to Paris and his mistress Gilberte. Jules and Catherine come to France and, following a reunion in the country, Jim tells them that he plans to marry Gilberte. Catherine invites him to take a ride in her car, and as Jules watches, she deliberately drives off a bridge into the Seine. Jules watches as his two friends are cremated, and then quietly leaves the cemetery.

COMMENTARY: "Visually, the film echoes Jean Renoir, and no film since *A Day in the Country* has been as charming as *Jules and Jim*," wrote Judith Shatnoff in *Film Quarterly* (Spring 1963). "It is delicately lighted; its historical atmosphere is effortlessly correct. There is only beauty in the landscapes, the architecture, the faces, the gestures, the period costumes—and for a reason: the visual loveliness contributes to the idyllic misrepresentation. It's a deft seduction. It prepares us to accept whatever unorthodoxy appears on screen."

Jules and Jim was Truffaut's third feature and his second to be released in the United States. An ironic and tragic tale, the film presents an adult study of love, based on the autobiographical first novel by Henri-Pierre Roché, written at the age of seventy-four. (Roché's other major claim to fame is that it was he who introduced Gertrude Stein to Picasso.) *Jules and Jim* is a new film, in a new style, but with a strong link to the past. Unlike the other filmmakers of the New Wave, François Truffaut understands that his work must rely as much on emotional impact as technique, and this is never more apparent than in *Jules and Jim;* as Dwight MacDonald wrote in *Esquire* (September 1962), Truffaut's film has "the emotional impact of *Blows* and the technical daring of [*Shoot the*] *Pianist.*"

"In Truffaut's work technique matters less than feeling," noted *Time* (May 4, 1962). "His feeling is spontaneous, sincere, generous, naive, natural. It bubbles up like the spring of life itself. A spectator who sits down to this picture feeling old and dry will rise up feeling young and green." Brendan Gill, in *The New Yorker* (May 5, 1962), felt the same way: "He makes the commonest things—leaves, tables, dominoes, a pair of spectacles, wind ruffling the grass of a mountain meadow—shine as if with their own light; he sings playful songs to them with his camera, and they respond by bestowing on him some secret means of deciphering what it is they signal to one another when our backs are turned, or say without words when no one is there to overhear their silences."

The emotion, the humanity is old, but the tragedy—and indeed the comedy of the relationship between Jules, Jim and Catherine—is distinctly *nouvelle*. "There are two themes," Truffaut has said, "that of the friendship between the two men, which tries to remain alive, and that of the impossibility of living à trois. The idea of the film is that the couple is not really satisfactory but there is no alternative." The three central players are at their best in the light and lively moments of the film. Oskar Werner was to work again for Truffaut in *Fahrenheit 451* (1966), but apparently the director's regard for the actor's work cooled somewhat after that particular experience. Jeanne Moreau (born 1928) gives one of the best performances of her career in *Jules and Jim;* in the early sequences she is young and lighthearted, reminiscent of Garbo as she first realizes her love for John Gilbert in *Queen Christina*. Moreau also has the face—certainly not overly attractive—that offers exactly the right enigmatic quality for the film's later scenes. She worked again with Truffaut, without the same impact, in *La Mariée Etait en Noir/The Bride Wore Black* (1967), and has been among the handful of French actresses of recent years with an international reputation, thanks largely to her work in *La Notte* (1961), *The Trial* (1962), *Viva Maria!* (1965), *The Sailor from Gibraltar* (1967) and *Monte Walsh* (1970).

Jules and Jim was not a total critical success in the United States; there were some reviewers who echoed Bosley Crowther's description of the film in *The New York Times* (April 24, 1962) as "an arch and arty study of the perversities of woman and the patience of men." However, the film consolidated Truffaut's reputation as a major, international filmmaker who, in the words of Dwight MacDonald, "is one of the handful of directors who have made contemporary cinema as original and exciting as it was in the Twenties."

ABOVE: A friendship develops between Jim (Henri Serre) and Jules (Oskar Werner). BELOW: Both Jules and Jim are captivated by Catherine (Jeanne Moreau).

ABOVE: Wife and Husband: Jeanne Moreau and Oskar Werner. BELOW: Wife and Lover: Jeanne Moreau and Henri Serre.

JUDEX

Producer: Robert de Nesles for Comptoir Français Films/Filmes Production. *Released:* 1963, CFF (France); 1966, Continental Distributing (U.S.). *Running Time:* 95 minutes (France); 91 minutes (U.S.).

Director: Georges Franju. *Screenplay:* Jacques Champreux and Francis Lacassin (based on the original screenplay of Arthur Bernède and Louis Feuillade). *Photography:* Marcel Fradetal. *Music:* Maurice Jarre. *Film Editor:* Gilbert Natot. *Art Director:* Robert Giordani. *Costumes:* Christine Courcelles. *Sound:* Jean Labussière.

CAST: Channing Pollock (*Judex/Vallière*); Francine Bergé (*Diana Monti/Marie Verdier*); Edith Scob (*Jacqueline*); Théo Sarapo (*Morales*); Sylvia Koscina (*Daisy*); Michel Vitold (*Favraux*); Jacques Jouanneau (*Cocantin*); Philippe Mareuil (*Amaury de la Rochefontaine*); Jean Degrave (*notary*); René Génin (*Kerjean*); Roger Fradet (*Léon*); Ketty France (*Jeanne-Marie Bontemps*); Luigi Cortese (*Pierrot*); Suzanne Gossen (*landlady*); André Méliès (*doctor*).

SYNOPSIS: By letter, Judex warns evil banker Favraux that he will die unless he makes recompense for his crimes, and at the appointed hour, at a masked ball in honor of his daughter's engagement, Favraux does, apparently, die. Upon learning from her father's faithful secretary, Vallière (whom she later discovers to be Judex in disguise), of how her father had acquired his wealth, daughter Jacqueline renounces her inheritance, resulting in her fiancé's walking out on her. Meanwhile the governess of Jacqueline's daughter by a previous marriage, Marie Verdier (the alias of adventuress Diana Monti), whom Favraux had once asked to marry him, is after the banker's fortune. Accompanied by her lover, Morales, she breaks into the house, and is about to kidnap Jacqueline when Judex appears on the scene. Diana Monti later initiates a second kidnap attempt, disguised as a nun, but Judex again comes to the rescue and, at the same time, Morales discovers he is the son of Réglisse, one of Favraux's victims who is now working with Judex. It transpires that Favraux is not dead, merely drugged, and has been sentenced to life imprisonment by Judex, but he is rescued by Diana Monti and the two of them, with Morales, hide out on the top floor of an abandoned tenement. They are tracked down by a private detective, Cocantin (who had been initially hired by Favraux to uncover the identity of Judex), aided by a young boy. Judex is captured by Diana Monti, but rescued by Cocantin's friend, Daisy, a circus performer, who happens to be passing by. Diana Monti stabs and kills Morales, thinking he is Judex, and, after a fight on the rooftop with Daisy, she falls to her death. Favraux shoots himself, and Judex and Jacqueline are last seen walking happily together on the beach.

COMMENTARY: Louis Feuillade (1873–1925) is best known to world audiences as the creator of a group of French serials—*Fantômas* (1915), *Les Vampires* (1915) and *Judex* (1916)—that are not quite as good as many contemporary critics would have us believe. In fact, they are rather dull and uninspired, and work only as melodrama in its most outrageous form. The American distributor of Georges Franju's *Judex* suggests that Feuillade was the D. W. Griffith of France, an outrageously ridiculous analogy. The closest equivalent to Feuillade in American cinema is Louis Gasnier, who directed the serials of Pearl White and Ruth Roland, and who happens to have commenced his film career in his native France.

Franju's *Judex* is a tribute to Feuillade's world and to 1914 cinema. It utilizes Feuillade's basic storyline, and presents it not as a parody but as a straightforward drama. The result is a magically entrancing production, one of Franju's greatest and certainly most entertaining achievements. Franju asks the viewer to accept his story as it is presented. Judex appears mysteriously, his background is never explained and, thanks to Franju's storytelling, the viewer never particularly questions Judex's background or his motivations. Here is a film where everything is, literally, in black-and-white. The morality is unsophisticated and strictly Victorian.

As played by American magician Channing Pollock, Judex seems somewhat lacking in heroic stance, except when seen as a masked figure—particularly in his first appearance wearing a decidedly sinister-looking bird mask, the effect of which is downplayed by his immediately performing conjuring tricks involving pure white doves. Channing Pollock is excellent in the makeup for Vallière, and it is interesting to note that at the point when the viewer and Jacqueline discover Vallière's true identity, the film loses some of its impact. Once the fantasy has been broached, reality seems rather dull.

Georges Franju (born 1912) has had a curious career in French cinema, which has included co-founding what became the Cinémathèque Française; making his first film, a 1934 short, *Le Métro*, with Henri Langlois; and achieving a name for himself as much for his shorts as for his features. One of the shorts that seems a direct antecedent to *Judex* is *Le Grand Méliès* (1952), Franju's tribute to France's legendary fantasy film pioneer; and *Judex* reminds one of that wonderful turn-of-the-century period in French filmmaking when Méliès, Ferdinand Zecca and Emile Cohl were making film history, when the Pathé company was releasing a steady stream of dramas and fantasies.

As Hollis Alpert wrote in *Saturday Review* (May 7, 1966), "Franju has attempted to make art out of those old days of the movies' innocence. He succeeds best not when he is mimicking the iris effects and the old-fashioned titles used between sequences—touches which he inserts as a kind of tribute to the past—but when he conceives freshly and inventively on his own, using techniques that would have been far too sophisticated for Feuillade."

Most critics did not agree with Hollis Alpert. Brendan Gill, in *The New Yorker*, found *Judex* "thoroughly silly," adding: "the fatal stamp of patronizing cloyness is on every frame of *Judex*, and it fails from first to last. The blame for the direction rests with Georges Franju."

The critics failed to appreciate *Judex* as a commercial film that is almost avant-garde in style, a film that pays tribute to, but does not overly borrow from, the past. *Judex* is a highly original work by a director who understands storytelling from both a commercial and artistic viewpoint.

LEFT: Judex (Channing Pollock) makes his first appearance (seen here in a rehearsal shot). BELOW: The dogs prevent Diana Monti (Francine Bergé) and Morales (Théo Sarapo) from kidnapping Jacqueline (Edith Scob).

ABOVE: Channing Pollock as Judex. BELOW: The climactic fight on the roof between Diana Monti (Francine Bergé) and Daisy (Sylvia Koscina).

THE UMBRELLAS OF CHERBOURG
LES PARAPLUIES DE CHERBOURG

Producer: Mag Bodard for Madeleine Films–Parc Films–Beta Film. *Released:* 1964, 20th Century-Fox (France); 1964, Landau Releasing Organization (U.S.). *Running Time:* 95 minutes (France); 90 minutes (U.S.).

Director: Jacques Demy. *Screenplay:* Jacques Demy. *Photography:* Jean Rabier. *Art Director:* Bernard Evein. *Music:* Michel Legrand. *Lyrics:* Jacques Demy. *Film Editor:* Anne-Marie Cotret. *Catherine Deneuve's Costumes:* Réal. *Other Costumes:* Jacqueline Moreau.

CAST: Catherine Deneuve (*Geneviève Emery*); Nino Castelnuovo (*Guy*); Anne Vernon (*Mme. Emery*); Ellen Farner (*Madeleine*); Marc Michel (*Roland Cassard*); Mireille Perrey (*Aunt Elise*); Jean Champion (*Aubin*); Harald Wolff (*Dubourg*); Dorothée Blanc (*woman in nightclub*).

SYNOPSIS: Madame Emery thinks her sixteen-year-old daughter Geneviève too young to marry her boyfriend Guy, who works in a garage. Guy is drafted, but before he leaves Cherbourg he and Geneviève make love. Geneviève discovers she is pregnant, and agrees to marry Roland Cassard, a wealthy young diamond merchant whom she and her mother had met at a jeweler's where Madame Emery had tried to sell her pearl necklace. Eventually Guy returns home after being wounded and hospitalized (and thus being unable to write to Geneviève). When his godmother Elise dies, Guy seeks consolation from her young companion Madeleine, and the two are married. At Christmas, three years later, Geneviève and Guy meet again when she comes to his garage for gas, accompanied by her young daughter. The couple have a desultory conversation, and after Geneviève leaves, Guy rushes happily to meet his wife and young son returning from a shopping trip.

COMMENTARY: "One day I confided to Michel Legrand that it was my ambition to make a film musical. A film that would owe nothing to American musical comedy or to French operetta. I had in mind a film entirely sung; the narrative in free verse, with clear and direct dialogue. A kind of opera in a way, in which all the words would be audible, without forcing the lyricism of the voice, and where the music sometimes would include traditional or well-known tunes. Rather as though opera had followed the evolution of jazz." Thus wrote Jacques Demy, continuing: "This would be a film where the direction was regulated by the music. The camera movements, the movements of the actors themselves would be guided by the musical rhythm, while always remaining close to reality."

The resultant film, based on an eight-month collaboration between Demy and Legrand and filmed entirely on location in Cherbourg, is *The Umbrellas of Cherbourg*, which had quite a reputation at the time, but now appears almost banal and ineffectual. First, *The Umbrellas of Cherbourg* indicates little debt to Demy's mentors, Max Ophüls, Robert Bresson and Jean Renoir, but, rather, owes something to those wonderfully appealing Hollywood musicals of the early Thirties: *This Is the Night* (1932), *Love Me Tonight* (1932), *The Phantom President* (1932) and *Hallelujah, I'm a Bum* (1933). Those films boasted rhyming dialogue and songs that moved the story along, and their stories were fantasies, ideally suited to this type of screen technique. Demy's story is ordinary, commonplace and uninteresting. Demy has a beautiful title for such a film, *The Umbrellas of Cherbourg*, but he has no plot to match the title, and a score that cannot be compared to Rodgers and Hart, who perfected this style of musical. (*The Umbrellas of Cherbourg* offers only one memorable tune, "I Will Wait for You," with English lyrics by Norman Gimbel, which was nominated for an Oscar; the film was also nominated for Best Foreign Language Film of the year.)

Jacques Demy (born 1931) tried unsuccessfully to match the commercial success of *The Umbrellas of Cherbourg* with *Les Demoiselles de Rochefort/The Young Girls of Rochefort* (1967). His one American feature, *The Model Shop* (1969), was not a success, either. Aside from *The Umbrellas of Cherbourg*, Demy's best-known film is *La Baie des Anges/Bay of Angels* (1963), starring Jeanne Moreau, made while he was trying to arrange financing for *Umbrellas*. Michel Legrand (born 1932) is possibly France's best-known composer, thanks to his scores for *The Thomas Crown Affair* (1968) and *Summer of '42* (1971). He wrote the score for Demy's first feature, *Lola* (1961), and for *Cléo de 5 à 7/Cleo from 5 to 7* (1962), directed by Demy's wife, Agnès Varda.

On the whole American critics were not wildly enthusiastic about *The Umbrellas of Cherbourg*. "True, *The Umbrellas of Cherbourg* has beautiful color-photography. But otherwise, rien," commented Adelaide Comerford in *Films in Review* (January 1965). In *Saturday Review* (January 30, 1965), Hollis Alpert wrote, "The story is sung in not always melodious recitatif, it is acted pleasantly, the color *is* nice, but I must confess it left me cold, a little bored, and rather annoyed at those who claim it to be an important film." Similarly, Stanley Kauffmann, in *The New Republic* (January 2, 1965), wrote, "The tired material might possibly have been freshened by sparkling music and direction, but Michel Legrand's score is wingless, and Jacques Demy, who made *Lola* and *Bay of Angels*, is one of the least stimulating directors in the recent New Wave."

Surprisingly, *The Umbrellas of Cherbourg* was honored at the Cannes Film Festival, and was also adapted for a 1979 off-Broadway musical, which even had a mild success that same year in Paris.

RIGHT: Catherine Deneuve: "A lovely, dewy child who grows, in the course of the picture, into a cool young matron"—Richard Oulahan in *Life* (December 11, 1964). BELOW: Madame Emery (Anne Vernon) with her daughter Geneviève (Catherine Deneuve).

ABOVE: Carnival time in Cherbourg, March 1958. BELOW: Christmas 1963: Guy (Nino Castelnuovo) and Madeleine (Ellen Farner).

KING OF HEARTS
LE ROI DE CŒUR

Producer: Philippe de Broca for Fildebroc–Les Productions Artistes Associés–Compagnia Cinematographica Montoro. *Released:* 1966, United Artists (France); 1967, Lopert (U.S.). *Running Time:* 100 minutes.

Director: Philippe de Broca. *Screenplay:* Daniel Boulanger (based on an idea by Maurice Bessy). *Photography:* Pierre Lhomme. *Music:* Georges Delerue. *Art Director:* François de Lamothe. *Film Editor:* Françoise Javet.

CAST: Alan Bates (*Private Charles Plumpick*); Pierre Brasseur (*General Geranium*); Jean-Claude Brialy (*the duke*); Geneviève Bujold (*Coquelicot*); Adolfo Celi (*Colonel Alexander MacBibenbrook*); Françoise Christophe (*the duchess*); Julien Guiomar (*Bishop Daisy*); Micheline Presle (*"Madame Eva"*); Michel Serrault (*the crazy barber*); Marc Dudicourt (*Lieutenant Hamburger*); Daniel Boulanger (*Colonel Helmut von Krack*).

SYNOPSIS: As the First World War comes to its grim conclusion, the Germans plant a large bomb in a small French town before retreating, in the hope that the explosion will destroy the Allied forces as they advance. When the townspeople learn of the bomb, they flee in terror, forgetting that the inhabitants of the lunatic asylum are still in the town. Private Charles Plumpick is sent by his Scottish regiment to locate and defuse the bomb. When he arrives in the town he finds that the inmates of the asylum have taken over. A duke and duchess are the community's social leaders, Madame Eva runs the brothel, and one of her most beautiful "girls" is Coquelicot. Plumpick only discovers the true identity of the "inhabitants" when he takes the nickname of "King of Hearts," is named king of the community and told to take Coquelicot as his queen. Eventually the two opposing armed forces march into the town and annihilate each other. Plumpick accidentally detonates the bomb, and the town is safe for the inhabitants' return, at which point the lunatics are returned to the asylum. The final scene is of the naked Plumpick standing, a bird cage in his hand, at the gates to the asylum, seeking sanctuary among the only people that he perceives of as sane.

COMMENTARY: It is unusual for a foreign-language film to become a cult favorite, but such is the case with Philippe de Broca's *King of Hearts*, which is the very antithesis of *Rocky Horror Picture Show*, but which has probably appealed to just as many young people through the years. Filmed in the spring of 1966, *King of Hearts* opened in New York, at the Festival Theatre, on June 19, 1967; it was the opening film at the new Granada Theatre on Sunset Boulevard in Los Angeles, on August 15, 1967. The Granada Theatre has long closed its doors, but *King of Hearts* is still playing somewhere in Los Angeles. The film achieved something of a record, playing continuously for five years, from 1971 to 1976, at the Central Square Cinema in Cambridge, Massachusetts. And, yet again, the Central Square Cinema has closed, but *King of Hearts* goes on forever.

All this might not be surprising if *King of Hearts* was a superb piece of filmmaking—along the lines, say, of *La Grande Illusion*—but it is not. One might find it easier to accept the film's enduring fame had it been well received by the American critics on its initial release, but the critics, on the whole, were only lukewarm in their reviews. Many found the film simplistic and uneven, with the best review probably coming from Vincent Canby in *The New York Times* (June 20, 1967), who thought "Mr. de Broca's parable . . . a funny and touching experience."

King of Hearts is a slow-moving film—another reason why it should *not* have been appealing to a young audience—and the antics of the lunatics become decidedly tedious after a while. Certainly there is a great deal of charm in the film, and Geneviève Bujold never was photographed more lovingly. The moralistic point that the insane are saner than those designated sane is made in a lighthearted, entertaining fashion. One critic suggested that René Clair would have appreciated this film, but I doubt he would have found the amount of killing particularly justified. *King of Hearts* seems to adopt a strangely immoral tone when it comes to dealing with the soldiers' killing each other.

It is all a little too simplistic, a little too pat. De Broca is giving the audience exactly what it wants to see, and letting it believe what it wants to believe. The film satirizes war and civilization. But, as Wilfrid Sheed wrote in *Esquire* (July 1967), "War may be intolerable, but it isn't basically crazy, any more than a natural disaster or a crop failure or an economic depression." The lunatics can be happy in this film, because the setting is the First World War. Could they have behaved in the same lighthearted way if *King of Hearts* were set during the Second World War?

More importantly, *King of Hearts* stays well clear of the truth concerning the mentally retarded. Institutions for such people are not happy places, and in America of the Eighties the mentally ill to be seen on any city street are not the happy band of *King of Hearts*.

Philippe de Broca (born 1933) would appear to have a strong romantic strain within him, despite beginning his career in the film industry as an assistant director to such men as François Truffaut and Claude Chabrol (who produced the first two films de Broca directed). "Film always has a moral, a responsibility to be altogether beautiful," de Broca has said, "and to make people better, more generous, more hopeful, full of love for what they have." Audiences do not appear to have gone along with de Broca's viewpoint, except in *King of Hearts*. The director's other features, including *Le Farceur/The Joker* (1961), *L'Homme de Rio/The Man from Rio* (1964), *Les Caprices de Marie/Give Her the Moon* (1970) and *Le Cavaleur/Practice Makes Perfect* (1979), have been remarkably unsuccessful in this country.

ABOVE: The inmates escape from the asylum . . . BELOW: . . . and enjoy themselves in the deserted town.

ABOVE: Geneviève Bujold as Coquelicot. BELOW: The final scene with Alan Bates as Private Charles Plumpick.

BELLE DE JOUR

Producer: Robert and Raymond Hakim for Paris Film–Rive Films. *Released:* 1967, Valeria (France); 1968, Allied Artists (U.S.). *Running Time:* 102 minutes.

Director: Luis Buñuel. *Screenplay:* Luis Buñuel and Jean-Claude Carrière (based on the novel by Joseph Kessel). *Photography:* Sacha Vierny. *Art Director:* Robert Clavel. *Set Designer:* Maurice Barnathan. *Film Editors:* Louisette Hautecœur and Walter Spohr. *Catherine Deneuve's Costumes:* Yves Saint Laurent. *Sound:* René Longuet.

CAST: Catherine Deneuve (*Séverine Sérizy*); Jean Sorel (*Pierre Sérizy*); Geneviève Page (*Madame Anaïs*); Michel Piccoli (*Henri Husson*); Pierre Clémenti (*Marcel*); Macha Méril (*Renée Févret*); Francisco Rabal (*Hyppolite*); Georges Marchal (*the duke*); Françoise Fabian (*Charlotte*); Maria Latour (*Mathilde*); Francis Blanche (*Monsieur Adolphe*); Iska Khan (*Asian client*); François Maistre (*the professor*); Bernard Fresson (*Le Grêle*); Dominique Dandrieux (*Catherine*); Brigitte Parmentier (*Séverine as a child*); Michel Charrel (*footman*); D. de Roseville (*coachman*); Marcel Charvey (*Professor Henri*); Pierre Marcay (*interne*); Adélaïde Blasquez (*maid*); Marc Eyraud (*barman*); Bernard Musson (*majordomo*).

SYNOPSIS: Despite affection for her husband Pierre, Séverine is unable to respond to his lovemaking; she fantasizes the enjoyment of a masochistic relationship with her husband, and rejects the advances of her husband's friend, Henri Husson. The latter mentions a local brothel run by Madame Anaïs, and Séverine eventually goes to work there each afternoon, from two to five, using the name of Belle de Jour. Séverine's relationship with her various clients helps improve her lovemaking with Pierre. However, one such client, a cheap hood named Marcel (brought to the brothel by another gangster, Hyppolite) becomes infatuated with her, and after Husson's discovery of her in the brothel has led to Séverine's quitting prostitution, Marcel goes to her home and shoots Pierre in a jealous rage, before being shot himself by the police. Husson reveals Séverine's secret life to the now blind and paralyzed Pierre. In the final scene Séverine imagines that Pierre is whole again and the two of them are happily married.

COMMENTARY: With its close links to *L'Age d'Or* and its blatantly commercial theme, *Belle de Jour* is certainly Luis Buñuel's most successful film, and also one of his most entertaining. It is cloyingly lush in its cinematography and in the Yves Saint Laurent wardrobe worn by Catherine Deneuve (although her short skirts now seem the most dated aspect of the production). Buñuel announced the film as his swan song—which it was not—and obviously had a great deal of fun in keeping both the audience and the critics guessing as to how much of the film was reality, and how much Séverine's fantasy world. The fact that many critics were confused, and *did* wonder if the entire prostitution story, including Marcel's shooting of Pierre, was nothing more than a figment of Séverine's imagination, shows how well Buñuel succeeded in the Surrealistic theory that reality and dreams are one. In a *New York Times* interview (August 18, 1968), Catherine Deneuve was able to confirm that the girl really did work in a brothel and really did have a gangster-lover, and that her husband really was shot. What Miss Deneuve was unable to clarify, and what has fascinated audiences, is what exactly the Japanese client at the brothel had in his lacquered box—was it a bee, and if so, what did he do with it?

The fantasy sequences are not that hard to identify, particularly if one bears in mind that the film opens with the best-known one: as Séverine and Pierre drive in a horse-drawn coach into a wood, Séverine is dragged from the coach, tied to a tree, stripped to the waist and whipped, and then, as the film suggests, raped by one of the coachmen. The presence of the coach and the sound of bells usually signify a fantasy (although, of course, the Japanese client *does* have a couple of bells). The one sequence that does give one pause is when Belle de Jour is picked up at an open-air café, taken by a duke to his château and placed in a coffin while the duke apparently masturbates underneath. Is this a fantasy or does it really happen to Séverine? The reference to letting out the cats, a reference also made in the opening sequence, would seem to imply this is fantasy. But who knows?

Belle de Jour is one of six films that Buñuel wrote with Jean-Claude Carrière, the others being *Diary of a Chambermaid* (1965), *The Milky Way* (1968), *The Discreet Charm of the Bourgeoisie* (1972), *The Phantom of Liberty* (1974) and *That Obscure Object of Desire* (1977). Buñuel did not care too much for Joseph Kessel's 1929 novel—"but I found it interesting to try and turn something I didn't like into something I did"—and considerably changed the ending, which originally had Marcel accidentally shoot Séverine's husband while attempting to kill Husson, who was about to reveal her secret life. Buñuel has described the film as "chaste eroticism," but by current standards *Belle de Jour* is exceedingly coy.

All in all, as Robert Hatch commented in *The Nation* (April 29, 1968), "Except that she needs to be raped daily, the heroine is a dull girl." And certainly Catherine Deneuve is not the most responsive of actresses. Her expression seldom changes; she may be "deliciously sumptuous" (as Penelope Gilliatt found her in the April 20, 1968 edition of *The New Yorker*), but she displays little sensuality and even less emotion.

American critics, perhaps because they could not decide what to make of *Belle de Jour*, were cautious in their praise. In *Esquire* (February 1968), Wilfrid Sheed had to admit, "The result, even in a relatively trashy film like *Belle de Jour*, is oppressively powerful. Like being buried alive in Sarah Bernhardt's dressing room."

RIGHT: Luis Buñuel and Catherine Deneuve. BELOW: A suggestion of a possible lesbian affection between Séverine (Catherine Deneuve) and Madame Anaïs (Geneviève Page).

LEFT: Séverine and her young gangster client/lover Marcel (Pierre Clémenti). BELOW: Catherine Deneuve as Belle de Jour.

Z

Producers: Jacques Perrin and Hamed Rachedi for Reggane Films–O.N.C.I.C. *Released:* 1969, Valeria (France); 1969, Cinema V (U.S.). *Running Time:* 128 minutes.

Director: Constantin Costa-Gavras. *Screenplay:* Jorge Semprun and Costa-Gavras (based on the novel by Vassili Vassilikos). *Photography:* Raoul Coutard. *Music:* Mikis Theodorakis (arranged and conducted by Bernard Gérard). *Production Supervisor:* Hubert Mérial. *Art Director:* Jacques d'Ovidio. *Film Editor:* Françoise Bonnot. *Sound:* Michèle Boehm.

CAST: Yves Montand (*the deputy*); Jean-Louis Trintignant (*the magistrate*); Jacques Perrin (*the journalist*); François Périer (*the district attorney*); Irene Papas (*Hélène*); Georges Géret (*Nick*); Charles Denner (*Manuel*); Bernard Fresson (*Matt*); Jean Bouise (*Pirou*); Jean-Pierre Miquel (*Pierre*); Renato Salvatori (*Yago*); Marcel Bozzufi (*Vago*); Julien Guiomar (*the colonel*); Pierre Dux (*the general*); Guy Mairesse (*Dumas*); Magali Noël (*Nick's sister*); Clotilde Joano (*Shoula*); Maurice Baquet (*the bald man*); Jean Dasté (*Coste*); Gérard Darrieu (*Baron*); José Artur (*the newspaper editor*); Van Doude (*the hospital director*); Eva Simonet (*Niki*); Hassan Hassani (*the general's chauffeur*); Gabriel Jabbour (*Bozzini*); Jean-François Gobbi (*Jimmy the boxer*); Andrée Tainsy (*Nick's mother*); Steve Gadler (*English photographer*); Bob de Bragelonne (*Under-Secretary of State*).

SYNOPSIS: In an unidentified European country, "Z," a member of the political opposition, is attacked at a rally and, after his speech, is knocked down by a van and taken to a local hospital, where he dies. Despite the efforts of the authorities, an examining magistrate and a newspaper photographer investigate, discovering that Yago, the driver of the van, was not drunk, as he claimed, but is the member of a right-wing political organization, and that witnesses have been bribed or intimidated. Concluding that "Z" was murdered, the magistrate—resisting the efforts of the district attorney—orders the arraignment of Yago, his passenger Vago and several high-ranking government officials. But Yago and Vago receive only light sentences and the charges against the officials are dismissed.

COMMENTARY: Greek-born Constantin Costa-Gavras (born 1933) is a propagandistic filmmaker. Outside of his first film, *Compartiment Tueurs/The Sleeping Car Murders* (1964), all of his features—*Un Homme de Trop/Shock Troops* (1966), *Z*, *État de Siège/State of Siege* (1972), *Section Spéciale/Special Section* (1975) and *Missing* (1982)—have been highly politically motivated, all espousing nationalistic or left-wing causes (the director is not always able to differentiate between the two). In an interview with *Cineaste* (Vol. 6, No. 1, 1974), Costa-Gavras explained, "The general public has become more political. The world has become much more open-minded. I think cinema has to follow this trend. More and more of our films will be political. I will make more political films. There's no doubt I have a penchant for this kind of film—for films with real subjects."

Vassili Vassilikos' novel Z interested Costa-Gavras because of his Greek origins and because he had long been concerned with the case of Grigorios Lambrakis, upon whose murder Z is based. (Lambrakis, a Deputy of the Union of the Democratic Left party, was killed in Salonika on May 22, 1963 under circumstances similar to those depicted in Z, and the postmortem on his death was handled in much the same way as it is in the film.) "Z," the Greek symbol for "Zei" (he lives), became a forbidden sign for Lambrakis' supporterrs.

No matter what one's political beliefs, Z is a powerful film—as powerful in its liberal fashion as is Leni Riefenstahl's *Triumph of the Will* as a piece of reactionary filmmaking. The violence accompanying the actions of the right-wing forces is brutally realistic, sickeningly frightful. Costa-Gavras manages, very skillfully, to depict the right-wing establishment as both quietly dangerous and later as ineffectual and silly (as at the film's close, when the general and the chief of police try to open a barred door). What he fails to do is to depict Z and his supporters as being particularly strong in numbers. The 200 supporters of Z at the opening rally seem particularly overwhelmed by both the right-wing populace and the riot police, and later, after Z's assassination, only a handful of students are seen protesting. If Z was such a popular figure, why does his support seem so meagre? Even those witnesses who come forward to support the assassination theory do so out of a desire to tell the truth, not because they support Z. Costa-Gavras' case is further weakened by one of the two assassins being a homosexual (and a particularly sadistic one, with a yen for young boys). It is doubtful that the right wing would embrace any homosexual, and in depicting a homosexual as a tool of the right wing, Costa-Gavras seems to be asking for a loss of credence from much of his liberal audience.

The director has talked of Z's being an adventure film, and it certainly has some exciting moments, notably the fight on the pick-up truck. The sharp cuts to flashbacks of Z's earlier life with his wife also add to the excitement and feeling of immediacy that the film generates. Regrettably, the film also contains a few too many clichés left over from Sixties cinema.

Yves Montand and Irene Papas lend their names and presence to the film, but little else. The acting honors go to Jean-Louis Trintignant as the investigating magistrate, to Georges Géret as the witness whose evidence first raises doubts in the magistrate's mind and to Marcel Bozzufi and Renato Salvatori, who give magnificently evil performances as the two assassins Vago and Yago. Although Z was shot entirely on location in Algeria, the speaking cast is all French.

Z was a major critical and box-office success in the United States. Stanley Kauffmann, in *The New Republic* (December 1969), hailed it as "An exciting film on an agonizing subject." Joseph Morgenstern in *Newsweek* called it "one of the best examples I know of great story-telling." Z received Academy Award nominations for Best Directing, Best Picture and Best Screenplay (based on material from another medium) and Oscars for Best Film Editing and Best Foreign Film. It was also named Best Film of the Year by the New York Film Critics.

ABOVE: The young photojournalist (Jacques Perrin) is removed from the scene of Z's later assassination. LEFT: A tender moment between Z and his wife (Yves Montand and Irene Papas), recalled in the film by the latter after Z's death.

ABOVE: Following her husband's shooting, Hélène (Irene Papas) is rushed to the hospital. BELOW: Jacques Perrin as the photojournalist whose investigation helps uncover the truth of Z's shooting.

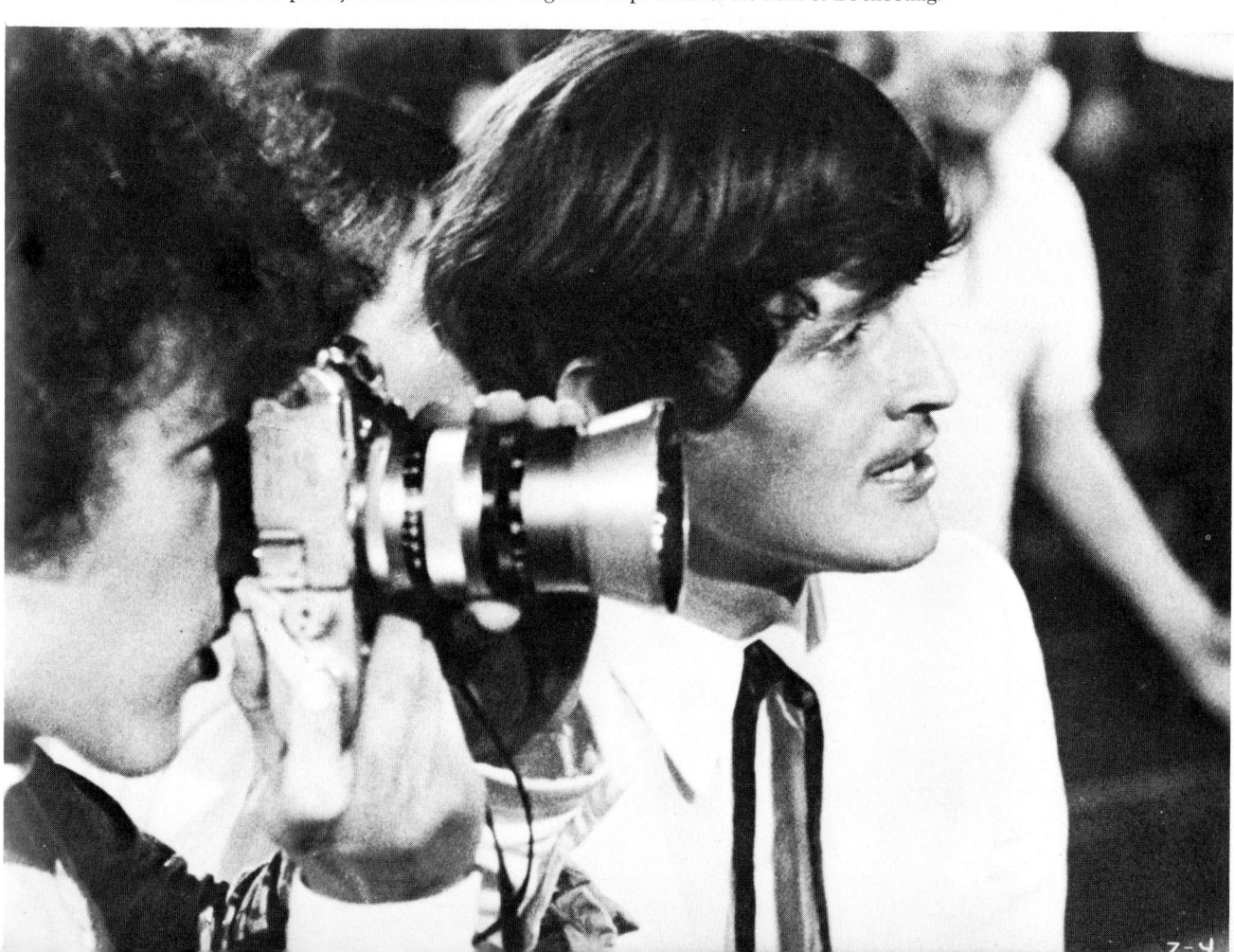

DAY FOR NIGHT
LA NUIT AMÉRICAINE

Producer: Marcel Berbert for Les Films du Carrosse-PECF-Produzione Internazionale Cinematografica. *Released:* 1973, Columbia-Warner (France); 1973, Warner Bros. (U.S.). *Running Time:* 120 minutes.

Director: François Truffaut. *Screenplay:* François Truffaut, Jean-Louis Richard and Suzanne Schiffman. *Photography:* Pierre William Glenn. *Art Director:* Damien Lanfranchi. *Costumes:* Monique Dury. *Film Editor:* Yann Dedet. *Sound:* René Levert.

CAST: Jacqueline Bisset (*Julie/Pamela*); Valentina Cortese (*Séverine*); Alexandra Stewart (*Stacey*); Jean-Pierre Aumont (*Alexandre*); Jean-Pierre Léaud (*Alphonse*); François Truffaut (*Ferrand*); Jean Champion (*Bertrand*); Nathalie Baye (*Joëlle*); Bernard Menez (*property man*); Nike Arrighi (*Odile*); Gaston Joly (*Gaston*); Jean Panisse (*Arthur*); Maurice Séveno (*TV reporter*); David Markham (*Dr. Nelson*); Zénaïde Rossi (*Gaston's wife*).

SYNOPSIS: The action takes place in and around the Victorine Studios in Nice, where a feature titled *Meet Pamela* is being filmed. Actor Alphonse has obtained a job as script girl for his girlfriend Liliane; Séverine is upset that her former lover, Alexandre, has been cast as her husband in the film; Alexandre keeps visiting the airport to await his "lover"; actress Stacey is discovered to be pregnant; director Ferrand is beset with various problems. Production gets under way with the arrival of the American actress Julie Baker, who is to play the title role, accompanied by her husband, Dr. Nelson. Alexandre's lover proves to be a young man named Christian. When Liliane deserts Alphonse for an English stuntman, he spends the night with Julie Baker and then telephones her husband with the news. Alphonse disappears, but returns later to apologize for his behavior; a reconciliation takes place between Julie and Dr. Nelson; Alexandre is killed in a car crash. Shooting is only completed by having a stand-in replace Alexandre in the final scene, after which the company disbands.

COMMENTARY: *Day for Night* is Truffaut's thirteenth film, and it marked a return to the director at his best, both artistically and commercially, a welcome change and relaxation from *L'Enfant Sauvage/The Wild Child* (1969) and *Les Deux Anglaises et le Continent/Two English Girls* (1971). *Day for Night* also presented François Truffaut with his second opportunity to work as an actor in one of his own films (following his starring role in *The Wild Child*), and the role Truffaut wrote for himself is that of director Ferrand. "I am playing what I have written and what I have personally experienced," commented Truffaut. "I am myself behind and in front of the camera."

The title *Day for Night* is the phrase used in the film industry to mean shooting night scenes during the day through the use of special filters. *Day for Night* is—as Gordon Gow wrote in *Films and Filming* (November 1973)—"a eulogy to cinema." It is François Truffaut, the film buff, paying tribute to the motion picture that he truly loves. There is the opening dedication to Dorothy and Lillian Gish. One of the streets through which the company passes is named Rue Jean Vigo (a real street in Nice). Ferrand makes reference to all of Nice's 37 theatres seemingly showing *The Godfather*. Actress Séverine asks if she may say numbers instead of her lines, in the manner in which Federico Fellini would make a film. Ferrand opens a package of books—monographs on Truffaut's favorite directors. We, the audience, are participating in the making of a film, not at just any studio, but at the Victorine Studios in Nice, where Rex Ingram shot some of his greatest productions, one of the most beautiful studios in the world (I recall British cinematographer Desmond Dickinson telling me that his fervent wish was to retire and become the gateman at the Victorine Studios).

François Truffaut was a frequent visitor at Jean Renoir's Beverly Hills home during the latter's final years, and most weekends Robert Gitt and I were also present, screening a different feature for Jean—the last film we showed him only days before his death was Fritz Lang's *M*. Truffaut would constantly surprise us not only with his knowledge of American cinema, but his choice of films that Renoir must see. *Sullivan's Travels* was one; Sturges' *Unfaithfully Yours* was another. I do not intrude myself lightly into this essay, but in so doing I can attest to the love and admiration that Truffaut felt for Jean Renoir and his work. And, as many critics have pointed out, *Day for Night* is comparable to Renoir's *Rules of the Game* in that both Truffaut and Renoir have put the best of themselves into each of the productions.

Filmed from September through November of 1972 on the French Riviera, at a reported cost of $800,000, *Day for Night* is unquestionably the best fictional film ever made about filmmaking. It is, as Jan Dawson wrote in *Sight and Sound* (Winter 1973/74), a record of "the trials and tribulations of his [Truffaut's] own love story." "It's a film," wrote Joy Gould Boyum in *The Wall Street Journal* (October 5, 1973), "that offers lots of lightweight pleasures in the very tradition of those 'Hollywood stamped' movies it both teases and commemorates." Its success was immediate. *Day for Night* was chosen for the Cannes Film Festival and to open the 11th New York Film Festival. It was voted Best Picture by the National Society of Film Critics and Best Foreign Language Film by the International Film Importers and Distributors of America. The Academy of Motion Picture Arts and Sciences nominated it for Best Supporting Actress (Valentina Cortese), Best Directing and Best Original Screenplay, and voted it Best Foreign Film.

ABOVE: François Truffaut shares a humorous moment on the set with Jean-Pierre Léaud. BELOW: Jean-Pierre Léaud, Jean-Pierre Aumont, Jacqueline Bisset and Valentina Cortese.

ABOVE: Julie (Jacqueline Bisset) leaves Alphonse (Jean-Pierre Léaud) after spending the night with him.
BELOW: Jacqueline Bisset and Jean-Pierre Aumont in a scene from *Meet Pamela*, the film within the film.

MADAME ROSA
LA VIE DEVANT SOI

Producer: Raymond Danon for Lira Films. *Released:* 1977, Warner Bros. (France); 1978, Atlantic Releasing (U.S.). *Running Time:* 105 minutes.

Director: Moshe Mizrahi. *Screenplay:* Moshe Mizrahi (based on the novel *La Vie Devant Soi,* by Emile Ajar). *Photography:* Nestor Almendros. *Production Designer:* Bernard Evein. *Costumes:* Jacques Fonteray. *Music:* Philippe Sarde. *Film Editor:* Sophie Coussein. *Sound:* Jean-Pierre Ruh and Louis Gimel.

CAST: Simone Signoret (*Madame Rosa*); Claude Dauphin (*Dr. Katz*); Samy Ben Youb (*Momo*); Gabriel Jabbour (*Hamil*); Michal Bat Adam (*Nadine*); Constantin Costa-Gavras (*Ramon*); Stella Anicette (*Madame Lola*); Mohammed Zineth (*Kadir Youssef*).

SYNOPSIS: An elderly retired prostitute, Madame Rosa, takes care of the children of her younger colleagues, but as her health deteriorates she is left with only one child, a fourteen-year-old Arab boy named Momo (short for Mohammed), who has lived with Rosa for as long as he can remember. Despite her Jewish ancestry and her being a survivor of Auschwitz, Madame Rosa has brought up Momo in the Islamic faith. When Momo's father, who had killed the boy's mother, comes to reclaim his son, Momo learns the truth about himself before Rosa sends the man away. As Madame Rosa becomes more ill, she begs Momo to help her die rather than be sent away to a hospital to die as a vegetable. When Dr. Katz decides it is time for Rosa to make the final trip to the hospital, Momo pretends that Rosa's family is about to send her to Israel, and helps her hide in a basement room which Momo has transformed into a Jewish shrine. Momo stays with Madame Rosa until she is dead, and then, upon being discovered, is sent to live with Nadine, a young married woman, who has always been interested in his well-being.

COMMENTARY: Moshe Mizrahi (born 1931) became an internationally renowned director thanks to *Madame Rosa*. However, long before he made the film, Mizrahi had been gaining acclaim. Born in Egypt of Jewish parents, he has said, "I was always a film freak." He came to Paris in 1958 to work as an assistant director in French television, and directed his first feature film, *Le Client de la Morte-Saison/The Traveller,* on location in Israel in 1969. Two of the more important of his pre-*Madame Rosa* features are *I Love You, Rosa* (1972) and *The House of Chelouche Street,* both of which were nominated for Academy Awards for Best Foreign Language Film.

Madame Rosa is based on the second, and best-selling, novel by Emile Ajar, which was published in France as *La Vie Devant Soi* and in the United States as *Momo*. Having sold more than a million copies in France, the novel has been translated into seventeen languages. The theme of both the novel and the film is: "It takes love." It is a curiously touching story of the relationship between an elderly prostitute and a young Arab boy, told without obvious emotion and in an almost matter-of-fact fashion. Mizrahi shot the film on location in the Arab quarter of Paris, giving the production a harsh, realistic look that helps offset any suggestion of cloying sentimentality. (The film was shot between May and July of 1977.) Mizrahi obviously has great empathy with the subject. His Arab-Jewish background is very apparent from one remark made by Madame Rosa: "Jews and Arabs are alike. That's why they're fighting." The director has tried, and almost succeeded, to resolve the Arab-Israeli conflict on a personal level.

As Vincent Canby wrote in *The New York Times* (March 19, 1978), *Madame Rosa* "is sweet and tough in conventional ways, but it also acknowledges something you don't often see except in the films of directors like Renoir and Truffaut, that the greatest courage may often be the will to go on, to continue, in the conviction that there is nothing but darkness beyond."

Both the sweetness and the toughness are represented in the portrayal of Madame Rosa by Simone Signoret (born 1921). A brilliant actress and one of the most sensually attractive stars of the Forties and Fifties, Signoret made films that included *Fantômas* (1947), *La Ronde* (1950), *Casque d'Or* (1952), *Les Diaboliques/Diabolique* (1955), *Room at the Top* (1958), *Term of Trial* (1962), *Ship of Fools* (1965) and *Games* (1967). With *Madame Rosa,* her career revived and she gave, arguably, one of her finest performances—it earned her a César. "As played by Simone Signoret," wrote Vincent Canby, "Madame Rosa is a tremendous character, an overwhelming mountain of worn-out flesh whose arteries are hardening, whose ankles are weak, and whose lungs are less dependable than a couple of ancient innertubes." In fact, Mizrahi—in the role of both director and scriptwriter—has changed the focus of the story from Momo (who is the storyteller in the novel) to Madame Rosa. It is a change that seems to have appealed to the American critics. Of the Simone Signoret character, Penelope Gilliatt wrote in *The New Yorker* (March 27, 1978), "This character has been through Auschwitz and life, not through a health farm, and her nobility is authentic." Signoret's attention had apparently first been drawn to the novel by director Constantin Costa-Gavras, who has a small part in the film, and by her husband, Yves Montand. When Claude Berri was initially named as director, Signoret turned the role down, but agreed to do it after Moshe Mizrahi spoke with her.

Madame Rosa was well received by American critics, but as Molly Haskell noted—in *New York* (April 24, 1978)—"critics are as irrelevant to *Madame Rosa* as they are to the Oscar ceremonies." It is a film that easily wins over an audience, and gains in strength through word-of-mouth reports. It succeeds very easily, perhaps so easily that one tends to overlook Moshe Mizrahi's contribution and give all the credit to Simone Signoret. Certainly Mizrahi gained partial recognition for his work when the film was named Best Foreign Language Film of the year.

ABOVE: Simone Signoret in the title role. BELOW: Dr. Katz (Claude Dauphin) and Madame Rosa (Simone Signoret).

ABOVE: Madame Rosa's apartment serves as both an unofficial nursery and a meeting ground for all racial and religious groups. BELOW: Madame Rosa passing into senility and Momo (Samy Ben Youb) passing through puberty.

LA CAGE AUX FOLLES

Producer: Marcello Danon for Les Productions Artistes Associés–Da Ma Produzione SPA. *Released:* 1978, United Artists (France); 1979, United Artists (U.S.). *Running Time:* 103 minutes (France); 99 minutes (U.S.).

Director: Edouard Molinaro. *Screenplay:* Francis Veber, Edouard Molinaro, Marcello Danon and Jean Poiret (based on the play by Jean Poiret). *Photography:* Armando Mannuzzi. *Art Director:* Mario Garbuglia. *Set Decorator:* Carlo Gervasi. *Costumes for Ugo Tognazzi and Michel Serrault:* designed by Piero Tosi and created by Carlo Palazzi. *Other Costumes:* Ambra Danon. *Music:* Ennio Morricone. *Film Editors:* Robert and Monique Isnardon.

CAST: Ugo Tognazzi (*Renato*); Michel Serrault (*ZaZa*); Michel Galabru (*Charrier*); Claire Maurier (*Simone*); Rémy Laurent (*Laurent*); Benny Luke (*Jacob*); Carmen Scarpitta (*Mme. Charrier*); Luisa Maneri (*Andrea*).

SYNOPSIS: Renato Baldi, owner of the nightclub known as La Cage aux Folles, has been living for twenty years, as man and wife, with the club's leading female impersonator, Albin, who performs under the name of "ZaZa." Renato has a son, as a result of a drunken evening spent with Simone Deblon, and the son, Laurent, is now engaged to Andrea, the daughter of Charrier, one of the prime movers behind the Union for Moral Order. Andrea has persuaded her parents that Renato is the Italian cultural attaché in Nice, and a dinner party is arranged at Renato's home, at which Simone will pretend to be Renato's wife and the black "maid," Jacob, is persuaded to give up "drag" for the night and masquerade as the butler (singing "Ol' Man River"). Chaos reigns that night as Albin also pretends to be Renato's wife and as the "boys" from La Cage aux Folles arrive with a cake in celebration of Renato and Albin's twentieth anniversary. Reporters learn that Charrier is dining at the home of the owner of La Cage aux Folles, and he is forced to don a dress in order to escape, undetected, from the apartment. A reconciliation of sorts takes place at Laurent and Andrea's wedding.

COMMENTARY: Jean Poiret's play *La Cage aux Folles* opened in Paris in 1973, and by 1976—when Gaumont initially announced it would be filmed—it had been seen by some 800,000 patrons at the Théatre du Palais-Royal. When it was eventually filmed in 1978, the film earned over five million dollars during the first 42 days of its release in France. On its American release, in the summer of 1979, *La Cage aux Folles* grossed almost two million dollars during its first thirteen weeks at only a dozen small art houses. The film eventually became the highest-grossing foreign-language feature in the history of the cinema. It ran for nineteen months at New York's 68th Street Playhouse, and only closed because the management had inadvertently booked in another film. Within one month of *La Cage*'s closing in New York—in January of 1981—a sequel opened to equally massive business. On August 21, 1983, the musical version of *La Cage aux Folles* opened at New York's Palace Theatre, starring George Hearn and Gene Barry, and was an immediate critical and commercial success, with two touring companies taking to the road a year later.

All this may sound impressive—even unique—in the annals of motion-picture history, but it is even more extraordinary in view of the fact that *La Cage aux Folles* is not only a non-American film and play, but also in that it deals openly and amusingly with the subjects of homosexuality and transvestism. It is not surprising that Michel Serrault, as the female impersonator Albin, should have won a César award for Best Actor; what is amazing is that the film picked up three Academy Award nominations—for Best Direction, Best Screenplay and Best Costume Design.

And yet, perhaps, much of *La Cage*'s success is not difficult to comprehend. For all its story's permitting the homosexual couple a happy ending, *La Cage aux Folles* presents a very stereotyped view of homosexuality. The "gays" are all limp-wristed, camp creatures, bordering on the tasteless in their behavior. The two central characters, Albin and Renato, are caricatures of homosexual lovers, created strictly to provide laughs for the middle-class viewer, presenting no threats to an audience, no hint of "gay power," no suggestion that a homosexual can be as "masculine" or as ordinary as the man next door. As Vincent Canby wrote in *The New York Times* (May 13, 1979), "*La Cage aux Folles* is naughty in the way of comedies that pretend to be sophisticated but actually serve to reinforce the most popular conventions and most witless stereotypes."

La Cage aux Folles offers no threats to a straight audience. It is very much in the tradition of the great French farces of the last century and of the superb British farces of Ben Travers. The men dress up as women, but it is all nothing more than a joke. Even the performers in the nightclub are pathetically amateurish, with none of them displaying the glamor of a Jim Bailey or the sauce of a Charles Pierce. They themselves are the joke, and the audience can savor the humor of their sad impersonations. The female impersonator, Albin, is presented at times as an almost sad character, and not once does the film address the question as to why homosexual Renato, who likes men, should want to spend twenty-five years of his life with a man who dresses like a woman. One cannot help but consider that the real thing would be a lot more attractive—and a lot less trouble. (Nor does the film indicate there is any difference between a homosexual and a transvestite!)

The film was shot at the Dear Studios in Rome and on location in the hills around the city and in Nice. The Cage aux Folles nightclub was, in fact, the Paradise disco club on Rome's Piazza di Spagna. Director Edouard Molinaro (born 1928) began his career as a director back in 1953, with his first feature film being *Back to the Walls/Dos aux Murs* (1958); a prolific director, Molinaro is noted more for the commercial success of his films than for their quality. Tom Allen, in *The Village Voice* (May 4, 1969), described Molinaro as a "French commercial director of no particular taste or personal signature who has had uncommon access to the American market."

On the whole American critics were not wildly enthusiastic about *La Cage aux Folles*. *La Cage aux Folles* is successful largely because of when it was made. Twenty years ago it would have been a disastrous failure, twenty years from now—hopefully—it will be considered a piece of offensive trash. In the Eighties it serves as a gentle rebuff to strident gay politics and the effect those politics can, and may, have on the community.

ABOVE: Jacob the maid (Benny Luke) receives his instructions for the day from Renato (Ugo Tognazzi).
BELOW: ZaZa (Michel Serrault) discovers that the apartment has been redecorated by Renato (Ugo Tognazzi).

ABOVE: Disguised as Laurent's mother, ZaZa (Michel Serrault) meets M. Charrier (Michel Galabru).
BELOW: In order to avoid the news media, M. Charrier (Michel Galabru) is forced to don female attire.

I SENT A LETTER TO MY LOVE
CHÈRE INCONNUE

Producer: Lise Fayolles and Giorgio Silvagni for Cineproductions, S.A. *Released:* 1980, Gaumont (France); 1981, Atlantic Releasing (U.S.). *Running Time:* 102 minutes.

Director: Moshe Mizrahi. *Screenplay:* Moshe Mizrahi and Gerard Brach (based on the novel by Bernice Rubens). *Photography:* Ghislain Cloquet. *Music:* Philippe Sarde. *Art Director:* Bernard Evein. *Film Editor:* Françoise Bonnot. *Sound:* Michel Vionnet and Claude Villand.

CAST: Simone Signoret (*Louise*); Jean Rochefort (*Gilles*); Delphine Seyrig (*Yvette*); Geneviève Fontanel (*Beatrice*); Dominique Labourier (*Catherine*).

SYNOPSIS: An aging brother and sister, Gilles and Louise, live together in their parents' old home by the sea. Gilles is confined to a wheelchair and Louise has devoted her life to taking care of him. Their only friend appears to be Yvette, who works in a local bakery and is obviously attracted to Gilles. The loneliness and frustration that Louise feels encourages her to place an advertisement in the personal column of the local newspaper, seeking to meet "a refined gentleman." The only response is from her brother, who she realizes is as lonely and frustrated as she, and the two carry on a correspondence, with Louise using the name of Béatrice Deschamps. When Gilles asks to meet Béatrice, Louise hires a local actress to play the role. The correspondence helps Gilles take a new lease on life; he is less slovenly and difficult with Louise and eventually asks Yvette to marry him. On the couple's wedding day, Gilles discovers the identification card that Louise had altered from her own name to that of Béatrice Deschamps in order to pick up the mail from the post office. At the church, as Gilles and Yvette take their vows, the former looks long and hard at his sister, perhaps revealing to her that he knows the truth.

COMMENTARY: After the success of *Madame Rosa*, it was, perhaps, not surprising that Moshe Mizrahi and Simone Signoret should be reteamed. What was surprising was that their new film, *I Sent a Letter to My Love*, was as successful and as superb a production as *Madame Rosa*.

I Sent a Letter to My Love is a slow-paced drama of an aging brother and sister in whose relationship there obviously exists an undercurrent of hatred. Louise has given up what chances she might have of a romance in order to care for her disabled brother Gilles. Gilles responds to her care by deliberately behaving in a slovenly fashion. Completing the picture is Yvette, romantically attracted to Gilles, whose looks are beginning to fade with age. When Louise advertises in the personal column of the local newspaper, seeking to meet "a refined gentleman," the only response is from Gilles, who writes: "My legs are paralyzed, but my heart is free and I know how to love." And so a strange, incestuous relationship by mail begins, ended only with Gilles's wedding to Yvette.

Moshe Mizrahi has created an enigmatic film, in which it is never clear whether Gilles is aware that his correspondent is Louise—after all, she makes no attempt to disguise her handwriting and surely he must have been familiar with his sister's penmanship. Perhaps the affection that the two feel for each other can only be expressed through the written word.

Above all, *I Sent a Letter to My Love* is a splendid example of ensemble playing. The three principals play their parts to perfection. Simone Signoret is a simply dressed, ordinary woman, and, as Richard Schickel commented in *Time* (August 10, 1981), "After 40 years in movies, Signoret has the sturdy, pouched, life-lined charm of an old duffel bag." From the favorite actress of Alain Resnais, Delphine Seyrig has matured into a fine middle-aged character actress, still beautiful but in a down-to-earth fashion. Similarly, Jean Rochefort, a leading man of French films of the Fifties and Sixties, has developed into a consummate character performer. "It's unlikely casting, and it works beautifully," commented Vincent Canby in *The New York Times* (May 3, 1981).

I Sent a Letter to My Love is based on a British novel, and was originally intended as a screen vehicle for Simone Signoret and Dirk Bogarde. It was filmed at St. Anne à Palud in Brittany (substituting for the Wales of the novel) in the winter of 1979–1980 at a budget of $2.3 million. The film opened in Paris in April of 1980, and was the official French entry at the Cannes Film Festival.

American critical reaction to the film was decidedly mixed, with many reviewers complaining that it was overly saccharine, with the plot far too simplistic and obvious. "Insensitive direction and unconvincing performances ruin an interesting dramatic idea," complained *Variety* (May 21, 1980). *Rolling Stone* (July 9, 1981) also complained: "There's something phony about Mizrahi's films: his compassion comes too easily, partly because he turns his lead characters into people who are supposed to be more 'human' than anyone else around them." Far more sympathetic was Guy Flatley, in *Cosmopolitan* (July 1981), who remarked: "This muted, smoldering French film first teases and eventually clutches our emotions." Judith Crist, in *Saturday Review* (May 1981), called *I Sent a Letter to My Love* "a 'small' film in the best sense and a triumph of ensemble playing." Carrie Rickey, in *The Village Voice* (June 12, 1981), thought the feature "so corny it qualifies for an agricultural embargo, but I loved every minute." Vincent Canby, in *The New York Times*, quite rightly pointed out: "It's a comedy of blithe spirit and uncommon sense."

ABOVE: Louise (Simone Signoret) considers pushing her brother (Jean Rochefort) over the cliff. BELOW: "As a comparatively commonplace woman," wrote Vincent Canby in *The New York Times* (May 3, 1981), Simone Signoret "discovers resources she never dreamed she possessed."

ABOVE: Yvette, Gilles and Louise (Delphine Seyrig, Jean Rochefort and Simone Signoret). BELOW: One of the few tender moments between brother and sister (Jean Rochefort and Simone Signoret).

DIVA

Producer: Irène Silberman for Les Films Galaxie/Greenwich Film Production. *Released:* 1981, GEF CCFC (France); 1982, United Artists Classics (U.S.) *Running Time:* 123 minutes.

Director: Jean-Jacques Beineix. *Screenplay:* Jean-Jacques Beineix and Jean Van Hamme (based on a novel by Delacorta). *Photography:* Philippe Rousselot. *Music:* Wladimir Cosma. *Art Direction:* Hilton McConnico. *Film Editors:* Marie-Josèphe Yoyotte and Monique Prim. *Sound:* Jean-Pierre Ruh.

CAST: Wilhelmenia Wiggins-Fernandez (*Cynthia*); Frédéric Andreï (*Jules*); Richard Bohringer (*Gorodish*); Thuy An Luu (*Alba*); Jacques Fabbri (*Saporta*); Gérard Darmon (*Spic, l'Antillais*); Chantal Deruaz (*Nadia*); Anny Romand (*Paula*); Roland Bertin (*Weinstadt*); Dominique Pinon (*Le Curé*); Jean-Jacques Moreau (*Krantz*); Patrick Floersheim (*Zatopek*).

SYNOPSIS: Jules, a young Parisian mailman, passionately in love with Cynthia Hawkins, a Black American prima donna, secretly records one of her concerts because she refuses to have her voice recorded. He accidentally acquires a second tape recording, this one by a murdered prostitute, Nadja, in which she names Inspector Saporta as the head of a crime ring. Two of Saporta's thugs are after the latter tape, while two Taiwanese businessmen seek the former to use on a pirated record. As Jules becomes the unwitting victim of a violent and insane chase, he is aided—albeit unknowingly—by Gorodish, the wealthy lover of a young Vietnamese girl, Alba, whom Jules had befriended. The two Taiwanese businessmen are killed by a bomb intended for Gorodish, who eventually kills Saporta as he is about to murder Jules and a policewoman, Paula. Jules has become friendly with Cynthia Hawkins after returning a dress he had stolen from her dressing room at the theatre, and the film concludes with the prima donna standing on stage and for the first time hearing her own voice on Jules's pirated recording. She is thrilled and kisses Jules.

COMMENTARY: If *La Cage aux Folles* has been the most popular French film of recent years, *Diva* has been the most critically acclaimed. It won four César Awards in France, and ran for more than a year in New York following its U.S. premiere on April 16, 1982, at the Plaza Theatre. American critics were fulsome in their praise. David Denby, in *New York* (April 19, 1982), described it as "one of the most audacious and original movies to come out of France in recent years." In *The Wall Street Journal* (May 7, 1982), Joy Gould Boyum hailed *Diva* as "an emphatic original, a charming, funny and thoroughly off-beat, off-the-wall movie." On a more serious note, J. Hoberman, in *The Village Voice* (April 20, 1982), wrote: "*Diva* is a film of considerable visual wit and style—full of pleasing symmetries and hairbreadth escapes—that consummately blends the old Paris with the new and, despite its engaging pop frivolity, makes several successful forays into the sublime." Perhaps closest to the truth was David Ansen with his backhanded compliment in *Newsweek* (April 19, 1982): "*Diva* demonstrates the depth of pleasure a shallow movie can provide."

Diva is, unquestionably, a delightful comic thriller in the best traditions of American films of the Thirties. Surprise follows surprise with the viewer given—or asking—little opportunity to consider the probability of the situations. Indeed it is a good thirty minutes at least into the feature before the viewer has much of a conception as to what connects all these apparently unrelated sequences. The theme may be old, but the surrounding characters and elements are definitely part of the pop culture of the Eighties. Record piracy is a current subject. Jules's apartment is decorated in a New Wave manner (and yet the beautiful voice of Wilhelmenia Wiggins-Fernandez, as Cynthia Hawkins, fits in perfectly with the wrecked cars and ultra-modern murals that dominate Jules's quarters). Alba, the Vietnamese girl, is a product—an irritating product—of the present, perfectly at ease roller-skating around Gorodish's apartment or stealing phonograph albums; while the character of Gorodish is a marvelous parody of all the meditating freaks that this generation has thrown up.

The chase sequences highlight *Diva*. They are as comic as those to be found in the Marx Brothers movies and as exhilarating as the one in *The French Connection*. They range from the urgency of a police detective chasing Jules through the Paris subway on a moped to the quietly sinister, slow-paced operation of Gorodish's planned handing over of the Nadja tape to Saporta.

The freshness of the story is matched by the unknown quality of the actors. Frédéric Andreï is a skinny, unprepossessing hero. First seen singing an aria from Catalani's 1892 opera *La Wally*, Wilhelmenia Wiggins-Fernandez upsets the old fallacy that opera stars cannot act—unless they happen to be named Geraldine Farrar—and gives the film a gentle note that helps break up the frenetic quality of much of the production. Equally excellent is Thuy An Luu as the Vietnamese girl, although one wonders what other parts she can possibly play.

Diva is based on one of a series of thrillers written by Delacorta, all featuring Serge Gorodish and Alba. (In a fascinating article by Lesley Hazleton in *Vanity Fair*, June 1983, it is revealed that Delacorta is the pseudonym of Daniel Odier, a Swiss novelist.) The film shows the remarkable talent of Jean-Jacques Beineix (born 1946), here making his directorial debut. Having entered the film industry in 1969 as a production assistant, Beineix worked as an assistant director to René Clément, Claude Berri and Willard Huyck, among others. "I have little hope for him," wrote Stanley Kauffmann in *The New Republic* (May 12, 1982), "*Diva* is such a cascade of (presumably) long-stored ideas that one or two films may drain him, as they have done other sparking debutants." Hopefully Kauffmann is wrong, for Beineix (certainly helped to a large extent by Delacorta's original novel) has brought to the French screen an originality and a vitality that are reminiscent, in the excitement they occasion, of the early work of Marcel Pagnol and Sacha Guitry.

ABOVE: Saporta's two thugs, Spic (Gérard Darmon) and Le Curé (Dominique Pinon). BELOW: Gorodish (Richard Bohringer) and his Vietnamese girlfriend (Thuy An Luu).

ABOVE: Gorodish meets up with the thugs. BELOW: Mortier (Patrick Floersheim) and Paula (Anny Romand) await Jules's return to his apartment.

SELECT BIBLIOGRAPHY

Abel, Richard. *French Cinema: The First Wave, 1915-1929.* Princeton, New Jersey: Princeton University Press, 1984.
Aranda, Francisco. *Luis Buñuel: A Critical Biography.* New York: Da Capo, 1976.
Armes, Roy. *French Cinema Since 1946.* London: A. Zwemmer, 1970.
Bandy, Mary Lea (editor). *Rediscovering French Film.* New York: Museum of Modern Art, 1983.
Bazin, André. *French Cinema of the Occupation and Resistance.* New York: Frederick Ungar, 1981.
Beylie, Claude. *Marcel Pagnol.* Paris: Editions Seghers, 1974.
Bond, Otto. *Fifty Foreign Films.* Chicago: The University of Chicago Press, 1939.
Bordwell, David. *The Films of Carl-Theodor Dreyer.* Berkeley, California: University of California Press, 1981.
Braucourt, Guy. *Claude Chabrol.* Paris: Editions Seghers, 1971.
Brownlow, Kevin. *Napoleon.* New York: Alfred A. Knopf, 1983.
Cameron, Ian (editor). *The Films of Robert Bresson.* London: Studio Vista, 1969.
Carné, Marcel, and Jacques Prévert. *Le Jour Se Lève.* New York: Simon and Schuster, 1970.
Chapier, Henry. *Louis Malle.* Paris: Editions Seghers, 1964.
Chazal, Robert. *Marcel Carné.* Paris: Editions Seghers, 1965.
Clair, René. "Nothing Is More Artificial Than Neo-Realism," *Films and Filming* (June 1957), pages 7 and 10.
Cocteau, Jean. "Beauty and the Beast," *Theatre Arts* (January 1948), pages 20-26.
____. *The Blood of a Poet.* New York: Bodley Press, 1949.
____. *Diary of a Film.* London: Dennis Dobson, 1950 (revised edition of translation: New York: Dover, 1972).
____. *Beauty and the Beast.* New York: University Press, 1970.
____. *Three Screenplays.* New York: Grossman, 1972.
The Complete Jean Vigo. London: Lorrimer Publishing, 1983.
de la Roche, Catherine. *René Clair: An Index.* London: British Film Institute, 1958.
Durgnat, Raymond. *Franju.* Berkeley, California: University of California Press, 1968.
Fowler, Roy. *The Film in France.* London: Pendulum Publications, 1946.
Harding, James. *Sacha Guitry: The Last Boulevardier.* New York: Charles Scribner's Sons, 1968.
Hazleton, Lesley. "Who Did Diva?," *Vanity Fair* (June 1983), pages 100-102.
Insdorf, Annette. *François Truffaut.* Boston: Twayne, 1978.
Jacobs, Lewis. "The Films of René Clair," *New Theatre* (February 1936), pages 12-13 and 31.
Jaubert, Maurice. "Music and Film," *World Film News* (July 1936), page 31.
Kriedl, John Francis. *Alain Resnais.* Boston: Twayne, 1977.

Lambert, Gavin. "Marcel Carné," *Sequence,* No. 3 (Spring 1948), pages 16-25.
____. "René Clair," *Sequence,* No. 6 (Winter 1948/9), pages 21-29.
Léaud, Jean-Pierre. "Getting beyond the Looking Glass," *Sight and Sound* (Winter 1973/74), pages 46-47.
Maddock, Brent. *The Films of Jacques Tati.* Metuchen, New Jersey: Scarecrow Press, 1977.
Masterworks of the French Cinema: The Italian Straw Hat, Grand Illusion, La Ronde, The Wages of Fear. New York: Harper & Row, 1974.
McGerr, Celia. *René Clair.* Boston: Twayne, 1980.
Moullet, Luc. "Jean-Luc Godard," *Cahiers du Cinéma in English,* No. 12 (December 1967), pages 24-33.
N.Y. Film Bulletin Special Issue: "Last Year at Marienbad," Vol. 3, No. 2 (March 1962).
Nolan, Jack Edmund. "Jean Gabin," *Films in Review* (April 1963), pages 193-209.
Paris, James Reid. *The Great French Films.* Secaucus, New Jersey: The Citadel Press, 1983.
Pilard, Philippe. *H.-G. Clouzot.* Paris: Editions Seghers, 1969.
Pye, Douglas. "Le Plaisir," *Movie,* No. 29/30 (Summer 1982), pages 80-89.
Renoir, Jean. *La Grande Illusion.* London: Lorrimer Publishing, 1968.
____. *My Life and My Films.* New York: Atheneum, 1974.
Roud, Richard. *Max Ophuls: An Index.* London: British Film Institute, 1958.
____. *Jean-Luc Godard.* Garden City, New York: Doubleday, 1968.
Sadoul, Georges. *French Film.* London: The Falcon Press, 1953.
____ (translated by Peter Morris). *Dictionary of Filmmakers.* Berkeley, California: University of California Press, 1972.
____. *Dictionary of Films.* Berkeley, California: University of California Press, 1972.
Sarris, Andrew. "Buñuel at the Beginning," *The Village Voice* (May 5, 1980), page 39.
Sesonske, Alexander. *Jean Renoir: The French Films, 1924-1939.* Cambridge, Massachusetts: Harvard University Press, 1980.
Smith, John M. *Jean Vigo.* New York: Praeger, 1972.
Stanbrook, Alan. "*The Passion of Joan of Arc,*" *Films and Filming* (June 1961), pages 11-13 and 40-41.
Truffaut, François. *Jules and Jim.* New York: Simon and Schuster, 1986.
Tyler, Parker. *Classics of the Foreign Film.* New York: Citadel Press, 1962.
Wood, Robin, and Michael Walker. *Claude Chabrol.* New York: Praeger, 1970.

ALPHABETICAL LIST OF FILMS

A Bout de Souffle, 112
Age d'Or, L', 19
Amants, Les, 100
Amours de la Reine Elisabeth, Les, 1
And God Created Woman, 97
Année Dernière à Marienbad, L', 115

Baker's Wife, The, 46
Beauty and the Beast, 67
Belle de Jour, 130
Belle et la Bête, La, 67
Blood of a Poet, The, 16
Breathless, 112

Cage aux Folles, La, 142
Carnival in Flanders, 31
César, 25
Chapeau de Paille d'Italie, Un, 7
Chère Inconnue, 145
Children of Paradise, 64
Cousins, Les, 103
Cousins, The, 103

Daybreak, 55
Day for Night, 136
Day in the Country, A, 34
Diary of a Country Priest, 79
Diva, 148

Enfants du Paradis, Les, 64
Et Dieu . . . Créa la Femme, 97

Fanny, 25
Femme du Boulanger, La, 46
400 Blows, The, 106
French Cancan, 84

Golden Age, The, 19
Grande Illusion, La, 37
Grand Illusion, 37

Hiroshima, Mon Amour, 109

I Sent a Letter to My Love, 145
Italian Straw Hat, The, 7

Journal d'un Curé de Campagne, 79
Jour Se Lève, Le, 55
Judex, 121
Jules and Jim, 118
Jules et Jim, 118

Kermesse Héroïque, La, 31
King of Hearts, 127

Last Year at Marienbad, 115
Lovers, The, 100

Madame Rosa, 139
Marius, 25
Marseillaise, La, 49
Million, Le, 22
Miracle des Loups, Le, 4
Miracle of the Wolves, 4
Monsieur Vincent, 70
Mouton a Cinq Pattes, Le, 91
Mr. Hulot's Holiday, 85

Napoléon, 10
Nuit Américaine, La, 136

Only the French Can, 94
Orphée, 73

Orpheus, 73

Parapluies de Cherbourg, Les, 124
Partie de Campagne, Une, 34
Passion de Jeanne d'Arc, La, 13
Passion of Joan of Arc, The, 13
Pearls of the Crown, The, 40
Perles de la Couronne, Les, 40
Pépé le Moko, 43
Plaisir, Le, 82
Port of Shadows, 52

Quai des Brumes, 52
Quatre Cents Coups, Les, 106
Queen Elizabeth, 1

Règle du Jeu, La, 61
Roi de Cœur, Le, 127
Ronde, La, 76
Rules of the Game, 61

Salaire de la Peur, Le, 88
Sang d'un Poète, Le, 16
Sheep Has Five Legs, The, 91

Umbrellas of Cherbourg, The, 124

Vacances de Monsieur Hulot, Les, 85
Vie Devant Soi, La,139
Volpone, 58

Wages of Fear, The, 88

Z, 133
Zéro de Conduite, 28
Zero for Conduct, 28

152